Feasting with Demons or with Christ?

An African Spiritual Reading of Ritual Meals
in 1 Corinthians 8:1–11:1 and 11:17–34

Samantha Chambo

© 2025 Samantha Chambo

Published 2025 by Langham Academic
An imprint of Langham Publishing
www.langhampublishing.org

Langham Publishing and its imprints are a ministry of Langham Partnership

Langham Partnership
PO Box 296, Carlisle, Cumbria, CA3 9WZ, UK
www.langham.org

ISBNs:
978-1-83973-952-1 Print
978-1-78641-184-6 ePub
978-1-78641-185-3 PDF
DOI: https://doi.org/10.69811/9781839739521

Samantha Chambo has asserted her right under the Copyright, Designs and Patents Act, 1988 to be identified as the Author of this work.

All rights reserved. No part of this publication may be reproduced, stored in a retrieval system or transmitted, in any form or by any means, electronic, mechanical, photocopying, recording or otherwise, without the prior written permission of the publisher or the Copyright Licensing Agency.

Requests to reuse content from Langham Publishing are processed through PLSclear. Please visit www.plsclear.com to complete your request.

Scripture quotations marked (NRSV) are taken from the New Revised Standard Version Bible, copyright © 1989 National Council of the Churches of Christ in the United States of America. Used by permission. All rights reserved.

Scripture quotations marked (RSV) are taken from the Revised Standard Version of the Bible, copyright © 1946, 1952, and 1971 National Council of the Churches of Christ in the United States of America. Used by permission. All rights reserved.

Scripture quotations marked (NIV) are taken from the Holy Bible, New International Version®, NIV®. Copyright © 1973, 1978, 1984, 2011 by Biblica, Inc.™ Used by permission of Zondervan.

Scripture quotations marked (ESV) are taken from The Holy Bible, English Standard Version® (ESV®), copyright © 2001 by Crossway, a publishing ministry of Good News Publishers. Used by permission. All rights reserved.

British Library Cataloguing-in-Publication Data
A catalogue record for this book is available from the British Library

ISBN: 978-1-83973-952-1

Cover & Book Design: projectluz.com

Langham Partnership actively supports theological dialogue and an author's right to publish but does not necessarily endorse the views and opinions set forth here or in works referenced within this publication, nor can we guarantee technical and grammatical correctness. Langham Partnership does not accept any responsibility or liability to persons or property as a consequence of the reading, use or interpretation of its published content.

Contents

List of Abbreviations ix

Abstract xi

Acknowledgements xiii

Chapter 1 1
Introduction
    1.1 Justification for This Study and Survey of Existing Research 4
    1.2 Interpretive Method 11
    1.3 Outline of Study 14

Chapter 2 19
Turner's Theory as a Lens to Study Ritual Meals in Corinth
    2.0 Introduction 19
    2.1 Overview of Turner's Ritual Theory: Liminality and
        Communitas 20
    2.2 Rituals and Symbol Analysis 23
    2.3 Sociological vs Religious Approach 25
    2.4 Conclusion 31

Chapter 3 33
Ritual Meals in the African Context
    3.0 Introduction 33
    3.1 Liminality and *Communitas* in the African Cultural Context 34
    3.2 The Ubiquity of Ritual Meals in Modern Africa 41
    3.3 Vertical *Communitas* during Ritual Meals 47
    3.4 Horizontal *Communitas* in African Ritual Meals 51
    3.5 Holiness in African Ritual Meals 54
    3.6 Conclusion 59

Chapter 4 65
Liminality, Communitas, and Holiness in Paul
    4.0 Introduction 65
    4.1 Liminality 66
        4.1.1 Liminality as between the Times 66
        4.1.2 Liminality: Between the Realm of the Flesh and the
            Realm of the Spirit 76
        4.1.3 Liminality and Anti-structure in Paul 79

4.2 *Communitas* 88
    4.2.1 *Communitas* as Participation in Christ................................89
    4.2.2 Analysing Participation "In Christ" through the
        Lens of African Vital Participation and
        Spirit Possession 97
    4.2.3 Horizontal *Communitas* 102
4.3 Holiness 105
    4.3.1 Holiness and Liminality..109
    4.3.2 Holiness and *Communitas*...110
    4.3.3 Holiness and Anti-structure 111
    4.3.4 Holiness and Aggregation 113
4.4 Conclusion 114

Chapter 5 117
Sociohistorical Context for Ritual Meals in 1 Corinthians 8:1–11:1 and 1 Corinthians 11:17–34
    5.0 Introduction 117
    5.1 The Use of Ritual or Ceremony 118
    5.2 Liminality and *Communitas* in 1 Corinthians 8:1–11:1 and
        1 Corinthians 11:17–34 120
    5.3 Defining the "Strong" and the "Weak" in Corinth......................122
    5.4 Meals in Corinth...127
    5.5 Conclusion 130

Chapter 6 135
Feasting with Demons in 1 Corinthians 8:1–11:1
    6.0 Introduction 135
    6.1 The Ritual Context of 1 Corinthians 8:1–11:1 137
    6.2 Defining Idolatry in 1 Corinthians 8:1–11:1.................................143
    6.3 The Exodus Narrative and Old Testament Covenant as
        Ritual Myth in Light of Christ's Sacrifice 149
        6.3.1 The Exodus Narrative to explain the believing
            communities new identity. 150
        6.3.2 References to the covenant in 1 Corinthians 8:11–11:1 152
    6.4 *Communitas* in 1 Corinthians 8:1–11:1 157
    6.5 Ritual Outcomes of Εἰδωλοθυτα 160
    6.6 Conclusion 163

Chapter 7 167
Feasting with Christ in 1 Corinthians 11:17–34
    7.0 Introduction 167
    7.1 The Ritual Context of 1 Corinthians 11:17–34.............................169

    7.2 Vertical *Communitas* during the Lord's Supper 174
    7.3 Horizontal *Communitas* during the Lord's Supper 181
    7.4 Conclusion 187

Chapter 8 193
  Inculturation of the Lord's Supper for the African Context
    8.0 Introduction 193
    8.1 Inculturation of the Lord's Supper for the African Context 194
    8.2 Inclusion of the Ancestors? 195
    8.3 Communication of the *Sacra* during the Lord's Supper 202
    8.4 *Communitas* during the Lord's Supper 205
    8.5 Practical Considerations 208
    8.6 Conclusion 209

Chapter 9 211
  Summary and Conclusions
    9.1 Summary 211
    9.2 Conclusions and Contributions 214
    9.3 Further Studies 217
    9.4 Implications for the Church Today 218

Bibliography 221

List of Abbreviations

AFER	*African Ecclesiastical Review*
AJWT	*Africa Journal of Wesleyan Theology*
AJRH	*African Journal of Reproductive Health*
ASR	*African Studies Review*
AT	*Anthropology Today*
ATR	African Traditional Religions
AQ	*American Quarterly*
BET	*Biblical Exegesis and Theology*
CBQ	*Catholic Biblical Quarterly*
CSSH	*Comparative Studies in Society and History*
CI	*Critical Inquiry*
ExpTim	*Expository Times*
FemTh	*Feminist Theology*
HBT	*Horizons in Biblical Theology*
HTR	*Harvard Theological Review*
IBC	*Interpretation: A Bible Commentary for Teaching and Preaching*
Int	*Interpretation*
IPA	*International Political Anthropology*
IST	*Issues in Systematic Theology*
JBL	*Journal of Biblical Literature*
JBP	*Journal of Black Psychology*
JIAI	*Journal of the International African Institute*
JRT	*Journal of Religious Thought*
JSNT	*Journal for the Study of the New Testament*

JSPL	*Journal for the Study of Paul and his Letters*
JSSR	*Journal for the Scientific Study of Religion*
JTSA	*Journal of Theology for Southern Africa*
NBBC	New Beacon Bible Commentary
Neot	*Neotestamentica*
NIGTC	New International Greek Testament Commentary
NovT	*Novum Testamentum*
NovTSup	Supplements to Novum Testamentum
NSBT	New Studies in Biblical Theology
NTS	*New Testament Studies*
PBM	Paternoster Biblical Monographs
PNTC	Pelican New Testament Commentaries
PP	*Political Psychology*
RCR	Reader in Comparative Religion
SAJE	*South African Journal of Ethnology*
SBL	Society of Biblical Literature
SBT	Studies in Biblical Theology
SNTSMS	Society for New Testament Studies Monograph Series
SP	Sacra Pagina
StBibLit	Studies in Biblical Literature
TynBul	*Tyndale Bulletin*
WATSA	What Are They Saying About
WeBC	Westminster Bible Companion
WBCAR	Wiley Blackwell Companion to African Religions
ZECNT	Zondervan Exegetical Commentary on the New Testament

Abstract

This study investigates ritual meals in 1 Corinthians 8:1–11:1 and 1 Corinthians 11:17–34 by using Victor Turner's ritual theory, paired with insights from an African cultural context, to shed new light on this conversation. It seeks to answer two questions that arise from this African context: Do continued practices of ritual meals to honour ancestors constitute idolatry? Can the Lord's Supper be used as a means of transformation for holiness in evangelical churches?

Part 1 explores Victor Turner's theory of liminality and *communitas* and the African cultural context, showing that this methodology illuminates the ritual and sacramental nature of Paul's admonitions. Part 2 looks at liminality and *communitas* in Paul and demonstrates that the holiness of the Corinthian community was a concern because they were living in liminal circumstances until the *parousia*. Part 3 looks at ritual meals in 1 Corinthians 8:1–11:1 and 1 Corinthians 11:17–34 and shows their impact on the nature of the ἐκκλησία. While participating in εἰδωλόθυτα may lead to a community shaped by an ethos of idolatry and self-elevation, celebrating the Lord's Supper in a worthy manner can create a community marked by holy love.

Part 4 applies these findings to the African context. This section shows that ritual meals in honour of ancestors constitute idolatry because they involve unfaithfulness to God when adherents turn to ancestors – rather than to God – for well-being in life and accept ancestors – rather than Jesus Christ – as mediators between humans and God.

This study concludes that ritual meals create a reciprocal dynamic between vertical and horizontal *communitas*. Paul emphasizes *communitas* with Christ in his discussion of ritual meals because he believed that the abuse and the disregard of the "weak" were evidence of a defective relationship with Christ.

Horizontal *communitas* – sacred, egalitarian relationships among believers – is thus an outflow of participating in the Lord's Table in a "worthy" manner. However, Paul also strongly highlights interpersonal relationships in the church because the mistreatment of the other can destroy *communitas* with Christ. This study thus shows that a biblical understanding of ritual meals as contextualized in African culture has the power to transform relationships with Christ and others.

Acknowledgements

I thank my primary supervisor, Dr. Kent Brower, for his consistent encouragement and guidance during this process. He has been a thought-provoking discussion partner, and his feedback has proved invaluable to the final thesis. I am also indebted to my secondary supervisor, Dr. Ayodeji Adewuya, for his guidance and helpful observations. His knowledge of the African Theology challenged me and proved advantageous to this research.

I express my sincere gratitude to the faculty, staff, and students of the Nazarene Theological College, Manchester. They welcomed me into their community and nurtured me with their encouragement and fellowship. In addition, I am incredibly thankful to my fellow PhD candidates, who generously shared information and strategies for success. I could not have made it to this point without all these Christlike people to cheer me on.

I am thankful to the Souter Charitable Trust Postgraduate Student Fellowship for supporting me financially. Without their generous contribution, this research would not have been possible. A special thank you to Debra Bradshaw, Director of Library Services, and the Nazarene Theological Seminary for providing me with resources during the Covid pandemic.

A special thank you to my family in Africa and my Nazarene family worldwide for their encouragement and prayers. I thank God every time I think of them. I thank God for his generous provision and empowerment because I am nothing without him.

Finally, I thank my husband, Filimão Chambo, and my children, Tsakani and Emanuel, for their generous love, patience, and support during this research. I am thankful for their faith in me and the sacrifices they have made during the past seven years. I dedicate this thesis to them.

CHAPTER 1

Introduction

Recent studies have shown that the way "the message of Christian holiness" is proclaimed by churches within the holiness movement has not connected well with an African cultural context.[1] One reason for this is that the articulation of this "message" has neglected the existing religious and philosophical world view of African converts. As a result, some Christians experience a significant dichotomy between religious beliefs and everyday life.

Kwame Bediako suggests that the vast number of Christians on the continent is evidence that African Christians have internalized the gospel.[2] However, he also draws attention to the integration of the gospel with African sensibilities, warning that

> if the Christian way of life is to stay in Africa, then African Christianity should be brought to bear on the fundamental questions of African existence in such a way as to achieve a unified worldview which finally resolves the dilemma of an Africa uncertain of its identity, poised between the impact of the West and the pull of its indigenous tradition.[3]

According to Bediako, there is a need for "Africanizing" the Christian experience in Africa.[4] Africanizing can be done through inculturation – that

---

1. See Chambo, "Doctrine of Christian Holiness," for evidence based on which this conclusion is drawn; see also Muzorewa, *Origins and Development*, x–xi. Muzorewa suggests that Western missionaries suppressed African religious expression, favouring an artificial Western form of decorum.
2. Bediako, *Christianity in Africa*, 5.
3. Bediako, 5.
4. Bediako, 5.

1

is, the integration of the Christian experience into the culture of the people. The lack of inculturation has led to a situation where the gospel appears powerless to address challenges faced by Africans. There is an apparent disconnect between their Christian beliefs and real life. The result of this dichotomy is that many Africans who profess to be Christians[5] still turn to African Traditional Religious practices – more specifically, to ritual meals to ancestors – in response to crises in life.[6]

Africa is a vast continent, with a wide variety of African Traditional Religious beliefs and practices. However, certain common threads can be identified across the continent. The traditional African belief is that ancestors are intermediaries between the creator and humans:[7] "The living dead and other departed convey human requests, needs, prayers, sacrifices and offerings to God, and sometimes relay His response back to humans."[8] In short, these ancestors are responsible for ensuring well-being in the community, which is achieved through ritual meals.[9] Though much of the continent is Christianized and Islamized, ritual meals for ancestor veneration, performed to assure well-being or avert evil, are still widely practised.[10]

Early evangelical missions neglected the African spiritual world view[11] and, therefore, the importance of rituals in African communities to address life issues such as illness, economic problems, or death. Unfortunately, this neglect resulted in confusion concerning the relationship between the African cultural past and Christian beliefs. According to Bediako, the combination of these two aspects are essential to describe the "nature and meaning of African Christian identity."[12] A conversation around their cultural past and Christian beliefs could have addressed questions of continuity and discontinuity with

---

5. Evidence for this assertion can be found in chapter 3 of this book.

6. Several theses have explored this problem. See Amadi, "Inculturating the Eucharist," 1–5; Banda, "Sufficiency of Christ," 1–9; Sipuka, "Sacrifice of the Mass," 1–9.

7. Mbiti, *African Religions and Philosophy*, 67.

8. Mbiti, 69.

9. Mbiti, 180.

10. See Ainslie, "Harnessing the Ancestors," 530–552; Bucher, *Spirits and Power*; wa Gatumu, Supernatural Powers; Gottlieb, *Sacred Earth*, Hamer, "Commensality," 126–144.

11. According to Mbiti, mission Christianity was not willing to have a serious encounter with Africa's traditional religions and philosophy, as a result of which the gospel did not go "deep into African traditional religiosity." Mbiti, *African Religions and Philosophy*, 226–232; see also Idowu, "Introduction," 9–16; Strayer, "Mission History in Africa," 1–15.

12. Bediako, *Theology and Identity*, 4.

pre-Christian traditions, thereby contributing to the satisfaction of the African religious consciousness. As it stands, the African religious experience was ignored.[13]

Several questions arise from this contextual problem: How should the church respond to this highly complex issue in the twenty-first century? How can the gospel of Jesus Christ address the spiritual needs of African Christians? Can the Lord's Supper be inculturated for the African context to better meet these spiritual needs?

To address these questions, we will consider Paul's discussion of ritual meals in 1 Corinthians 8:1–11:1 and 1 Corinthians 11:17–34. Ritual meals are defined as meals performed in reference to beliefs in spiritual powers or deities.[14] This discussion is a resource for two reasons. First, as shown later, there appears to be a commonality between the African cultural context and the Corinthian cultural context. Both contexts are communal cultures with a spiritual world view. Re-reading Paul through a cultural lens that is closer to his own may help shed light on these passages. Second, Paul addresses the same fundamental problem in Corinth that African Christians face today: How should they relate to their cultural context now that they have been included in the holy people of God? The Corinthian discussion could thus be very significant for contemporary rituals in African churches because it addresses similar questions.

Paul discusses ritual meals in 1 Corinthians 8:1–11:1 and 11:17–34 in the light of ethical problems in the church at Corinth. These concerns relate primarily to their relationships with Christ and fellow believers, and, in both cases, Paul refers to the Lord's Supper as the epitome of proper relations. What can we learn from these passages about the nature of idolatry? According to Paul, what endows the Lord's Supper with the capacity to transform the community?

All these questions can be subsumed under the focus of this research, which aims to address the following question: If Paul attributes to the Lord's Supper a function similar to that of meals offered to idols or demons (1 Cor 10:16–17),[15] does this signify that Paul sees commonality in how both types

---

13. Bediako, 2.
14. Turner, "Social Dramas," 159.
15. Ehrensperger, "Eat or Not to Eat," 114–133.

of ritual meals function? If so, how does the practice of ritual meals impact the community? The underlying primary question is this: In Paul's view, what is the nature and impact of ritual meals – be it meals offered to idols or the Lord's Supper – and how do these meals affect the holiness of the believing community?

1.1 Justification for This Study and Survey of Existing Research

Previous research on these passages has diverse intentions, methodologies, and outcomes. The principal focus has been on resolving the problems of interpretation present in these passages or examining the sociological impact of these ritual meals. This focus on the social implications of ritual meals has led to neglect of the religious implications. As a result, scholars have not sufficiently explored either the nature of idolatry and holiness in the context of ritual meals or the transformative capacity of these meals.

In what follows, I will offer a brief survey of scholarly interpretations of the role and nature of idolatry and the nature and function of the Lord's Supper in these texts. First, I will refer briefly to a sample of studies that deal with our passages, as well as Pauline studies that employ ritual theory.

One particularly influential thesis on 1 Corinthians 8:1–11:1 is that of Wendell Lee Willis. His examination of "Cultic Meals and Association in Hellenistic life"[16] addresses the question of "idol food" in Corinth and gives valuable information about the sociohistorical situation at the time. However, Willis concludes that most pagan meals did not have sacramental significance, arguing that the evidence indicates that first-century Graeco-Roman meals were "occasions of good company, good food, and good fun."[17] Thus, Willis concludes that the Lord's Supper is also an expression of the communal nature of κοινωνία and that viewing 1 Corinthians 10:16–17 as sacramental can be misleading.[18] However, Willis's study fails to take into account Paul's broader use of κοινωνία and the ritual context of the passage. His emphasis

---

16. Willis, *Idol Meat in Corinth*, 5.
17. Willis, 63.
18. Willis, 284.

on the sociological impact may lead to neglecting the ritual and theological implications present in the passage.

Peter D. Gooch, who also reviewed Graeco-Roman cultic meals, comes to the opposite conclusion. According to Gooch, Paul affirms both that εἰδωλόθυτα can be harmless (1 Cor 8:8) and that it does have a religious effect (10:20).[19] According to Gooch,

> Paul believed that the Christian rite carried something akin to infection: he believes improper eating cause illness and even death (11:30). It can be asserted, then, that Paul believed idol-food to carry the contagion of demons in the same way that the meal of the Lord infects with the Lord's blessing.[20]

Concerning Paul's apparent allowance of eating food offered to idols in chapter 8, Gooch suggests that Paul does not condemn the eating of εἰδωλόθυτα because he was employing a rhetorical strategy and was unwilling to reveal his strong stance against it at the outset of his argument.[21] Although I am not convinced that Paul only allowed participation in εἰδωλόθυτα because he was attempting to be persuasive, I do agree with Gooch on the sacramental nature of the meal and will elaborate on these sacramental aspects in chapter 6.

Other interpreters fall on a spectrum between the two views described above. Khiok-Khng Yeo, for instance, accepts the sacramental view but interprets 1 Corinthians 10:16–18 in communal terms, viewing κοινωνία as happening among worshippers.[22] For Yeo, participating in the bread and cup is synonymous with participation in the love of Christ, implying that participating in the Lord's Supper is a means to have κοινωνία in God's love, and should result in exclusive loyalty to God.[23] Once again, the neglect of the ritual context leads to a reductionist interpretation of the text. The ritual context depicts the Lord's Supper as a cultic meal, with Jesus as the deity being honoured,[24] suggesting that a more sacramental view may be justified.

---

19. Gooch, *Dangerous Food*, 56.
20. Gooch, 56.
21. Gooch, 84.
22. Yeo, *Rhetorical Interaction*, 173.
23. Yeo, 173.
24. Fuad, "Lord's Supper," 202–214.

Derek Newton, who postulates that Paul's principal and consistent warning in 1 Corinthians 8:1–11:1 is against idolatry, affirms the sacramental nature of ritual meals and explores idolatry in this passage.[25] Newton argues that the Corinthian believers – like the Torajanese people of Indonesia whom Newton studied – probably had diverse beliefs about idolatry. Newton suggests that it was this lack of a clear definition of idolatry that led Paul to focus on the ethical and relational responsibilities of the believers.[26] However, there are problems with this view. The fact that the Corinthians seemed to have disagreed on what constitutes idolatry does not signify that Paul was confused about the matter. On the contrary, Paul's references to the wilderness generation (1 Cor 10:1–10) and his emphatic command to "flee from idolatry" (1 Cor 10:14) suggest that he had a clear understanding about the nature of idolatry. My research defines idolatry as unfaithfulness to God, whether by worshipping other gods, approaching God through a medium other than Jesus Christ, or misrepresenting God through wrong intentions or wrong actions. I will define idolatry more fully in section 6.2.

Other monographs that see idolatry as central to Paul's discussion include those of A. T. Cheung[27] and Joop Smit.[28] Cheung focuses on Paul's Jewish background and concludes that Paul consistently rejects the consumption of εἰδωλόθυτα on the basis that it violates a believer's allegiance to Christ. Smit comes to the same conclusions by using a rhetorical approach. I concur with both works but see a need for a more in-depth exploration of the nature of idolatry and the perceived impact of ritual meals on the holiness of the community.

Richard Phua offers an interesting discourse on the nature of idolatry in 1 Corinthians 8:1–11:1.[29] He compares the Jewish diaspora communities to the Corinthians to demonstrate that all the parties represented in the Corinthian church were "Jewish in varying ways."[30] Although this argument is not convincing, his discussion of idolatry proves most enlightening. Phua uses the work of Halbertal and Margalit as a tool to survey the Septuagint

---

25. Newton, *Deity and Diet*, 331–342.
26. Newton, 40–78.
27. Cheung, *Idol Food in Corinth*.
28. Smit, *About the Idol Offerings*.
29. Phua, *Idolatry and Authority*.
30. Phua, 27.

and other Second Temple Jewish texts to examine the diverse facets of idolatry.[31] This approach offers helpful insights, which will be explored in more detail below.

In recent times, "rituals" as a research category have generated significant interest within Pauline studies. The nomenclature used is as diverse as the ritual theories applied by Pauline scholars. The anthropological approaches employed by scholars are varied and focus on distinct aspects of rituals in Pauline churches. Themes that emerge describe rituals as illuminating existing ideologies, generating new ideologies, or both. Rituals are portrayed as a means to create a communal identity, organize society, provide control, and maintain boundaries with the surrounding cultures. Rituals also affirmed the early church's mission by enacting sacred mandates. I mention below a few works that utilize ritual theory.

There are many studies utilizing ritual theory, among which those of Christian Strecker[32] and Stephen Richard Turley[33] are particularly relevant to this research. Strecker uses Victor Turner's theory of social drama to explore Paul's *Transformationstheologie* (Transformation Theology). According to Strecker, Paul's letters present four levels of transformation: Paul's personal transformation, Christ's transformation from his crucifixion to his elevation (Rom 6:3; Phil 2:6–11), the transformation of the aeons, and the transformation of the new believing community.[34] Strecker makes a significant contribution by underscoring the liminal circumstances of the early church and highlighting the role of rituals in its transformation. However, the scale of Strecker's research limits the amount of space devoted to ritual meals, revealing a need for further discussion. We will engage more with his research below.

Turley explores ritual washings and meals in the Pauline corpus through the lens of performance- and practice-based theories, as exemplified in the work of Roy Rappaport.[35] According to Turley, rituals are a means to shape believers and the community. His practice-based theory focuses on time, space, and cosmology during the ritual process. As far as ritual meals are

---

31. Phua, 30.
32. Strecker, *Die Liminale Theologie*, 324–226.
33. Turley, *Ritualized Revelation*, 99–172.
34. Strecker, *Liminale Theologie*, 82.
35. Turley, *Ritualized Revelation*, 26.

concerned, he contends that eating in idol temples reflects a cosmology contrary to Christ's and, in turn, results in ethics contrary to that represented in the Lord's Supper. Turley's research proves to be very effective in exploring the sociological aspects of the problem of ritual meals.

Other studies highlighting the pervasiveness and importance of rituals in the early church include that of Jerome Neyrey, who utilizes Mary Douglas's anthropological model of bodily control as a cross-cultural model to analyze Paul's exhortations concerning the body in 1 Corinthians.[36] According to Douglas, the physical body is a means of expressing society's perceptions, norms, and values.[37] Neyrey proposes that Paul was advocating strong bodily control instead of the lax attitude of the *pneumatics* in Corinth.[38] Neyrey's study highlights the vital aspect of holiness and the call to communal cohesion in Corinth. However, his focus on the body limits his interpretation of the theological significance of ritual meals in Corinth.

According to Wayne Meeks's classical study *The First Urban Christians*,[39] rituals function as a form of communication. They not only convey the values and beliefs of a society but also have a social function. The principal question for Meeks is this: "What do they do?"[40] Meeks differentiates between the "two great ritual complexes, baptism and the Lord's Supper"[41] and various minor rituals mentioned and sometimes alluded to in the Pauline corpus. For example, possible ritual actions might have included meeting together (1 Cor 11:17, 18, 20), the reading of Paul's letters (1 Thess 5:27), and the presenting of psalms, teachings, revelations, and prayers by congregation members (1 Cor 14:26).

According to Meeks, meetings, "besides exposition of scripture, preaching in the assemblies must have included other things, pre-eminently statements about Jesus Christ, and inferences, appeals, warnings, and the like, connected logically and rhetorically with those statements."[42] Meeks suggests that the Pauline corpus contains various verbal formulas such as exhortation "in the

---

36. Neyrey, "Body Language," 129.
37. Neyrey, 131.
38. Neyrey, 129.
39. Meeks, *First Urban Christians*.
40. Meeks, 142.
41. Meeks, 142.
42. Meeks, 146.

name of Jesus," greetings, or giving a holy kiss.[43] He also suggests that there must have been a variety of other rituals – such as ceremonies of burial and marriage – of which we have no record: "Acts and the Pauline letters provide only tantalising glimpses of the rituals practised by the Pauline groups, but those glimpses are enough for us to see that they had adopted or created a rich variety of ceremonial forms."[44] Meeks's observations indicate the vital importance and the pervasiveness of rituals in the early church. Although this research will focus on ritual meals, we do so within the broader context of ritual in the early church.

Gerd Theissen uses Turner's theory of symbols as a "cultural sign system"[45] for his inquiry into the life of the early church. According to Theissen, early Christian symbols should be understood in the light of the sign language of Judaism. Therefore, he compares Christian rites with Judaism's sacrificial system. Religions have a socializing function: they help individuals internalize values and beliefs and make them functional members of society. Religions also helps to regulate conflict in society. The rites of baptism and the Lord's Supper should be understood in the light of the prophetic actions of Jesus and John the Baptist.

Theissen's work underscores that early Christianity does emerge from an existing narrative – that of Judaism. This signifies that researchers may make assumptions concerning the myths regulating Christian rituals based on this background knowledge. The assumption that the birth of the Christian church forms part of God's salvation narrative that has its origin in the Old Testament can thus aid in interpreting early Christian rituals. However, this research does not preclude the importance of the apocalyptic perspective but, rather, argues that both salvation history and the apocalyptic are essential for interpreting ritual meals in Corinth.

Stanley K. Stowers prefers Catherine Bell's concept of ritualization, where the ritual action itself generates new ideologies and practices.[46] Stowers suggests that the Lord's Supper should be studied within the context of the Graeco-Roman world – that is, in the light of the common meal, meals

---

43. Meeks, 150.
44. Meeks, 163.
45. Theissen, *Earliest Churches*, 2.
46. Stowers, "Elusive Coherence."

involving animal sacrifices, and memorial meals for the dead. He argues that Paul's apparent contradiction between eating and not eating meat offered to idols favours the idea that their eating was a ritualized action: "Paul and the members of his communities may instinctively have sensed but did not see that their eating was negotiating a new place in the larger code of eating."[47] Stowers's challenge to coherence theories alerts us to the importance of individualized responses of participants during rituals and provides a convincing proposal to explain the varied responses of the Corinthians to the problem of εἰδωλόθυτα in their community.

B. J. Oropeza, in his discussion of 1 Corinthians 10:1–12, highlights the liminal nature of the Corinthians' situation by using Victor Turner's ritual process theory.[48] Oropeza investigates the dangers of apostasy in Corinth and concludes that Paul's analogy of the exodus event warns that those Corinthians (the "strong") who do not remain faithful and persevere during the liminal phase of their pilgrimage would suffer the same fate as the Israelites in the wilderness.

This sample of previous research affirms the comprehensive treatment of ritual meals in biblical scholarship. It shows that the interpretive questions and the sociohistorical and ritual contexts have been addressed from various angles. It also reveals the increased use of ritual theory in Pauline studies. However, there appears to be a deficiency in exploring the theological context, leaving a gap in research where a new theological basis for the discussion might be helpful. My use of the African cultural world view will provide a new lens that underscores the theological significance of ritual meals.

This research endeavours to contribute to this body of work by using ritual theory, paired with the African cultural context, to illuminate the sacramental (theological) aspects of ritual meals and their ability to transform. By sacramental, I simply mean "something spiritual being mediated by something material."[49] The sacramental thus points to the symbol's ability to connect humans to the spiritual or the divine, as well as to the symbol's capacity to mediate spiritual gifts to humans. However, the subject of ritual meals as a

---

47. Stowers, 78.
48. Oropeza, "Apostasy in the Wilderness," 69–86.
49. Schweitzer, *Mysticism of Paul*, 229.

means of transformation has not received enough attention, and this research aims to contribute to this discussion.

1.2 Interpretive Method

This research will take an interdisciplinary approach to studying ritual meals and their impact in Corinth. First, we will use a social scientific approach that uses tools from cultural anthropology to study ritual meals in Corinth. Victor Turner's classic expansion in *The Ritual Process* – particularly his concept of *communitas*[50] – will be used as a heuristic device to shed new light on the spiritual significance and transformational impact of rituals in 1 Corinthians 8:1–11:1 and 1 Corinthians 11:17–34 in building or destroying a holy community. We will expand on Turner's theory in chapter 2.

Second, we will utilize inculturation hermeneutics to arrive at a fresh understanding that is informed by the African cultural world view. Inculturation seeks to make Christianity relevant to indigenous people's social, cultural, political, and economic life situations:[51] "This method seeks to consciously and overtly study biblical texts with regard to indigenous socio-political/economic and religio-cultural context."[52] It is my hope that reading the text from an African cultural context would lead to further illumination of the text. According to Eugene Uzukwu, "To inculturate Christianity into Africa would mean a confrontation at depth level between the fundamental message of Christianity and the foundations of African life."[53]

Inculturation hermeneutics thus uses a cultural context – in this case, the African context – as a resource to facilitate the encounter with the text:[54] "The aim is to facilitate the communication of the biblical message within the African milieu, and to evolve a new understanding of Christianity that would be African and biblical."[55] Inculturation hermeneutics evaluates the theological underpinning that results from the encounter between African religion and culture and the Bible to determine the challenge of the biblical

---

50. Turner, *Ritual Process*, 94–97.
51. wa Gatumu, *Supernatural Powers*, 19.
52. wa Gatumu, 20.
53. Uzukwu, "Reconciliation and Inculturation," 275–279.
54. Ukpong, "Biblical Interpretation in Africa," 14.
55. Ukpong, 16.

text for the African context. It also determines possible African contributions to biblical studies.[56]

Rituals – that is, the repeated behaviour recognized in a group to express and embody the symbols and stories central to religion[57] – have the capacity to build or weaken holy community. This is apparent from Paul's comprehensive discussion of ritual behaviour in 1 Corinthians. Paul's response to the question of eating εἰδωλόθυτα (food offered to idols) in 1 Corinthians 8:1—11:1 and the ritual practices during the Lord's Supper (1 Cor 11:17–32) are examples of the possible impact of ritual meals on the community.

David Horrell asserts that focusing on rituals can help us to remember that the "Christian faith was practised and performed as well as 'believed.'"[58] The modern tendency to focus on the cognitive aspects of beliefs to the neglect of practice is anachronistic and will result in the loss of valuable information concerning the early church's life and Paul's teachings.[59] It makes more sense to prioritize the bodily aspects when studying Paul's letters since these are occasional in nature. Gorman states that "the purpose of Paul's letters generally, and of the various kinds of narratives within them, is not to teach theology but to mould behaviour, to affirm or more often – to alter patterns of living, patterns of experience."[60] The Pauline Epistles address practical problems that existed in churches, and Paul points to beliefs and the ritual practices that embody these beliefs in order to correct them.

This focus on the pragmatic aspects of worship ties in well with an inculturation approach because inculturation pertains to internalizing and living the biblical teaching.[61] This approach relates to making the Christian faith culturally permissible and acceptable in Africa.[62]

The African context demands a pragmatic approach since there is no dichotomy between the physical and the spiritual in the African world view.[63]

---

56. Ukpong, 16.
57. Horrell, *Social Ethos*, 80.
58. Horrell, *Solidarity and Difference*, 91. See also Hurtado, *Origins of Christian Worship*, 2–3.
59. Horrell, 91.
60. Gorman, *Cruciformity*, 3.
61. wa Gatumu, *Supernatural Powers*, 20.
62. Nche, Okwuosa, and Nwaoga, "Inculturation in Modern Africa," 1.
63. Bediako, *Christianity in Africa*, 95.

Pobee aptly describes African religious life in this manner: "In any case, it has been said that *homo Africanus* dances out religion. In other words, propositional statements of reality are less important for Africa than the living experience of it."[64] Thus, in ritual performance, experiences are created that instil axioms through bodily ways of knowing.[65]

The African context can provide critical resources for biblical interpretation in this discussion of ritual meals.[66] In chapter 3, I will discuss the African cultural context in detail, underscoring what Bediako refers to as the "sacramental universe."[67] In this world view, there is no separation between the physical and the spiritual.[68] Bediako argues that one of the problems of Western Christianity is that the epistemological dichotomies have drained Christian theology of its vital power.[69] He suggests that this African sacramental world view can help to "restore the ancient unity of theology and spirituality."[70] This book will expose the spiritual nature of ritual meals by creating a dialogue between the Corinthian text and the African context.[71]

This book will argue that Paul's directives for the problem of εἰδωλόθυτα in 1 Corinthians 8:1–11:1 and the Lord's Supper (1 Cor 11:17–34) underscore the vital importance of ritual meals, especially the Lord's Supper and its impact on the holiness transformation of the church. Correct participation – that is, observance of the ritual regulations during the Lord's Supper – will activate transformation that should lead to separation from the Graeco-Roman value system and its religious practices in Corinth and to the ethos of a holy community governed by love. Idolatrous participation in εἰδωλόθυτα, on the other hand, can lead to disruption of *communitas* with Christ, destruction of holy community among believers, and impede the proclamation of the gospel.

Implications gleaned from these findings will then be applied to the question of syncretism in Africa. Anita Leopold defines syncretism as "the negotiations and interaction of new elements into a particular group or domain

---

64. Pobee, "African Theology Revisited," 141.
65. Grillo, "African Rituals," 114.
66. Ukpong, "Biblical Interpretation in Africa," 23.
67. Bediako, *Christianity in Africa*, 95.
68. Bediako, 95.
69. Bediako, 104.
70. Bediako, 105.
71. Nyiawung, "Contextualising Biblical Exegesis," 3–4.

that stem from essentially different groups."[72] In the case of religion, it refers to the mixing of different religions.[73] According to Linda Thomas, syncretism in Africa – more specifically, in South Africa – resulted from a revolt against the colonial missionary enterprise that showed disregard for the religious life already existing in Africa.[74] The way organized religion responded to existing religious beliefs during Islamification and Christianization affected the manner and degree of syncretism.[75]

While inculturation is necessary to make Christianity relevant to the African cultural context, it must be differentiated from syncretism. Elizabeth Isichei asserts that while there is a dialectical relationship between the cultural presuppositions and practices of a new context into which Christianity enters (inculturation), care must be taken to ensure that this does not lead to syncretism, where the core identity of the church is eroded and blurred.[76] Syncretism happens when the central Christian identity and practices that are based on Scripture and accepted by Christian tradition disappear and a new and unrecognizable religion emerges. In contrast, inculturation is the continued dialogue between Christianity and the African cultural context, and its principal objective is to answer questions that arise from this context.

Therefore, this study will examine whether the continued practice of ritual meals to ancestors constitutes syncretism or whether it is an instance of inculturation of the gospel for the African context.

1.3 Outline of Study

This book is divided into four parts. Part 1 explores Victor Turner's ritual theory of social drama in chapter 2 and the African cultural context in chapter 3. These chapters are important as they elaborate on the interpretive method of this research.

Part 2 focuses on liminality and *communitas* in Corinth. Chapter 4 discusses liminality and *communitas* in the Pauline Epistles as life between times,

---

72. Leopold and Jensen, *Syncretism in Religion*, 4.
73. Leopold and Jensen, 2.
74. Thomas, "South African Independent Churches," 39–50.
75. Simpson, "Syncretism," 61–64.
76. Isichei, *History of Christianity*, 4.

between the realms of the flesh and the spirit, and as anti-structure. It also discusses *communitas* as manifested vertically – between God and believers – and horizontally among believers. Chapter 5 looks at the sociohistorical context of ritual meals in 1 Corinthians 8:1–11:1 and 1 Corinthians 11:17–34. Chapters 4 and 5 provide the foundation for a reflective theological study of ritual meals in Corinth.

Part 3 studies εἰδωλόθυτα in 1 Corinthians 8:1–11:1 and the Lord's Supper in 1 Corinthians 11:17–34. Chapter 6 focuses on pagan ritual meals in 1 Corinthians 8:1–11:1. It designates participation in εἰδωλόθυτα in pagan temples as idolatry and indicates that Paul's primary concern was for the holiness of the congregation that was threatened by it. Chapter 7 discusses the Lord's Supper in 1 Corinthians 11:17–34. It underscores the importance of the ritual nature of the passage and suggests that the Lord's Supper is sacramental in that it facilitates *communitas* between Christ and believers and among believers. The Lord's Supper is described as a re-enactment of the believer's union in the death and resurrection of Christ by participating in the narrative of Christ crucified through the ritual conditions, actions, and words. Participating in the Lord's Supper worthily thus creates the potential for community transformation.

Part 4 contains the applications and conclusions of this study. Chapter 8 discusses the inculturation of the Lord's Supper in the African context. It explores how the Lord's Supper can be made relevant to the African cultural context by considering the existing world view, the possibility of including ancestors, adapting liturgy, and reconsidering the frequency and location of the Lord's Supper.

Chapter 9 summarizes and draws conclusions in the light of the previous discussion. It concludes that the African cultural perspective provides an effective lens to enhance the understanding and interpretation of Scripture. It also concludes that the Lord's Supper should be used more effectively as a means for holiness transformation in evangelical churches.

Part 1

Ritual Theory and the African Cultural Context

In the previous chapter, I justified this research, introduced my methodology, and outlined the project. This section will expound on the methodology of this research by elaborating on Turner's ritual theory and the African cultural context. Findings in this section will be applied to the reflective theological discussion of ritual meals in 1 Corinthians 8:1–11:1 and 1 Corinthians 11:17–34.

In chapter 2, I briefly discuss Victor Turner's ritual theology of liminality and *communitas*. This theory provides the tools to explore the spiritual aspects of ritual meals by allowing for the importance of qualitative data because it accepts belief as a valuable source of information for ritual studies. In addition, Turner's theory will facilitate the intersubjective reflective discussion between the text and the African cultural context, emphasizing liminality and *communitas*.

Chapter 3 discusses the African cultural context. The African world view is, above all, spiritual and communal. The similarities between the African world view and Paul's world view make it an excellent lens through which to study ritual meals in Corinth.

The premise of part 1 is that combining Turner's theory of liminality and *communitas* with the African world view of spirituality and communalism may provide an effective means to explore the theological and sacramental nature of Paul's discussion of ritual meals in Corinth.

CHAPTER 2

Turner's Theory as a Lens to Study Ritual Meals in Corinth

2.0 Introduction

This chapter shows how Victor Turner's ritual theory is a viable heuristic device for this research question. Turner's concepts of liminality and *communitas*, along with his emphasis on belief as a cardinal element for ritual studies, provides an ideal means to study ritual meals in Corinth.

This chapter will briefly introduce Turner, give an overview of his ritual theory, and discuss liminality. It will then elaborate on the nature of *communitas*, the communication of the *sacra*, Turner's discussion of anti-structure, and his method for analysing symbols. Finally, the chapter will examine the potential of liminality and *communitas* as conditions conducive to transformation during ritual meals. This chapter is not a full-scale review of Victor Turner's work or criticism of his work but merely an overview of the elements particularly relevant to this research.

Victor Witter Turner (1920–1983) was a British cultural anthropologist who played a significant role in the "radical reconception of ritual."[1] Turner and his wife, Edith Davis, moved to Makanza Village in the Mwinilunga district of Northern Rhodesia (now Zambia), where they worked among the Ndembu people.[2] Most of Turner's ritual theory results from the fieldwork

---

1. Grimes, *Deeply into the Bone*, 121.
2. Deflem, "Ritual, Anti-structure, and Religion," 2.

carried out during this period (December 1950–February 1952 and May 1953–June 1954). Turner veers from the traditional notion – propagated by Emile Durkheim – that ritual serves to maintain social structure. Instead, he portrays ritual as "deeply subversive and creative."[3] Turner's numerous writings illustrate the importance he placed on ritual in religious studies, as his statement below demonstrates:

> If you wish to spay or geld religions, first remove its rituals, its generative and regenerative processes. For religion is not a cognitive system, a set of dogmas, alone; it is meaningful experience and experienced meaning. In ritual one lives through events or through the alchemy of its framing and symbolings; one relives semiogenetic events, the deeds and words of the prophets and saints or if these are absent, myths and sacred epics.[4]

Turner's method includes investigating and exegeting symbols and symbolic behaviour, while also listening to all the voices present in the narrative with respect for the spiritual world view it presents. It emphasizes respect for the religious content of the text, instead of "analyzing away"[5] the spiritual world view in favour of an overemphasis on social significance. This requires accepting that, within the ritual context, religious phenomena must take precedence.

2.1 Overview of Turner's Ritual Theory: Liminality and *Communitas*

Turner's ritual theory of social drama is an adaptation of van Gennep's *Rites of Passage*.[6] This theory suggests that three phases mark all rites of passage: separation, which indicates detachment from an existing state; liminality, a "Betwixt and Between"[7] state; and aggregation, referring to incorporation into

---

3. Grimes, *Deeply into the Bone*, 121.
4. Turner, "Social Dramas," 161.
5. Ezzy, "Faith and Social Science," 313.
6. Van Gennep, *Rites of Passage*.
7. Turner, *Forest of Symbols*, 94

the new state.[8] Turner advances this theory by expounding on the liminal phase, revealing its potential to effect transformation.[9]

According to Turner, the liminal state is ambiguous because it is an in-between state, somewhere between the previous state and the desired state. During transitional rituals, a person goes through a "cultural realm" that is very different from the previous or future state.[10] Participants are portrayed as sexless, positionless, and placeless within the ritual context.[11] People in liminality fall outside customarily accepted classifications and are portrayed as having no possessions or status.[12]

Turner creatively demonstrates that these characteristics might also apply to people experiencing liminality apart from ritual events. According to Turner, the qualities of liminality are evident in religious movements and other cultural movements, and this liminality can become a permanent condition.[13] In such situations, liminality is exemplified in the myths or doctrines and the values or properties of such movements. Turner differentiates between the properties of liminality and status systems: transition/state; homogeneity/heterogeneity; equality/inequality; absence of property/property; and absence of status/status, among others.[14] Turner thus expands on liminality to explain a broader range of in-between circumstances.

Communitas characterizes *the liminal phase*. This quality of relationship embodies the desired values that allow for functional societies. According to Turner, *communitas* is a modality of social relationship and includes a sacred component.[15] Social hierarchy and difference are put on hold during *communitas*, and all participants are equal. "Society is seen as a seamless and structureless whole, rejecting alike status and contract."[16] According to Edith Turner, *communitas* is almost impossible to define, but she describes it as "togetherness itself" and likens it to the African communal philosophy of

---

8. Turner, *Ritual Process*, 94.
9. Strecker, *Liminale Theologie*, 48.
10. Turner, *Ritual Process*, 94.
11. Turner, 95.
12. Turner, 95.
13. Turner, 107.
14. Turner, 106.
15. Turner, 96.
16. Turner, 135.

ubuntu.[17] *Ubuntu* means "humanness or being human,"[18] and it is exemplified in the African proverb "a person is a person through other persons."[19] *Ubuntu* includes values such as "sharing, belonging and participating in collective affairs."[20] We will explore the concept of *ubuntu* in chapter 3.

People in liminality live anti-structurally in relation to the dominant culture of their society. Anti-structure refers to a situation where "behavior and symbolism are momentarily enfranchised from axioms and values that govern the public lives of incumbents of structural positions."[21] During the liminal phase of rites, neophytes go through conditions where hierarchy and social structure fall away, excluding the ritual elders who preside over the proceedings. Anti-structure thus refers to the intentional exclusion of structural categories such as caste, rank, gender, or other political or social classifications that typically divide society.[22] The purpose of such exclusion is to help participants to reflect on their society. Such reflection might encourage them to affirm, reclassify, or act to change structural categories.[23]

According to Turner, there is a constant dialectic between social structure and *communitas*, where anti-structure occurs because one needs the other to become apparent or understandable.[24] Humans are thus temporarily released from structure into *communitas*, only "to return to structure, revitalised by their experience of *communitas*."[25] Society is thus the result of a dialectical relationship between structure and anti-structure.[26]

Transformation happens during the liminal period through "the communication of the *sacra*,"[27] which Turner terms "the heart of the liminal matter."[28] The *sacra* are the sacred information, myths, or ideologies communicated to neophytes during the liminal period. This sacred information serves as the

---

17. Turner, *Communitas*, 9.
18. Khoza, *Attuned Leadership*, xxxvii.
19. Khoza, xxxvii.
20. Khoza, xxxvii.
21. Turner, *Ritual Process*, 166.
22. Turner, 126.
23. Turner, 129.
24. Turner, 128.
25. Turner, 129.
26. St John, *Victor Turner*, 4.
27. Turner, *Forest of Symbols*, 239.
28. Turner, 239.

divine mandate that will obligate the correct relationships and behaviours in neophytes. The communication of the *sacra* has three main components: "(1) exhibitions, 'what is shown'; (2) actions, 'what is done'; and (3) instructions, 'what is said.'"[29] Exhibitions work by provoking thought by exaggerating features or realities or contrasting realities.[30] They challenges participants to think about their society's axioms and their own place in it.

According to Turner, "The neophytes are also told that they are being filled with mystical power by what they see and what they are told. Depending on the purpose of the initiation, this power confers on them capacities to undertake successfully the tasks of their new office, in this world or the next."[31] Thus, the communication of the *sacra* encourages participants to think about their society, conveys what is expected of them, and empowers them to accomplish the mandates given.

The characteristics mentioned above are what make liminality such an effective environment for change. As Grimes affirms, "It [liminality] was the generative, creative principle of ritual in particular and culture in general."[32] During liminality, participants and society experience egalitarian relationships, which aid the development of alternative lifestyles and encourage communal values. Liminality can become the engine of transformation in social structures.[33]

2.2 Rituals and Symbol Analysis

Another of Turner's innovative contributions to ritual studies is his analysis of symbols. Turner defines a symbol as a "storage unit" that contains valuable information about the possible significance of the ritual.[34]

Turner uses language borrowed from Freud's *The Interpretation of Dreams*[35] to describe the qualitative aspects of symbols. The language he borrows from Freud includes "multi-vocality," indicating that a symbol can have many

---

29. Turner, 239.
30. Turner, 240.
31. Turner, 242.
32. Grimes, *Deeply into the Bone*, 122.
33. Strecker, *Liminale Theologie*, 47.
34. Turner, *Drums of Affliction*, 1–2.
35. Freud, *Interpretation of Dreams*.

meanings, "polarity," referring to the two poles of symbols – the physiological pole and the ideological pole of meaning – and "sublimation," referring to the ritual action's ability to suppress anti-social behaviour. According to Turner, ritual language is often a commentary on the non-ritual social life of society.[36]

Ritual symbols transmit the themes present in any given culture. Turner defines themes as "a postulate or position, declared or implied, and usually controlling behavior or stimulating activity, which is tacitly approved or openly promoted in a society."[37] Symbols may express multiple themes, even contradictory ones.

Symbols can carry and transfer energy or power. According to Turner, "The objects and activities in point are not merely things that stand for other things or something abstract, they participate in the powers and virtues they represent."[38] Turner uses the example of the *Mudyi* tree, which is used by the Ndembu of Zambia. The leaves and scrapings of the tree are administered to afflicted persons and are believed to transmit the "life-giving powers thought to inhere in certain objects under ritual conditions."[39] The power of the symbols is derived from their relationship to the principal *significata*.[40] *Significata*, according to Turner, are entities the symbols represent. So, for example, the *Mudyi* tree's *significata* is the life that it represents.

Symbols have three dimensions: the exegetic, the operational, and the positional. The exegetic refers to the meaning ascribed to it by practitioners. Thus, interviewing leaders and laypeople is important to exegete symbols. The operational includes studying what is done with the symbol, and the positional refers to locating the symbol's place within the ritual process and its relationship to other elements in the ritual.[41]

Symbols and their related themes may or may not convey myths. Where myths are absent, meaning is generated by the interaction between the symbol's nominal, substantial, or artefactual aspects:

---

36. Turner, *Blazing the Trail*, 23–24.
37. Turner, "Symbols in African Ritual," 101.
38. Turner, 102.
39. Turner, 103.
40. Turner, 103.
41. Turner, 103.

The nominal basis is the name of the symbol, an element in an acoustic system; the substantial basis is a symbol's [sensorily] perceptible physical or chemical properties as recognised by the culture; and its artifactual basis is the technical changing of an object used in ritual by human purposive activity.[42]

Together, these symbols, themes, and myths form a matrix for cosmologies. Cosmologies are malleable, depending on a society's life, circumstances, and survival needs. A reciprocal relationship exists between myths and rituals – myths can be affirmed through rituals while rituals are the means to create and adjust myths and, by extension, cosmologies.[43]

2.3 Sociological vs Religious Approach

Regarding his approach, Turner wrote, "One has to consider religious phenomena in terms of religious ideas and doctrines, not only, or principally, in terms of disciplines which have arisen in connection with the study of secular institutions and processes."[44] Unfortunately, as the literature review demonstrates, this has not always been the case in scholarly approaches to 1 Corinthians 8:1–11 and 11:17–34. Nevertheless, Turner's approach to religious phenomena proved to be groundbreaking in its comprehensive approach to religious rituals.[45]

Turner's writing reveals a development in his interpretative method. This shift moves from a strictly structuralist framework to one that includes belief as an element in his method.[46] Thus, Turner sees the practitioners' beliefs as invaluable for interpreting the rituals they performed and suggests that researchers would be more effective in their analysis if they considered the belief system of the context they were studying. This position is exemplified in his research and writings. In his doctoral thesis – accepted by the University of Manchester in 1955 and later published as *Schism and Continuity in an*

---

42. Turner, 104.
43. Turner, 105.
44. Turner, *Revelation and Divination*, 195.
45. Ezzy, "Faith and Social Science," 313.
46. Engelke, "Problem of Belief," 3–8.

African Society[47] – Turner follows Durkheim in portraying ritual as merely social phenomena. However, he changed his views after conducting fieldwork among the Ndembu and became explicit in his criticism of the structuralist method of his time, as revealed by the quote below:

> At one time I employed a method of analysis derived essentially from Durkheim via A. R. Radcliffe-Brown. I considered the social function of *Chihamba* concerning the structural form of Ndembu society. However, this method did not enable me to handle the complexity, asymmetry, and antinomy that characterise real social processes, of which ritual performances may be said to constitute phases or stages. I found that ritual action tended thereby to be reduced to a mere species of social action, and the qualitative distinctions between religious and secular custom and behaviour came to be obliterated. The ritual symbol, I found, had its own formal principle.[48]

As we will see below, Turner's willingness to confront qualitative data set him apart as an innovative anthropologist for his time. Matthew Engelke uses Turner's work to address the problem of belief in religious studies and to consider whether neglecting belief can result in the loss of vital information for the anthropologist. Engelke suggests that belief "became an element of method"[49] for Turner and that, for Turner, "religious belief carries with it a certain privilege to understand religious experience – that one's inner life provides the key to explaining the inner lives of other."[50] Engelke notes that Turner's personal life, his acceptance of Catholicism, and his daughter's death played a vital role in his perspective during this period (1957).

This religious approach to ritual studies is evident in Turner's exegesis of the Ndembu ritual of *Chihamba*, a ritual of divination to uncover hidden causes of ills. Here, Turner's explanation of the importance of respecting practitioners' beliefs is evident.

---

47. Turner, *Schism and Continuity*.
48. Turner, *Revelation and Divination*, 186.
49. Engelke, "Problem of Belief," 4.
50. Engelke, "Problem of Belief", 8.

Turner suggests that *communitas*, as the locale of ritual change, does manifest the supernatural power to effect change in participants.[51] He refers to this supernatural power as "the primary act-of-being."[52] Moreover, he compares it to the "I am who I am of Exodus."[53] He suggests that the symbolism of whiteness used during the ritual of *Chihamba* among the Ndembu points to the mystical nature of the "act-of-being" and cautions that any attempt to gain understanding should be made with spiritual reality as the guiding paradigm: "In studying religious symbols, the product of humble vision, we must ourselves be humble if we are to glimpse if only to fully comprehend, the spiritual truths represented by them. In this realm of data only innocence can hope to attain understanding."[54]

Apart from the divine "act-of-being," Turner also gives attention to the role of the dead in *communitas*. In "Death and the Dead in the Pilgrimage Process,"[55] Turner compares African initiation rituals to pilgrimage in the Roman Catholic Church. He points out that the two religious practices differ: African initiation is for the preservation of the community, while Catholic pilgrimage is for personal salvation. However, the two have crucial aspects in common: both give vital importance to the role of the dead in *communitas*.

In African traditional religion, the departed are called upon for physical or biological well-being, such as good crops and human fertility, while Catholics pray for their dead in purgatory and appeal to the dead for help to get to heaven and even for well-being in life.

> In both types of religion, normative *communitas* is postulated among the living and the dead. The dead need the sacrifices and prayers of the living; the living need the fructifying powers of the dead, either as mediators with divinity for the living or as direct emission from the benevolent dead themselves.[56]

The studies mentioned above are examples of Turner's religious framework, which he used in his field research. He did not shy away from belief in

---

51. Turner, *Revelation and Divination*, 23.
52. Turner, 180.
53. Turner, 181.
54. Turner, Revelation and Divination, 197.
55. Turner, *Blazing the Trail*, 29–49.
56. Turner, 42.

the supernatural but insisted that this is essential in analyzing what happens during rituals.[57]

Turner's inclusion of belief as an element of research did draw some criticism from scholars.[58] Engelke, who lauds Turner for his innovative approach, highlights the difficulty of including beliefs in scientific research. He cautions that there is a danger in Turner's emphasis that you must be an insider or practitioner to understand religion since this could diminish the value of the outsider view, which is the general place of an anthropologist.[59]

This raises some critical questions: To what extent does being an insider prevent the researcher from weighing alternatives that seem different from their own views? Could an equal danger present itself in the case of those who approach a text or a context with unyielding scientific methods? An unyielding scientific approach may be limited precisely because it ignores cultural belief systems. Ultimately, all research represents specific viewpoints and belief systems about reality.[60]

This approach, where academic research requires scholars to "sequester their religious experience,"[61] is also present in biblical scholarship and has impacted the study of ritual meals in 1 Corinthians 8:1–11 and 11:17–34. This thesis follows Turner in asserting that "we must not dismiss what cannot be framed within our cognitive traditions as 'non-sense'"[62] and proposes that consideration of religious phenomena can enrich the study of ritual meals in Corinth.

Other criticisms levelled at Turner include concerns about the possible adverse effects of *communitas* and the possibility that liminality may affirm the status quo and, in so doing, marginalize transitional groups such as immigrants or historically oppressed groups such as women or minority communities.

---

57. Turner, *Revelation and Divination*, 195.

58. For examples of works that engage with Turner's contributions, see Rosaldo, Lavie, and Narayan, *Creativity/ Anthropology*; St John, *Victor Turner*; Salamone and Snipes, *Victor and Edith Turner*.

59. Engelke, "Problem of Belief," 8.

60. Ezzy, "Faith and Social Science," 312.

61. Ezzy, 314.

62. Turner, *Revelation and Divination*, 22.

First, we will address the possibility that *communitas* can emerge from negative motivation and hate agendas, ultimately leading to destructive situations. Bjørn Thomassen, for example, cautions that liminality can "become extremely dangerous."[63] This happens when negative *communitas* occurs, which "may also result from liminal moments, dominated by resentment, envy, and hate."[64]

Agnes Horváth also addresses the possible political devastation that liminal conditions may create.[65] She suggests that the liminal conditions created in Hungary by the end of World War II facilitated the acceptance and deep-rootedness of communism in this country.[66] Horváth uses the speeches of Mátyás Rákosi, a communist party leader, to demonstrate how the liminal circumstances facilitated change. According to Horváth,

> The speeches of Rákosi are messages about a common liminal state, communitive information sent to evoke the sympathy of other defenceless human beings sharing the tenderness of the same position of the outcast and sending relief from the pressures of concern and care by substituting their own version of vigilance that is centralised and mechanical, and where they serve as the guides.[67]

These examples underscore the generative potential of liminality and *communitas* for positive or negative change. In this regard, Edith Turner's caution may prove helpful. She states that a distinction should be made between *communitas* and "Emile Durkheim's 'solidarity,' which is a bond between individuals who are collectively in opposition to some other group."[68] As defined by the Turners, *communitas* is by its very nature selfless and willing to put the well-being of the community first.

---

63. Thomassen, "Liminality," 22.
64. Thomassen, 22.
65. Horváth, "Position of the Outcast," 331–347.
66. Horváth, 331.
67. Horváth, 339.
68. Turner, *Communitas*, 5.

The second question relates to the situation of marginal groups such as immigrants, minorities, and previously disadvantaged groups.[69] Jan Berry, writing from a feminist perspective, argues that although Turner discusses female rituals extensively, he does so from a male perspective and thus does not consider the experience of females as a marginal group in society.[70] Berry also points out that Turner's functionalist approach aims at cohesion in society, while the feminist's principle desire is to overturn the status quo. "They [women] do not envisage or ritualise a reversal of power and exploitation, but a different ordering of society, in which hierarchies are not reversed, but abolished."[71]

Objections from this perspective point out that Turner's liminality does not give sufficient consideration to the reality of those who will remain in perpetual liminality – such as those with non-binary gender identities[72] – and the struggle of liminal groups for political and narrative power.[73]

Turner does not expand significantly on the role of political power in liminality or the status of the permanently marginal. However, his theory of liminality provides a helpful framework for scholars interested in these aspects of liminality and *communitas*. The critiques point to areas of potential development in Turners theory, including the fact that not all social dramas result in, or should result in, cohesion, the importance of considering the role of political power when analysing liminal situations, and the place of narrative privilege in the analysis of social dramas.

Despite these cautions, Turner's ritual theory remains helpful for analysing rituals. Moreover, Turner's insistence on an insider view places him ahead of his time since current scholarship advocates for a self-reflective methodology – "a state of being in culture while looking at culture."[74] Reflexivity refers to the researcher's intentional engagement with their relationship to the study they undertake. It "describes the capacity of language and of thought – of any system of signification – to turn or bend back upon itself to become an

---

69. For more examples, see Robertson, "Power and Subjection," 45–59; Bynum, "Women's Stories," 27–51; Weber, "Limen to Border," 525; Ortner, "Theory in Anthropology," 126–166.
70. Berry, "Whose Threshold?," 273–288.
71. Berry, 276.
72. Robertson, "Power and Subjection," 45–59.
73. See Ortner, "Theory in Anthropology," 131; Rosaldo, *Culture and Truth*, 97.
74. Weber, "Limen to Border," 532.

object to itself and to refer to itself."[75] According to Turner, social life is "only comprehensible by the investigator as lived experience, *his/hers* as well as, and in relation to, *theirs*."[76] Such "intersubjectivity"[77] creates a possibility for enhancing research.

Because I undertake this study as an African Christian woman, Turner's theory is the ideal "analytical model"[78] for this study because it will facilitate the reflexive theological dialogue between the texts of 1 Corinthians (8:1–11:1 and 11:17–34) and the African cultural context. Turner's framework will be helpful in analysing the role of supernatural powers during ritual meals and the potential transformation within the Corinthian community because of these processes. This can be done without imposing anachronistic interpretations onto the original participants.

2.4 Conclusion

To summarize Turner's ritual theory of social drama, all rituals are divided into three phases: separation, liminality, and aggregation. Liminality is the phase that creates conditions for transformation because it is during this phase that participants experience *communitas* and receive the sacred information necessary for change. Liminality is an in-between stage, where participants are unclassified and in a process towards their desired condition. People in liminality live anti-structurally to the dominant culture.

Communitas is a sacred relationship that arises during ritual participants' liminal phases. It is an egalitarian relationship, where participants are stripped of status, belongings, and their previous identities and can experience what Turner calls the "essential and generic human bond."[79]

The *sacra* are sacred information imparted to participants in exhibitions, actions, and instructions. This information provokes participants to re-evaluate themselves and their society through exaggerated displays and the mystical

---

75. Babcock, "Reflexivity," 1–14.
76. Turner, "Dramatic Ritual/Ritual Drama," 80–93.
77. Turner, 93.
78. Bell, *Ritual*, 40.
79. Turner, *Ritual Process*, 97.

power they believe in during the ritual. The combination of these factors has ontological value and reshapes the being of participants.[80]

Turner's method of symbol analysis provides valuable tools for the interpretation of rituals. Symbols are storage units that contain information necessary for transformation. Symbols transmit themes that influence human behaviour in a society. Symbols and themes may or may not convey myths. Symbols, themes, and myths make up the network for desired cosmologies in society.

Participants' belief in supernatural power should not be neglected during ritual studies as this provides valuable data for the accurate analysis of ritual and may avoid a reductionist approach that neglects the religious nature of rituals.

This survey suggests that Turner's innovative ideas are still applicable today. However, important cautions are raised in light of postmodern society, where the voices of those previously on the margins demand attention, requiring consideration of the role of political and narrative power. This caution is vital for research that focuses on liminality outside of ritual studies.

Turner's method of symbol analysis provides a framework to explore Paul's discussion of how the consumption of εἰδωλόθυτα in 1 Corinthians 8:1–11:1 and the abuse of the Lord's Supper (1 Cor 11:17–34) might transform the community. It suggests that rituals may effectively create new myths, cosmologies, and, consequently, renewed societies.

In the next chapter, I will discuss ritual meals within the African cultural context.

---

80. Turner, 103.

CHAPTER 3

Ritual Meals in the African Context

3.0 Introduction

The previous chapter provided a brief overview of Victor Turner's ritual theory and suggested that the liminal phase of rituals makes transformation possible because participants experience *communitas*, receive sacred information, and receive spiritual power for change during rituals.

This chapter will discuss liminality, *communitas,* and ritual meals in the African cultural context. An analysis of the African cultural world view is important because a basic understanding of this world view is necessary for any attempt to inculturate Scripture for the African context. Additionally, appreciation of the African context can enhance the understanding of ritual meals in Corinth because the African context has much in common with the first-century Graeco-Roman world view. Using Turner's theory and reading the passage (1 Cor 8:1–11:1 and 1 Cor 11:17–34) from an African cultural world view may thus create new combinations of data that may contribute to a fresh interpretation of ritual meals in Corinth.[1]

This chapter will first discuss liminality and *communitas* in the African cultural context; second, it will explore the ubiquity of ritual meals in modern Africa; third, it will discuss vertical and horizontal *communitas* during ritual meals; and, finally, it will discuss holiness in the context of African ritual meals. This analysis of the African context can answer some aspects of the thesis question: To what degree are rituals still relevant in modern Africa,

---

1. Elliott, *Social-Scientific Criticism*, 15.

and what is the continued impact of ATR on the African Christian church in the twenty-first century? What elements of the African cultural context are helpful for our interpretation of ritual meals in Corinth? How do ritual meals influence change in society?

3.1 Liminality and *Communitas* in the African Cultural Context

In chapter 2, we observed that liminality refers to an in-between state. The African world view of spirituality and communalism creates such liminal conditions. According to Jacob Olupona, the common denominator among African religious beliefs and philosophy is a belief in a three-tiered model of the world where "humans are sandwiched between the sky and the earth (including the underworld)."[2] He explains,

> A porous border exists between the human realm and the sky, which belong to the gods. Similarly, although ancestors dwell inside the earth, their activities interject into human space. African cosmologies portray the universe as fluid, active, and impressionable, with agents from each realm constantly interacting with one another. This integrated worldview leads many practitioners of African religions to speak about the visible in tandem with the invisible.[3]

This belief in the continued connection between the realm of the living and the spiritual realm[4] creates liminal conditions where humans can experience *communitas* with other humans and with the supernatural world where the gods and ancestors reside. This supernatural world is populated with the creator or supreme God and lesser spiritual beings such as ancestors, deities, and heroes.[5] Belief in a creator god is common to most Africans. This creator

---

2. Olupona, *African Religions*, 4.
3. Olupona, 4.
4. Olupona, 4.
5. Olupona, 4.

god, who goes by various names in different tribes,[6] is the most significant spiritual power, generally approached through the mediation of ancestors.[7]

In the African world view, the ancestors are deceased family members who continue to play a central role in the daily lives of their kin.[8] There is a reciprocal relationship between ancestors and the living.[9] While the ancestors act as intermediaries between God and the living and can provide blessings or curses, they depend on the living to remember them through ancestral veneration.[10] These ancestors fade into the obscurity of the spiritual realm when their living kin forget them.[11] The relationship between the ancestors and believers will be discussed in more detail in section 8.2.

Mbiti describes the "living-dead" – as he calls ancestors – as bilingual because they can speak the languages of both the spirits and people.[12] They are "partly human and partly spirit"[13] and, therefore, able to mediate between the living and the divine. They can visit family members and request ritual meals through dreams or divination. Ancestors generally appear to the oldest living relatives.[14] They have the power to influence the lives of families negatively or positively, which causes fear among practitioners of ATR. The living are required to appease the ancestors through rituals, and neglect of this responsibility can lead to calamity in the family.[15] Misfortunes such as sudden death or illness signify that the ancestors have been offended by a person or a family, and such problems can only be resolved by utilizing rituals.[16] This cosmology and attendant practices are still prevalent in Africa.[17]

---

6. Isichei, *History of Christianity*, 6.
7. Olupona, *African Religions*, 22.
8. Muzorewa, *Origins and Development*, 13.
9. Olupona, *African Religions*, 32.
10. Triebel, "Living Together," 189.
11. Mbiti, *African Religions and Philosophy*, 83.
12. Mbiti, 82.
13. Mbiti, 83.
14. Mbiti, 83.
15. Triebel, "Living Together," 189.
16. Triebel, 181.
17. Studies from diverse disciplines and different countries in Africa demonstrate the pervasiveness of ritual practices in urban Africa between 2008 and 2019. See Kepe, McGregor, and Irvine, "Rights of 'Passage,'" 91–111; Simões and Alberto, "Family Rituals and Routines," 454–493.

Kwame Bediako – borrowing from Harold Turner's concept of primal religion[18] – affirms these liminal conditions. Bediako observes that a central aspect of the African world view is "the conviction that man [sic] lives in a sacramental universe where there is no sharp dichotomy between the physical and the spiritual."[19] Accordingly, the physical acts as a vehicle for spiritual power "whilst the physical realm is held to be patterned on the model of the spiritual world beyond."[20] For Bediako, this feature, where the universe is an essentially spiritual unified cosmic system, is the key to the African world view.[21]

The nature of this cosmos and the liminal place occupied by humans, while making it possible for humans to experience the divine presence and live in relationship with the divine, also allows for this continuity of relationship with the ancestors; in other words, it creates the necessary conditions for *communitas*. These sacred relationships are what Vincent Mulago calls "vital participation."[22] The community thus becomes a "transcendent community in which the human components experience and share in divine life and nature."[23] This transcendence takes the community to a higher level: their relatedness is grounded in their union with the divine.[24]

Rituals are of vital importance in such a spiritual cosmology. The belief that spiritual beings can provide happiness and the fear that malignant spirits can bring calamities necessitates rituals that are believed to influence these spiritual beings. Wa Gatumu notes that this relationship consists of two aspects. The first is theoretical and is concerned with beliefs in supernatural powers. The second is practical and seeks to appease supernatural powers through rituals and practices to avert their hostile influence, to help practitioners cope with life pressure, and obtain favours from them.[25]

---

18. Turner, "Primal Religions," 27.
19. Bediako, *Christianity in Africa*, 96.
20. Bediako, 96.
21. Bediako, 196.
22. Bediako, 103.
23. Bediako, 103.
24. Dube, "Postcolonial Feminist Perspectives," 127.
25. Wa Gatumu, *Pauline Concept*, 13.

Africans thus use various rituals to maintain a harmonious relationship between the world of the living and the supernatural world of the spirits.[26] As Laura Grillo notes, "Ritual is the means to negotiate a responsible relationship with the human community, with the ancestors, spirits, divinities and cosmos. African rituals are reflexive strategies seeking practical ends: They establish identity, elicit revelation, access divinity to foster empowerment and effect transformation."[27] Rituals and practices infuse this community life with symbolic meaning, serve as acts of worship, mark significant life changes, and have educational purposes. Rituals thus serve a liminal purpose. As Mudimbe and Kilonzo say, "Rituals bring together interacting universes, a visible and an invisible one; the primacy of the invisible universe and the existence of a supreme being and points to an immanent principle of solidarity between the universes."[28]

Diviners and traditional healers are central figures who oversee rituals. In addition, supernatural spirits can inhabit the bodies of diviners to convey their messages when invoked.[29] Common rituals include pregnancy and birth rites, puberty and initiation rites, death rites, and a host of everyday rites required for daily living. Performing rites may include eating, drinking, dancing, and copulating. The most significant rites result in markings on the body, which inform the rest of the community of the individual's compliance with required rituals and rites and serve as identity markers among various tribes. Consequently, children and youth are introduced and assimilated into the community through rituals of birth, puberty, and an array of threshold rites, which are also the means by which they receive the myths and knowledge needed for life in the community.[30]

Personhood is achieved within communal life. Personal development occurs through various rituals and fulfilling obligations to the community.[31] The person's significance within the community highlights the life-altering power that ritual meals hold in African communal life. We will explore various rituals in more detail in the following sections.

---

26. Mudimbe and Kilonzo, "Philosophy of Religion," 53.
27. Grillo, "African Rituals," 112.
28. Mudimbe and Kilonzo, "Philosophy of Religion," 53.
29. Mbiti, *African Religions and Philosophy*, 74.
30. Mbiti, 118.
31. Menkiti, "Person and Community," 172.

The African world view is communal and is best described by the African adage "A person is a person through other persons."[32] According to John Mbiti, community is the common world view that undergirds African life. He contends that this sense of kinship is "one of the strongest forces in traditional African life."[33] The sense of community or kinship includes immediate family and people from the same tribe, animals, plants, and objects. Strangers are included in this circle because of the belief that all people originate in the great creator. Kinship also includes those not yet born and the deceased or ancestors.[34] Mbiti explains that "only in terms of other people does the individual become conscious of his own being, his own duties, his privileges, and responsibilities towards him and towards other people."[35] This means that all suffering and misfortune, as well as good fortune, are experienced as affecting the community.

A belief in actual relatedness undergirds this communalism. Thus, in the eSwatini culture, the first duty of two strangers who meet on the road is to determine how they are related. Musa Kunene explains that such strangers will share their surnames to determine whether they share a common ancestor.[36] If they find that they are related, they will relate to each other accordingly and intermarriage will be discouraged. However, failure to find a connection does not imply that people are not related because Africans believe that all humanity originates in the creator or the supreme God.[37] All humanity is thus related because of their common origin and are, therefore, included and welcomed as kin.

The universe is also part of kinship relationships, which requires humans to live in harmony with the earth. Like every other aspect of their lives, Africans view nature through a religious lens. Human beings are at the centre of creation and are, therefore, responsible for its care. Order in nature is essential, and divergence from familiar patterns can be a source of great

---

32. Tutu, *God Is Not a Christian*, 21.
33. Mbiti, *African Religions and Philosophy*, 105.
34. Mbiti, 135.
35. Mbiti, 106.
36. Kunene, *Communal Holiness*, loc. 2595, Kindle.
37. Kunene, loc. 2606, Kindle.

distress. Thus, human beings uphold the moral order to maintain harmony and peace within the community.[38]

Africans maintain religious order by honouring moral codes and taboos. They believe in a mystical order that must be upheld. This order includes both power from the creator and dark powers that can cause havoc in society. Supernatural powers are also believed to inhabit inanimate objects in nature. Everything in the universe is generally viewed in terms of their usefulness to the advancement of humanity and contributes to the African communal life. Bediako affirms this view, stating that the objectives of African religions are this-worldly – focusing on the perpetuation of humanity in the present rather than on their eternal destiny – and that "this-worldliness encompasses God and man [sic] in an abiding relationship which is the divine destiny of humankind, and the purpose and goal of the universe."[39]

Moral and social order in society are achieved by individual and community regulations that dictate a code of conduct,[40] and hardships are believed to be the result of neglecting communal responsibilities to the ancestors, the elderly, and family shrines.[41] For example, the Ndembu of Zambia see illness as "a communal condition caused by imbalances in relationships with spirits, kinfolk, and members of one's community."[42] Healing is thus a result of curing the underlying social and spiritual disruption. The profoundly spiritual nature of these kinship relationships guides how kinsfolk relate to one another.

The intersection between communalism and a spiritual world view creates vital participation or, to use Turner's terminology, *communitas*. According to Mulago, vital participation is "the vital link which unites vertically and horizontally the living and departed; it is the life-giving principle which is found in them all. It results from a communion or participation the same reality, the same vital principle, which unites a number of beings with one another."[43] He further explains that this includes a union of the whole person

---

38. Musopole, *Being Human in Africa*, 10.

39. Bediako, *Christianity in Africa*, 101. This view is also taken by Mbiti, *African Religions and Philosophy*, 5; Ezeanya, "Spirit World," 36.

40. Space does not allow for a full discussion of African community ethics. See Mbiti, *African Religions and Philosophy*, 199–210; Kalu, "Gods as Policemen," 109–131; Adegbola, "Theological Basis of Ethics," 116–136.

41. Olupona, *African Religions*, 2.

42. Olupona, 3.

43. Mulago, "Vital Participation," 138.

and all that belongs to them and that it also includes all that belonged to the ancestors. Thus, those who are later added by marriage or, for example, by becoming blood brothers,[44] share in the same benefits as the family. Such a union is "not a merely legal, political or social result, but one which influences being (*ntu*)[45] itself, and modifies it intrinsically."[46] The inclusion of physical items has cosmological implications because it signifies that land, animals, and other resources are available to all who share in this participation.

This participation is a union with the life-force or "defused life," as Mulago describes it. This life-force can, by extension, reside in a person's belongings or in a departed spirit. It can increase, for example, when a person is appointed as king or healer. In such an instance, that person receives all the vital energies of the ancestors, which strengthens their being (*ntu*), making them a "synthesis of the ancestors and the living expression of the supreme being and his divine bounty."[47] The living must continually receive the vital force of the ancestors through religious activities, thus increasing their life-force.

This life-force can also decrease, for instance, when humans practise malice, as in the case of sorcery, or violate the rights of others. The prime evil, according to Mulago, is to "disregard someone's vital rank" in the community.[48] Thus, honouring all participants – visible and invisible – in the kinship and complying with social responsibilities and rituals increases life-force, while neglecting these duties decreases and diminishes the vital participation of the offender in the community. Therefore, practical life consists of "maintaining solidarity between the members of the community, improving solidarity between the members of the community, improving the communication and circulation of life, increasing vital force and preventing the diminution of life."[49] This is done through the ancestor cult, the hero-cult,

---

44. Some tribes affirm covenants by consuming blood – their own or that of their fellow participants. To cite an example from the Gbaya of Congo, when young men complete the initiation rituals, they make a cut on their stomach, dip a piece of manioc root in the blood, and eat it. Boys may exchange roots with a close friend or drink their blood. This covenant is a covenant to keep the secrets of the ritual experience from those who are yet uninitiated. Christensen, *African Tree of Life*, 24.

45. *Ntu* is a word found in many Bantu languages and can be translated as a person, personhood, or human being.

46. Mulago, "Vital Participation," 142.

47. Mulago, 146.

48. Mulago, 147.

49. Mulago, 149.

and the maintenance of social order. According to this belief, ethics and law flow from the ontic connection between humans, creation, and the spiritual world.[50] According to Mulago, all taboos and prohibitions in society can be explained in the light of vital participation.[51]

This section has explored liminality and *communitas* in the African context. Liminality results from the belief that humans live between the physical and the spiritual realms. Africans believe that the cosmos is filled with spiritual powers. *Communitas* refers to the vital participation of people, both vertically – when humans participate in the supernatural world of the ancestors – and horizontally – when they participate with one another in the same earthly reality, which includes components such as land and belongings. People participate in the spiritual realm through rituals. Therefore, rituals are a means to achieve *communitas* with those who reside in the spiritual world – including the ancestors – and are central to the African cultural context.

3.2 The Ubiquity of Ritual Meals in Modern Africa

This section – which will discuss the nature and pervasiveness of ritual meals for ancestral veneration in modern Africa – has several objectives. First, it will discuss the nature of ritual meals in the African context. Second, it will explore whether Christianization and Islamification of the continent has impacted the practice of ritual meals for ancestral veneration. Finally, it will consider whether ancestral veneration is viewed as worship – and thus, idolatry – or seen simply as paying homage to departed loved ones.

The following anthropological studies and personal examples will draw from various African societies, including the Xhosa and Northern Sotho people of South Africa, the Gbaya from Cameroon and the Central African Republic, and the Sadãma from Southwest Ethiopia. The hypothesis is that ritual meals still play a pivotal role in the development and transformation of persons and communities within various contexts.

It is necessary to begin with a discussion of the nature of ritual meals in the African context. Meals are foundational and serve various functions within African communities. While the nature and functions of ritual meals

---

50. Mulago, 150.
51. Mulago, 150.

in the African culture is diverse, several commonalities can be outlined.[52] The place and role of food and drink in African communities is an outflow of the philosophy of spirituality and communalism. According to Izunna Okonkwo, "A meal appears to be the most basic and most ancient symbol of friendship, love and unity within the traditional African context. Most Africans believe that when food and drinks are shared, it is a sign that life is shared."[53] This sharing includes people from one's homestead, the extended community, visiting strangers, and departed family members – who are all kinship members, as explained earlier. For example, among the Gbaya people, meals unify the community, and this unity is exemplified in how people eat. The rich meal traditions of the Gbaya from Cameroon and the Central African Republic provide valuable insights into the nature of ritual meals; like other African peoples, they share a spiritual world view that is reflected in their religious life and language.

The Gbaya believe in sharing meals, and eating alone is strongly discouraged. People in a household generally eat together from the same bowl, although adult men eat with boys while girls eat with their mothers. Meals have a three-part structure that includes washing hands, eating together from the same bowl, and washing hands at the end of the meal. Like all other aspects of Gbaya life, meals are viewed as religious activities.[54] Therefore, kinship and friendship meals endeavour to maintain peace between the living and the ancestors who are believed to be responsible for the safekeeping of the community.[55]

Spiritual power is also central to African meals. As Adewuya explains, "In the African consciousness, a strong sense of mystical power is attached to the human action of sharing a meal. The universe is imbued with a powerful energy, which may be tapped by spirits, medicine men, witches, priests and rainmakers."[56] Therefore, the meal can become an occasion to participate in the transference of spiritual power and communion with spiritual beings such as deities and the ancestors and is thus an opportunity for *communitas*.

---

52. Sekhukhune, "Symbolism," 64–68.
53. Okonkwo, "Eucharist," 112.
54. Christensen, 15.
55. Christensen, 16.
56. Adewuya, "Revisiting 1 Corinthians 11:27–34," 107.

The ancestors are included in meals through ritual sacrifices and offerings of food and libations. Mbiti asserts, "The food and libations so offered, are tokens of the fellowship, communion, remembrance, respect and hospitality, being extended to those who are the immediate pillars or roots of the family."[57] All meals generally include some way to invite and acknowledge the spiritual. This might take the form of saying a blessing over the meal, leaving food on your plate after eating, or dispensing drink on the floor for the departed.

The next main point for discussion is the question whether modernization dispensed with ancestral ritual meals.? The following examples suggest that ritual meals to petition ancestors are still present in various rural and urban communities in Africa.[58] A recent study by Phatudi Sekhukhune describes the prevalence of ritual meals among the North Sotho people of South Africa.[59] Sekhukhune suggests that food symbolism can be divided into transactional, sacrificial, communal, and restrictive symbolism. He suggests that these functions are present in all African societies, particularly in the Northern Sotho community. Sekhukhune states that although sacrificial meals are more directly aimed at ancestor veneration, all ritual meals include the recognition and inclusion of the ancestors as they are still a part of the community.[60]

Another example is the Xhosa-speaking people of the Peddie District in Eastern Cape Province, South Africa. Andrew Ainslie describes the pivotal role of ritual meals in distributing and maintaining power or social influence among this post-colonial South African tribe. Ainslie suggests that rituals practised by rural and urban people are performed as a means to contest two cultural tropes – intra-homestead, *ukwakh'umzi* (to build the home) and inter-homestead, *masincedisane* (let us help each other).[61] According to Ainslie, "Their activities and interaction in the consumption of traditional beer, brandy and the meat of ritually slaughtered animals are geared towards

---

57. Mbiti, *African Religions and Philosophy*, 105.
58. Due to limitations of space, I cannot discuss more examples. For further examples from diverse disciplines and countries in Africa that demonstrate the pervasiveness of ritual practices in urban Africa between 2008 and 2019, see Kepe, McGregor, and Irvine, "Rights of 'Passage,'" 91–111; Simões and Alberto, "Family Rituals and Routines," 454–493.
59. Sekhukhune, "Symbolism," 65.
60. Sekhukhune, 64.
61. Ainslie, "Harnessing the Ancestors," 530–552.

performing and contesting these to cultural scripts."[62] By contesting, he means that ritual meals are used to contest traditional social structures, as when female heads of households initiate ritual meals – a task that traditionally belonged only to males.

Ainslie observes that older Xhosa men maintain their social stature during ritual practices, both because they generally own the livestock needed for sacrifices and because it is their ritual responsibility to slaughter the animals. Another aspect that reinforces the position of these older men pertains to the issue of sacred spaces. Rituals may only be performed at the *imizi* (homestead), and a dwelling only qualifies as an *imizi* if a male homestead head is present, which means that many women-headed households are not considered *imizi*.[63] These factors allow older men in the Peddie District to maintain some level of control over the homestead, even over family members who have moved away to cities in search of employment. Although some rituals do take place in townships and urban homes, the *imizi* remains the primary place for effective rituals.

The belief in the importance of sacred space can bring homestead members, scattered by industrialization and migrant labour, back to the homestead. Family members return from various places to participate in rituals, motivated by fear that calamity might strike if they fail to honour their ancestors. During these rituals, strict adherence to regulations concerning gender, generations, and spaces is paramount because failure to do so might displease the ancestors, who may then reject the sacrifices. The approval of the ancestors is signified by the bellowing of the sacrificial animal. All ritual regulations are rigorously observed because all the time, money, and personal sacrifices of the participants would be in vain if the animal does not bellow. The sacrifice would be invalid, and the entire ritual would have to be repeated.[64]

Ainslie describes how costly and time-consuming these ritual practices have become over time but also stresses that they are still faithfully adhered to, even by those claiming to be Christians. Most Christians, except for members of a few denominations, continue to participate in rituals, justifying their

---

62. Ainslie, 530.
63. Ainslie, 537.
64. Ainslie, 540.

participation by drawing a distinction between their traditional responsibilities and their religious beliefs.[65] Ainslie says,

> I found that Christian belief did not always mean that people felt barred from conducting the rituals that are specifically linked to the ancestors, just that they had to finesse their reasons for doing so. However, for the members of some denominations, notably the Seventh Day Adventists, hosting slaughter ritual is unacceptable.[66]

Thus, ritual meals still take place regularly. It is reported that more than 103 separate rituals were held in Hobana village, South Africa, between November 2000 and October 2001.[67] This suggests that ritual practices are still essential for the Xhosa-speaking people of the Peddie District. Although there have been some modifications made to these rituals due to the demands of the twenty-first century, they are still governed by communalism and a spiritual world view. The negative aspects of these rituals include the fear that ancestors might bring calamity upon the living if they do not faithfully practise these rituals, the role played by rituals in maintaining social hierarchies, and the conflict for believers between participation with ancestors and their relationship with Christ. For a more detailed discussion, see chapters 6 and 8.

Another example is the Sadăma of Southwest Ethiopia, food rituals are dynamic means to navigate relationships, teach community values, create distinctions between social classes, generations, and genders, and connect with the spiritual realm.[68] Food rituals are also used in cases where sorcery is suspected and the elders are called in to curse the sorcerers.[69]

For the Gbaya, their spiritual world view is reflected in their language. For instance, the word *So*, meaning soul or spirit, is prevalent in their language. *So* is best understood in its compound form: "So-daa, soul or spirit of the father (ancestor); so-naa, soul or spirit of the mother; so-dan, spirit of twins; so-fio, spirit of death or of the dead (again, a term for ancestors)."[70] When joined to

---

65. Ainslie, 544.
66. Ainslie, 544.
67. Ainslie, 546.
68. Hamer, "Commensality," 128.
69. Hamer, 135.
70. Christensen, *African Tree of Life*, 28.

a compound word, *So* depicts the wide variety of spirits that require Gbaya rituals. The Gbaya do not have priests, but they have seers who serve various purposes such as consulting the spirits to find the cause of problems and representing the community in ritual functions. Space is also critical because spirits have their own spaces where they dwell. *So-kao*, the territorial spirits, dwell in the savanna bush, while the *so-daa* dwell in the villages. Sacrifices to the *so-daa* are made at a shrine next to the house on the right-hand side, customarily by the man of the house. Ritual meals are a means of navigating the relationship with the spiritual world.

Apart from these anthropological studies, my personal experience as a minister in both South Africa and Mozambique affirms that the practice of ritual meals to ancestors is widespread. Among my congregation members who participated in ritual meals to petition ancestral spirits was an older woman who wanted to obtain guidance from the ancestors because the hospitals could not diagnose or heal her disease. This lady was a long-time member of the church where I served as a local pastor. I also ministered to a young couple who called upon their family to participate in ritual meals because their marriage was in trouble and they wanted the blessing of the ancestors. They believed that their misfortune resulted from the fact that they had failed to perform rituals to petition their ancestors when they first got married.

Another case involved a teenage girl who sought "deliverance" because she had been dedicated as a bride to her ancestors. This incident took place while I was a teacher in a secondary school in Johannesburg, South Africa. The young girl fainted in class and would not wake up. She was taken to the hospital, where she was informed that nothing was physically wrong with her. The doctor who attended the girl advised me to take her to her pastor. I began questioning the girl, who told me a story that seemed rather farfetched. She admitted that as a very young girl, she had been dedicated as a bride to her ancestors during a family ritual. According to her, this was the beginning of her suffering. She confessed to sleepwalking to the graveyard, having dreams and visions, and becoming very sick when she entered into romantic relationships with boys. This dependence on the ancestral cult can be a source of suffering. In the example cited above, the young woman suffered immensely. Her sleepwalking put her in danger of physical harm, her affliction affected her performance in school, and she was unable to maintain normal relationships with the opposite sex.

In my own family, those who have turned to Christ have had no association with ancestral veneration. However, as a child, I have attended rituals in the homes of unbelieving families. During these rituals, animals were slaughtered, their blood was cooked and eaten, drinks were poured on the ground for the departed family members, and trips were made to the graveyard on special occasions to ensure the family's well-being.

Ritual meals continue to be a foundational element of communal life in many African communities. Ritual meal practices are rooted in the African cultural philosophy of spirituality and communalism, serving various functions within the communities. Spiritual power plays a key role during ritual meals, and the function of these meals is to maintain relationships with the spiritual world and shape the community. The examples of the Sotho, Xhosa, Gbaya, and Sadãma peoples, along with my personal experiences, affirm that ancestor ritual meals are still prevalent in both rural and urban areas in Africa. This raises important questions: Are there circumstances in which Christians can continue to practise ritual meals to ancestors? If so, how would these rituals need to be transformed so that they are appropriate for the Christian context?

3.3 Vertical *Communitas* during Ritual Meals

In African society, ritual meals serve as a context for *communitas* with the supernatural world and fellow community members. It is challenging to separate vertical from horizontal interaction in ritual meals because *communitas* with the supernatural and with participants is integrated or simultaneous. However, dividing it in this manner helps to examine its different aspects. Africans believe that participation with spiritual powers during rituals creates conditions for transformation. We will now look at how the supernatural connects with participants during ritual meals.

3.3. 1. Ancestral spirits may request or mandate a ritual meal.

Ainslie notes that various ritual practitioners among Xhosa women testified that they had dreams in which the ancestors mandated ritual slaughter.[71] These women would then seek permission from the male elders of their homestead to carry out these rituals since they are not authorized to perform

---

71. Ainslie, "Harnessing the Ancestors," 545.

these sacred duties. Rituals requested by women include rites of passage, rites associated with marriages, funerals, or graduations, and many other rituals associated with significant life stages.

Dreams are also the usual means by which the Sadãma ancestors mandate sacrifices. For example, a dream about a deceased father always signifies that a bull, a ram, or honey should be offered to the ancestors. According to Hamer, "Dreaming is considered one of the most important channels of communication with the supernatural world and to fail to honour the request of a dead father is to risk an untimely death."[72] This belief emphasizes the importance of continuing to offer ritual sacrifices amid changes in society, especially with increasing numbers of the Sadãma obtaining a Western education.

For the Gbaya from Cameroon and the Central African Republic, meal rituals are also performed in response to directions from the ancestral spirits. According to Christensen, a household head might have a dream in which his *so-daa* (ancestral spirit) instructs him to perform a ritual.[73] This ritual would be performed in the shrine next to the homestead by the community's priest. Christensen uses the term "priest" to include medicine men, diviners, and other ritual specialists who have been dedicated to the *so-daa*. The sacrifice involves a chicken – preferably one that is white and in perfect condition.

The priest first ties the rooster's legs together and hit its head against the altar while praying prayers of praise and petition for the family. He pours the chicken's blood over the termitaries, the wood, and the ground around the fireplace. Then he cooks the rooster in a pot and adds some salt and sesame oil. The priest's wife brings a container of *kam* (manioc root), and the priest uses the *kam* to look for the chicken's gizzard in the pot. He then throws the meat and manioc on the ground while reciting a prayer of dedication to the ancestor. Finally, the priest eats the rest of the chicken and cleans the shrine. Later, he returns to the shrine and eats any remaining food.[74]

People use rituals to invite the ancestors to intervene in their lives. Such rituals often follow life cycles or seasonal cycles. According to Olupona, "Divinities and ancestors have personalised yearly festivals during which

---

72. Hamer, "Commensality," 328
73. Sekhukhune, "Symbolism," 30–31.
74. Sekhukhune, 30.

adepts offer sacrificial animals, libations and favoured foods."[75] These regular rituals enable the supernatural to bless the community with needed resources for life.

People call on the spirits of the ancestors in times of existential crisis such as chronic illness, suspicion of witchcraft, or natural calamity.[76] They consult diviners to diagnose the problems and prescribe the necessary rituals. "Diviners in Africa, whether female or male, are perceived by their communities as mediums of spiritual 'forces'."[77] Spiritual entities can express themselves through the diviner's body and answer the questions of the living.[78] The presence of a diviner is a way by which supernatural entities can manifest during rituals.

3.3.2. Participating in meal rituals is believed to be a means of *communitas* with the ancestral spirits.

This is reflected in the prayers inviting the ancestral spirits to be present during the ritual meal, offering food portions to the ancestors while eating a portion, petitions and requests made to the ancestors during a meal, and the formal closing prayers. Physical signs – such as the noise made by the animal to be slaughtered in the Northern Sotho rituals – are essential to signify the presence of spirits. An example of this is the ritual performed by the Gbaya following an unsuccessful hunt. The hunters gather around a *kolo* or *gété* tree, performing purification rites as they offer the spirits salt, dried manioc, and tobacco. The hunters "wash their livers" by admitting their wrongs and anger, mixing water and manioc to form a white liquid that represents purity. The hunters then stand around in a circle and pass a calabash around while saying these words: "We wash away our anger . . . we wash it away right before you! Grant us animals for the hunt."[79] If the hunt is successful, another sacrifice is made the following day, offering the raw liver to the *so-daa* with these words: "Here is your part! Eat your part first, then we'll eat ours! Now grant us another animal, still bigger than this one!"[80] This thank offering, the words "right before you," and the sharing of the meat with

---

75. Olupona, *African Religions*, 56.
76. Devisch, "Divination in Africa," 80.
77. Devisch, 80.
78. Devisch, 80.
79. Christensen, *African Tree of Life*, 32.
80. Christensen, 32.

the spirits reveal the Gbaya's belief that the spirits are present and participate with them in this ritual meal.

Participation with the ancestors is also reflected in words uttered by the Gbaya during the offering of the first fruits of the harvest. For example, a son might present some corn from his first harvest to his father with these words: "Father, here are the first fruits of my cornfield, which I've brought for you to eat! Give *so-daa*, the spirit of [your] father, his part so that I may eat mine, too!"[81] The son's words point to the belief that the *so-daa* must eat first before the rest of the family participates. The father then grinds the corn, mixes it with water, and pours it over the family shrine dedicated to the *so-daa*, saying, "Father, look at my child's corn, which he was able to produce because you gave him health and strength. The corn grew well. And he brought your part to me so I can offer it to you! I hereby give you your part! Here it is!"[82] Finally, the family roasts some corn over an open fire, and everyone is free to eat. The whole family, along with the departed, participates in the Feast of the First Fruits.

The burial ritual – also known as the cooling of the ancestral spirit – practised by the Shona of Zimbabwe reflects fellowship between the living and the departed: "According to Shona informants, the purpose of "cooling" the spirit is to help the deceased to settle down in his new mode of existence as a member of the spirit world, without severing of any of the bonds with kin and friends left among the living."[83] In order to "cool" the spirit, the funeral must take place during the early morning or late afternoon hours. First, water and a very thin maize porridge are poured over the gravesite, and a tree is then planted to provide shade. Next, participants eat roasted, unsalted meat during the ceremony, which is followed by washing rituals. This ritual aims to make the spirit comfortable in the world of the spirits while still maintaining communion with living relatives through the shared meal.[84]

3.3.3. Spirits exercise power over the outcome of ritual meals.

It is believed that the spirits exercise power over the outcome of ritual meals and this outcome is dependent on the intention and disposition of

---

81. Christensen, 33.
82. Christensen, 33.
83. Bucher, *Spirits and Power*, 58.
84. Bucher, 59.

the spirits. Participants should ensure meticulous observance of rules and regulations during the ritual to avoid angering the spirits. For example, the Xhosa people take great care to avoid offending the ancestors, which could result in the sacrificial animal being rejected by the ancestors. Procedures, roles, spaces, and regulations are observed meticulously, including food distribution after the ritual slaughter.

The division of meat, brandy, *mqombothi* (homemade traditional beer), and purchased or bottled beer is done based on age and gender, overseen by a respected man who hold the position of *injoli* (apportioner). *Amaxhego* (old men) get the biggest share of the available brandy and *mqombothi*. In general, *abafazi* (women) are treated as an undifferentiated group when the *injoli* makes his allocations.[85] Rituals must be repeated if the regulations regarding roles, gender, space, and so on are not followed meticulously.

Supernatural powers are believed to play a pivotal role during African ritual meals. They may mandate rituals or be invited by people to meet a personal or communal need. Such supernatural powers infuse rituals with spiritual powers and determine the outcome of these rituals. Depending on adherence to ritual regulations, the supernatural powers may respond favourably or reject the ritual meals offered by the living kin.

3.4 Horizontal *Communitas* in African Ritual Meals

Ritual meals are effective means to create *communitas* among participants and bring about community transformation. First, meals provide a means for *communitas* among members, thus strengthening the community.

Among the Gbaya, there are different types of kinship and friendship meals, which have various functions. For instance, they may be used to set apart and consecrate a newlywed couple's home. A ritual meal also marks the stage when a woman is permitted to eat with her husband's mother, which can only happen once she has given birth to a child. The wife offers a meal to her mother-in-law, signifying that they may share such meals in the future. These rituals mark and celebrate significant transformations in relationships and, in the case of a home, even people's property.

---

85. Ainslie, "Harnessing the Ancestors," 541.

Meals are also used to mend relationships and make amends. The words "now we can eat together again"[86] are frequently used to mark the end of a quarrel. Meals are also a significant tool to build relationships with the broader community. The Gbaya also celebrate farewell meals, which could be before a person leaves home on a journey or when a family member is about to die. In the case of death, an older man might call his family together and ask them to share one final meal with him. This is an opportunity to say their final goodbyes and for the dying man to bless the family and share vital information with them. The dying man greets his family with these words: "When you eat together again, remember me!"[87] Eating together underscores the change but also the continuity of these relationships.

Second, ritual meals provide the opportunity to effect transformation within the community. For instance, ritual meals among the Xhosa of South Africa reflect the impact of the changing times. Women may utilize ritual meals to challenge the patriarchal system and gain some power in this traditionally patriarchal culture. According to Ainslie, women are increasingly initiating rituals – which is contrary to tradition – on the basis that the ancestors instructed them in a dream to do so.[88] Historically, only men could initiate ritual meals. Therefore, when women initiate rituals, this affects the distribution of power within the tribe, illustrating the potential of ritual meals to transform power dynamics within a community. Although women continue to adhere to all the ritual regulations concerning their role and place, they are empowered by initiating and financing rituals.

Social class systems are also addressed, with the poor being cared for during ritual meals among the Xhosa. Ainslie notes that women from lower social classes or poorer homesteads are often invited to work with the higher class family during ritual celebrations. This invitation creates an opportunity for those of higher and lower social ranks to interact on an equal footing, which is something that does not typically happen. Ainslie explains, "Thus ritual 'work parties' serve as important sites of sociality by providing the space, especially for women, to socialise and work together."[89]

---

86. Christensen, *African Tree of Life*, 4.
87. Christensen, 24.
88. Ainslie, "Harnessing the Ancestors," 545.
89. Ainslie, 543.

Non-kin are included in rituals because they serve as witnesses, thus legitimizing the ritual event. Their presence also bolsters the male host's stature within the community and makes the ritual more acceptable to the ancestors. Ainslie explains that "through their attendance and participation, non-kin local people thus contribute to 'building the homestead' by recognising the host homestead (and its ancestors) as one of their own, legitimising its members and their activities, and bearing witness to ritual and moral projects."[90]

This inclusion of non-kin reveals the broader impact of rituals on the community and the mutual uplifting of homesteads. For example, during these ritual work parties, poor people receive homemade nutritional beer, meat, and vegetables. In this way, these meals provide food for people suffering from food insecurity.

Third, ritual meals function to uphold and perpetuate existing social relationships, as in the case of the Sadāma of South West Ethiopia. *Halōli* is the social code by which the Sadāma live. The elders – both the living and the departed – are responsible guardians of this social code. *Halōli* can be interpreted as "'the true way of life' and, depending on the context, could concern honesty in giving evidence, adherence to the principle of mutuality, generosity and the avoidance of greed."[91] This code is taught within families and reinforced in the community through various methods. A foundational principal of *Halōli* is that self-worth is based on the accumulation of wealth and power but that such wealth and power can only be acquired through the practice of self-restraint and the generous sharing of resources, especially food, with the community.[92]

Food rituals are fundamental in developing and maintaining cohesive communalism for the Sadāma.[93] According to John Hamer, the elders – those who are living and the deceased forefathers – must be honoured first at every meal, and certain words should be avoided while the elders are eating so that their position of authority will not be contaminated.[94] There are also

---

90. Ainslie, 543.
91. Hamer, "Commensality," 128.
92. Hamer, 130.
93. Hamer, 126–44.
94. Hamer, "Myth," 328.

rules of etiquette that must be observed during ceremonial meals to honour these elders.

Food plays a vital role in negotiations during elder councils because food production, ownership, and distribution are paramount to self-worth and communal well-being. Gatherings are organized where the elders preside to hear cases and offer solutions based on the *Halōli* code.[95] Therefore, it is not surprising that there are stringent rules governing the preparation and distribution of food at these council meetings. According to Hamer, presenting or withholding food serves as a sign of acceptance or rejection during council meetings.[96] This leads to competition among community members, who use food offerings as a means of gaining the favour of the elders. The privileges of commensality may be withdrawn in the case of those who transgress this code. Food sharing or abstinence creates a clear distinction between social classes, generational categories, and even gender.

This section discussed the impact of African ritual meals on the community. These meals mark and celebrate the transformations of individuals and relationships. Communities may use ritual meals to mend relationships or deal with past transgressions. Meals also signify changes in relationship status among participants. Ritual meals provide the opportunity to challenge and change existing status and class systems in the community and allow for interaction and mutual upliftment among communities or homesteads. On the other hand, people may also employ ritual meals to uphold and perpetuate the existing social hierarchy. The regulations governing food distribution and seating during rituals may lead to corruption and abuse because participants may vie for the best positions during ritual meals and, by extension, within the community.

3.5 Holiness in African Ritual Meals

This section will examine the idea of holiness in African ritual meals. Such a discussion is essential to answer this question: What aspects of African ritual meals may aid in understanding holiness in ritual meals in 1 Corinthians 8:1–11:1 and 11:17–34?

---

95. Hamer, "Commensality," 133.
96. Hamer, 134.

According to Mbiti, holiness in ATR is exhibited primarily in moral and ritual matters.[97] In ATR, holiness is viewed as an essential element in a functional relationship with the spiritual world. As mentioned in section 3.1, ATR holds a spiritual view of the universe and see rituals as the primary means of relating to the spiritual realm. Therefore, we can say that the objective of most ritual practices in African culture is the sanctification of life.

According to Evan M. Zuesse, Africans view all of life as both sacred and ordinary and "all energies are directed to the ritual sustenance of the normal order."[98] Zuesse states that ATR are religions of structure, meaning that their "religious intentionality" is not to be saved from this life to an other-worldly place but, rather, to experience the transcendental in everyday life.[99] He explains,

> The religious intentionality centred on holy structure seeks to actualize this structure in all aspects of experience; its goal is the active sanctification of life, not escape from it as "illusory," "evil" or "sinful." [It] rejoices in the sanctification of everyday life, and finds eternity in the midst of change.[100]

Zuesse further states that rituals are employed in ATR to interrelate the spiritual and physical spheres and, in so doing, to "transform and renew the universe."[101] Zuesse's comments give valuable insights into the concept of holiness in ATR.

First, holiness encompasses all of life because life is lived in relation to the transcendental. According to Mbiti, Africans believe that God is holy and that the creator God is good and cannot do evil.[102] God's holiness requires that he be approached with care, and this is achieved by adhering to purity rules during rituals.[103] By extension, this also applies to the ancestors, who act as intermediaries between God and people. Ayodeji Adewuya suggests that many purification rites are concerned with the community's relationship to

---

97. Mbiti, *Concepts of God*, 41.
98. Zuesse, *Ritual Cosmos*, 3.
99. Zuesse, 5.
100. Zuesse, 7.
101. Zuesse, 9.
102. Mbiti, *Concepts of God*, 41.
103. Mbiti, 41.

the deity and usually fall into three categories: taboos, the holiness of God, and relationship with the deity.[104] According to Adewuya, "The discussion about holiness in African traditional life is cognizant of the concept of ritual dirt and ensuing purification."[105] This cleansing involves symbolic actions resulting in "spiritual inner cleansing."[106]

The hunting ritual of the Gbaya, which was referred to earlier, demonstrates the interplay between practical considerations and purity concerns, as well as the focus on moral integrity. These purity concerns go beyond the superficial, emphasizing a concern not just for physical purity but also moral and ethical purity. Blood plays a vital role during this ritual, being used to purify both the shrine and the cooking utensils used for the sacrifices. Water is also central to rituals and is used in various purification rites. A priest may also use hot oil to anoint someone who is believed to be afflicted by *Simbo*. *Simbo* happens when a person violates the gift of life – that is, by spilling blood or stepping over a *soré* leaf. The hot oil cleanses the violator from guilt and, hopefully, averts negative consequences such as illness or death.

Second, holiness is inherently practical and is achieved and maintained by ritual practices. Jacob Olupona's summary of the significance of transitional rites in ATR underscores this sanctification of life.[107] According to Olupona, puberty rites mark the transition from children to adulthood, calendrical rites facilitate important transitions between seasons and harvest or planting time, and burial rites help the deceased transition to the realm of the ancestors or the afterlife. Similarly, marriage rituals serve to unite individuals, families, and communities.[108] All these rites demonstrate the scope of ritual practices in African culture, where life – from birth to death – is sanctioned by ritual practices.

Many insights can be gleaned from ATR holiness rituals. First, cultic purity rules and regulations are a recurring theme, as in the Sadāma meal rituals.[109] According to Hamer, the motivation underlying these rituals is to petition

---

104. Adewuya, "2 Corinthians 7:1," 68.
105. Adewuya, 68.
106. Adewuya, 68.
107. Olupona, *African Religions*, 56
108. Olupona, 56–66.
109. Hamer, "Myth," 327–339.

for wealth, children, or improved health.[110] These petitions can be made to the "creator sky god, powerful possession spirits, and occasionally other clan founders."[111] For the Sadāma, their most common rite is performed in honour of Abo, their founding ancestor; these rites, also known as the feeding of the ancestors, are performed at Abo's burial site against the side of the mountain. Women and those belonging to lower social classes – such as leather workers and pottery makers – are expected to maintain a respectful distance from the sacred grounds because they are considered impure. Only men may sacrifice at Abo's grave, and even they must offer sacrifices according to the level of closeness of their relationship to Abo.

Participants must sprinkle themselves with the blood of a lamb before they set off in procession to the burial site and again when they arrive at the site. The bulls for slaughter are cleaned with water from the river before the ceremony, and the ritual site is divided into four enclosures. The most unworthy can enter the first enclosure, the slaughter of the bull happens in the third enclosure, and the grave of Abo is found in the first enclosure where the actual offering takes place. Only officiants and elders can pass the second enclosures.[112] After the slaughter of the bull and the offering at Abo's grave, men are expected to visit the gravesites of at least fifteen of their ancestors, where they must pour out a bit of honey mead on each grave. Graves of the long-departed are marked with trees. When the sacrifice is completed, the people partake in the meat of bulls, and the members of the pottery caste – who are known for their enormous appetites – help to consume most of the leftover meat. This meticulous division of space, functions, and food points to the need for purity to maintain the relationship with the spiritual realm. Those closest to Abo in terms of bloodline are considered the most pure. The use of blood and water to "wash" people and sacrificial animals all underscore the importance of purity for the success of the rituals.[113]

Second, prayers offered during ritual sacrifices and dedications demonstrate the need for purity when approaching the spiritual realm. Worshippers pray for their purification in preparation for their journeys to shrines, praying

---

110. Hamer, 328.
111. Hamer, 328.
112. Hamer, 334.
113. Christensen, *African Tree of Life*, 42.

for the cleansing of the land and their homes. Fire is used symbolically to cleanse impurities associated with witchcraft, hatred, and wrongdoing.[114] The following prayer from the Didinga of South Sudan illustrates an appeal for purity, where the means to achieve this purity is fire and the prayer appeals to the ancestors to spare the sick person's life.

> Burn, fire: rise sparks: for our brother Lokwerabok lies ill, and they are calling him. Burn red for the life that is in him. Burn bright, O fire, and take to thyself that which afflicts our brother that, rising with the smoke, it may vanish as the smoke vanishes, and he may be left purged of his affliction and whole of the sickness which would destroy him. By our great ancestors I adjure thee, O fire, that seeing thee and savouring they smoke, the smoke which carries our entreaties, they may be content and grant that our brother remain.[115]

Third, sacred spaces emobody the idea of holiness. These spaces, where the ancestors and spirits are believed to reside, are sites for ritual practice. For the Sadāma, it is the gravesite of Abo;[116] for the Gbaya, a shrine next to the family homestead;[117] and for the Xhosa of South Africa, it is the *imizi* (a homestead where a male head is present).[118] Like the temples of the first-century Roman Empire, these spaces are considered the dwelling places of the gods and ancestors and viewed as hallowed ground where rituals are believed to be effective.

Fourth, the desired outcome of ritual practices is ethical changes that will lead to peaceful, harmonious, and prosperous communities. According to Grillo, rituals are always pragmatic.[119] She suggests that rituals achieve ontological change, shaping people, circumstances, and the community.[120] An example of such an ethical change is found in Turner's study of the installation

---

114. Mbiti, *Prayers of African Religion*, 23.
115. Mbiti, 121.
116. Hamer, "Myth," 338.
117. Christensen, *African Tree of Life*, 32.
118. Ainslie, "Harnessing the Ancestors," 530.
119. Grillo, "African Rituals", 121.
120. Grillo, 121.

rite of the senior chief among the Ndembu of Zambia.[121] According to Turner, the desired ethical outcome of this rite is that the chief should act for the community's well-being and act in "whiteness."[122] Whiteness represents the seamless web of connection that ideally ought to include both the living and the dead. It is the opposite of pride (*winyi*), secret envies, lusts, and grudges that result in the practice of witchcraft (*wuloji*), theft (*wukombi*), adultery (*kushimbana*), meanness (*chifwa*), and homicide (*wubanji*).[123] All these characteristics underscore the ritual purpose of being cleansed of vices and endowed with the ethical qualities that will prepare the chief to act for the common good of the community.

According to Augustine Musopole, the goal of rituals in African culture is humanness. He says that "humanness is that essential character defined by our culture as the sum of what makes a person authentically human."[124] This humanness encompasses the ethical qualities that lead to sacred relationships with other human beings and the cosmos.[125] This character should be lived out in concrete situations, thereby combining the ontological change that is believed to take place during rituals with moral conduct.[126] There is no dichotomy.

3.6 Conclusion

This section discussed liminality, *communitas,* and ritual meals in the African context. The African world view, with its rich spiritual and communal nature, offers a possible lens through which to interpret ritual meals in 1 Corinthians. It was affirmed that ritual meals for ancestral veneration are still prevalent in Africa today, which raises crucial questions for the church in Africa since this means that evangelical churches can no longer ignore the seriousness of ritual practice in modern, urban Africa. Therefore, biblical scholarship must engage in meaningful discussions that endeavour to address the impact and implications of continued ancestral veneration for African Christians. This

---

121. Turner, *Ritual Process*, 97–102.
122. Turner, 104.
123. Turner, 104.
124. Musopole, *Being Human*, 3.
125. Musopole, 9.
126. Musopole, 10.

implies that a re-reading of the text from an African rather than a Western world view is needed to address the complex relationship between culture and Christian beliefs and practice. Paul's discussion of ritual meals, idolatry, and Christian holiness in 1 Corinthians 8:1–11:1 and 11:17–34 promises to be helpful in this discussion.

Examples from the Xhosa and Sotho of South Africa, the Shona of Zimbabwe, the Sadāma of Ethiopia, and the Gbaya of Cameroon and the Central African Republic demonstrate that ritual meals to ancestors are still prevalent in modern Africa.

The African world view can be interpreted as liminal in its belief that humans live in an in-between condition – between the world of the sky, where the gods reside, and the earth, where the ancestors reside. Humans are thus able to live in *communitas* with the supernatural world. Rituals are the means that enable humans to cross this divide, thereby maintaining order in society. The belief in the liminality between the world and the sky forms the spiritual essence of the African worldview by positioning humans in an intermediary state between the divine and the ancestral realms

Communalism is the second pillar that undergirds the African world view. Africans believe that an individual is intrinsically tied to the community and cannot achieve full personhood in isolation. This communalism includes all humanity, the created world, and the spiritual realm because all these find their origins in the creator God. The combination of spirituality and communalism create vital participation or *communitas*. *Communitas* unites humanity vertically with the spirit world and horizontally with one another, as well as with all living and non-living aspects of the earth.

Holiness in African culture is, therefore, holistic. It is based on the philosophy that all of life is sacred and lived in relationship with the transcendental. ATR employ a myriad of rituals to achieve the right relationship with the ancestors, the community, and the cosmos. These rituals encompasses purification from defilement, moral and ethical demands, and right relationships. The problem with this high and sometimes divine perception of the ancestors is that it may confuse adherents concerning the appropriate approach to ancestors in relation to God. It also complicates the discussion concerning how people should relate to their ancestors because it requires recognizing that the responsibility for the well-being of the living does not lie with ancestors but with God. Furthermore, this view could lead to syncretism, particularly when rituals simulate worship practices – for example, addressing the ancestors instead of God during prayers and petitions – or when fear motivates rituals.

In this chapter, I have reconstructed an African world view based on which I will re-read Paul's Corinthian correspondence. As we will see in chapter 4, the African context has much in common with the religious environment of first-century Christians, and understanding this will help us to better appreciate the cultural world view of Paul and the Corinthians. This, in turn, will shed light on the sacramental and transformative capacity of ritual meals in Corinth.

Part 2

Liminality in Paul and in Corinth

This section seeks to establish the theological and sociohistorical context of ritual meals in the Corinthian ἐκκλησία (church) because this information is crucial for my analysis of the Corinthians passages.

Chapter 4 explores liminality and *communitas* in the Pauline Epistles. The hypothesis is that Paul believed that believers lived in liminal circumstances as they awaited the *parousia* of Christ and that the holiness of the congregation was vital during this time. Paul's admonitions concerning ritual meals will be read within the spiritual context of liminality and *communitas*.

Chapter 5 discusses the sociohistorical background of the Corinthian ἐκκλησία. This sociohistorical background answers crucial questions for this study, including the importance of ritual meals in the first century, defining the "strong" and the "weak" in Corinth, and establishing the place of rituals in the early church.

Chapters 4 and 5 provide the theological and sociohistorical background essential for a faithful interpretation of 1 Corinthians 8:1–11:1 and 1 Corinthians 11:17–34.

CHAPTER 4

Liminality, *Communitas*, and Holiness in Paul

4.0 Introduction

In this chapter, we will consider whether the themes of liminality and *communitas* can help to interpret Paul's admonitions regarding ritual meals. The critical question is this: What are the implications of liminal circumstances for the communal holiness of believers?

Previous research shows that first-century believers lived in a liminal situation as they awaited the second coming of Christ.[1] It demonstrates that baptism was a threshold ritual[2] and that the infilling of the Holy Spirit served as the principal identity marker of this liminality. It also shows that believers lived in *communitas*, living anti-structurally to the pagan world.[3] All of this took place within the context of Paul's inaugurated eschatology; the coming of Christ in the middle of time and the outpouring of the Holy Spirit created

---

1. See Russell, "In the World," 42; Meeks, *First Urban Christians*, 87; Strecker, *Liminale Theologie*, 50; Fee, *Corinthians*, 17; Wright, *Faithfulness of God*, 1043–1049; Campbell, *1 Corinthians*, 30; de Boer, *Paul*, 9.

2. Meeks, *First Urban Christians*, 90; Theissen, *Earliest Churches*, 123; Brower, *God's Holy People*, 67; Turley, *Ritualized Revelation*, 100; Moule, "Judgement Theme," 464–481; Hurtado, *One God, One Lord*, 108.

3. Johnson, *Religious Experience*, 100; Turley, *Ritualized Revelation*, 36; Meeks, *First Urban Christians*, 88; Strecker, *Liminale Theologie*, 300; Russell, "In the World," 224.

a liminal period – the age of the Spirit – that will reach completion at the second coming of Christ.[4]

This chapter will further the discussion by suggesting that holiness was an essential characteristic of liminality in Paul's writings. It argues that God's principal objective during this liminal period was to create a holy people, characterized by holy *communitas*, who would impact the cosmos on behalf of Christ by living anti-structurally with regard to the surrounding pagan value system. Ritual meals served to advance these purposes as they created *communitas* (1 Cor 10:16–17) while proclaiming the good news of Jesus Christ (1 Cor 11:26).

Context is crucial to interpreting any ritual because a ritual is never performed in a vacuum.[5] Although ancient Mediterranean culture and the Graeco-Roman world provide the physical context for Paul's discussion of ritual meals, liminality provides the spiritual context. The premise is that the liminal situation of the believers demanded that they practise rituals with the utmost seriousness because these could shape them negatively or positively as they anticipated the *parousia*. Their current circumstances were temporary and passing away (1 Cor 7:31), and they had to live their life in preparation for the day of the Lord, who could return at any time (1 Thess 5:1–4). This chapter will show that liminality and *communitas* create a spiritual framework that aids in the interpretation of the effect and significance of consuming εἰδωλόθυτα in 1 Corinthians 8:1–11:1, as well as the correct way of participating in the Lord's Supper in 1 Corinthians 11:17–34.

4.1 Liminality

4.1.1 Liminality as between the Times

Liminality in Paul will be discussed within the context of "participatory eschatology."[6] Participatory eschatology proposes that being "in Christ" is

---

4. See Strecker, *Liminale Theologie*, 212–245; Sampley, *Walking between the Times*, 7–24; Vos, *Pauline Eschatology*, 36–38; Beker, *Paul's Apocalyptic Gospel*, 39–44; Fee, *Paul*, 49–52; Fee, *God's Empowering Presence*, 13; Wright, *Faithfulness of God*, 477–479, 1101.

5. DeMaris, *New Testament*, 7.

6. Space only allows for a summary of the debate concerning what is central to Paul's theology. Participatory eschatology is a strand in the stream that sees apocalyptic as central to Pauline theology. This view generally gained acceptance in scholarship since Johannes Weiss, Albert Schweitzer, and Ernst Käsemann featured apocalyptic as the central point of Paul's

Paul's principal way of describing salvation.⁷ The Christ-event marks the point

---

theology. It was later advanced by J. Christiaan Beker, J. Louis Martyn, and Martinus C. de Boer. Apocalyptic is a complex concept in Pauline studies, and the various proponents focus on different aspects of it. According to Blackwell et al., "All viewpoints stress both eschatology – that is, Paul's two ages paradigm (temporal/horizontal axis)- and revelation – that is, the intersection of heavenly and earthly realms by way of God's redemptive activity and Paul's mystical experiences (spatial/vertical axis)." Blackwell, Goodrich, and Maston, *Apocalyptic Imagination*, 5.

This position marks a deviation from the stance that "righteousness by faith" was the centre of Paul's gospel, as proposed by Bultmann and those of his school – for example, Conzelmann and Bornkamm. Bultmann takes an existentialist approach to Paul's letters by focusing on the human problem of sin as his starting point. Bultmann, *Theology*, 270–285. This approach received criticism in scholarship for being too individualistic and anachronistic. Krister Stendahl, for instance, suggests that Paul did not have the "introspective conscience" evident in Western scholarship and, therefore, could not have had "justification by faith" as his central concern. According to Stendahl, Paul was grappling with the place of Gentiles in the church and the final salvation of the Jews. Stendahl proposes that the framework of "social history" would open new insights into Pauline theology. Stendahl, "Apostle Paul," 199–215. Another approach is that of "salvation history." This view holds that Paul saw the coming of Christ as the fulfilment of Judaic promises and the church as the new people of God. Campbell, *Quest for Paul's Gospel*, 56. This view is advanced by Oscar Cullmann and N. T. Wright. According to Cullmann, human history is linear, and the incarnation, death, and resurrection of Jesus constituted the midpoint in salvation history. The Christ-event – rather than "justification by faith" or the *parousia* as emphasized by Schweitzer and other apocalyptic scholars – should thus be of central significance in Pauline theology. Cullmann uses the analogy of D-Day and V-Day to demonstrate the tension between the already and the not yet in Paul's gospel. The resurrection of Christ ensured victory over the powers, but the actual day of the end of the war against the powers of death would only arrive at the *parousia*. Cullmann, *Christ and Time*, 84. N. T. Wright seems to prefer "inaugurated eschatology." He underscores that although the coming of Christ has inaugurated the new age of the Spirit, salvation is not yet complete because the final enemy, death, has not yet been destroyed. Although Wright also adopts a "salvation history" approach, he disagrees with Cullmann's V-Day analogy. For Wright, there is no evidence of a steady advance to victory in Paul's writing as Cullmann proposes; rather, the *parousia* would be a dramatic inbreak into human history, just like the resurrection day. Wright, *Faithfulness of God*, 548–562. Salvation history and apocalyptic are not mutually exclusive. According to J. P. Davies, salvation history is not antithetical to Paul's apocalyptic motifs. Davies argues based on Jewish and Christian apocalyptic by focusing on Paul's metaphors of childbirth. He demonstrates that "the 'punctiliar' and the 'linear' are not antithetical. Such false dichotomies are called into question by the evidence of a creative tension between continuity and discontinuity found in the apocalypses, particularly in their use of the childbirth metaphor." Davies, "What to Expect," 312. Davies's book *The Apocalyptic Paul: Retrospect and Prospect* was published too late for consideration in this study.

7. Albert Schweitzer refers to Paul's "in Christ" language as Paul's mysticism. According to Schweitzer, understanding Paul's usage of being "in-Christ" would lead to understanding all of Paul's theology. Schweitzer, *Mysticism of Paul*, 3. Although Schweitzer's use of "mysticism" created a negative response from some scholars, the centrality of participation "in Christ" in Paul's soteriology is currently commonplace in Pauline scholarship. Douglas Campbell notes that the sheer concentration of the term "in-Christ" and other related terms in the Pauline letters testify, to some degree, to its significance in Paul's thought. Campbell, *Quest for Paul's Gospel*, 39; see also Sampley, *Walking between the Times*, 12; de Boer, *Paul*, 87–88.

where God intervenes in human history to end the old age and usher in the new age of the Spirit.[8] Believers are thus unified with the death and resurrection of Christ through baptism.[9] They enter a new existence "in Christ," freed from the power of sin.[10] This condition is entered into by faith (Gal 3:1–5).[11] Believers are thus transferred from the realm of sin and death into the new reality in Christ. We will discuss participation in Christ in section 4.2: *Communitas*.

The use of participatory eschatology is intended to highlight participation "in Christ" because this is essential for this study, but it is not intended to exclude other aspects of Paul's soteriology, such as salvation history.

---

8. Käsemann, "Justification and Salvation History," 67; Blackwell, Goodrich, and Maston, *Apocalyptic Imagination*, 10; Sanders, *Paul and Palestinian Judaism*, 440; Campbell, *Quest for Paul's Gospel*, 39.

9. While it is beyond the scope of this research to provide a complete analysis of baptism, a brief discussion is warranted because Paul alludes to baptism in our passage (1 Cor 10:1–2). Although Paul often uses baptism as a metaphor for salvation (Rom 6:1–23), consideration of baptism as a ritual helps us to gain insight into Paul's view on the significance of rituals and how they affect the ethical and moral life of the church. For a detailed ritual analysis of baptism, see Turley, *Ritualized Revelation*, 29–99. Paul's explanation that believers die and are raised with Christ during baptism suggests a transformational process whereby the initiates are not just transferred from one state to another but undergo total personal and social transformation (Rom 6:3–6; 1 Cor 12:13; Gal 2:20; Gal 3:27). This initiation separates them from the "world" and adds them to the sanctified community. Theissen, *Earliest Churches*, 128. This death to their old lives was even more acute for Gentile believers. They were not just repenting and returning to the God of their ancestors, as in the case of their Jewish counterparts, but had to make a total break from their old belief systems and way of life and embrace the new life of the believing community. The death, resurrection, and the ascension with Christ is a purification ritual that moves believers from a state of "defilement and blemishes to a state of cleanness and wholeness." deSilva, *Honor, Patronage, Kinship*, 307. This holy state is in itself a liminal place, where believers will suffer much but will enjoy the blessing of access into the holy presence of God. Baptism is characterized by liminality. During the ritual, time converges as believers appropriate the past crucifixion of Jesus Christ by dying with him, are sanctified in the present, and are made righteous at the final resurrection at the *parousia*. Baptism is eschatological because it anticipates the judgement of the last days. Thus, as Moule suggests, since judgement is associated with the forgiveness of sins, the baptized community "escapes" the final judgement because of their union with Christ. Moule, "Judgement Theme," 464–481. This assertion makes sense from a ritual perspective. Theissen suggests a theory of ritual sacrifices where the victim is taken at the expense of the participant's life. Theissen, *Earliest Churches*, 124. In the case of baptism, the sacrifice of Christ ensures escape from the final judgement for believers because they were united in his death and resurrection. Therefore, believers appropriate this freedom from judgement when they are baptized into Christ and raised with him during their baptism. This acquittal, however, is conditional. According to Paul, believers can lose their salvation if they do not live according to the new life they have received in Christ. We will discuss this further when we look at the ritual of the Lord's Supper.

10. Campbell, *Quest for Paul's Gospel*, 39.

11. Sanders, *Paul and Palestinian Judaism*, 440.

Participatory eschatology creates the framework to interpret Paul's comments concerning participation with Christ and eschatological judgement during ritual meals in 1 Corinthians 8:1–11:1 and 1 Corinthians 11:17–34. Participatory eschatology highlights the cosmic significance of the coming of Christ and points to liminality in Paul's emphasis on the temporal – that is, life between the ages – and the spatial – "that is, the intersection of the heavenly and the earthly realms by way of God's redemptive activity and Paul's mystical experiences."[12] Sections 4.2 and 4.3 will show how these aspects are important pointers to the liminal situation of the early church.

Participatory eschatology, as used in this study, includes aspects of apocalyptic and salvation history in Paul's theology. According to Horrell, Paul perceived the Christ-event as an apocalyptic event; it is not just a punctiliar event but one that Paul casts within the narrative framework of God's salvific action begun in Genesis.[13]

Therefore, participatory eschatology is to be understood in the light of God's complete salvation story. Although God created humanity for communion, they fell into sin, and their relationship with God was marred. Thus, participatory eschatology points to the time when God will act to restore creation, especially humanity, to himself. Paul interprets history in the light of the coming of Christ,[14] and, according to Michael Gorman, Christ fulfilled the anticipated salvation proclaimed by the prophets.

> Paul understands the coming, death, resurrection, and exaltation of Jesus as the inauguration of the prophetically promised age of peace, justice, and salvation – the-age-to-come, or the new creation. Of course, "this age" – the era of sin and death – persists, and will do so until the parousia, or return of Christ. Therefore, interpreters of Paul refer to this phenomenon as the "overlap" of the ages (see 1 Cor 10:11).[15]

---

12. Blackwell, Goodrich, and Maston, *Apocalyptic Imagination*, 5.
13. Horrell, *Solidarity and Difference*, 95–97.
14. Fee, *Paul*, 50.
15. Gorman, *Becoming the Gospel*, 16.

Paul's understanding concerning eschatology is thus rooted in the Hebrew Scriptures.[16] According to N. T. Wright, Paul's understanding was in continuity with the Jewish eschatological expectation that God would bring an end to the present age by the coming of the Messiah and that this would initiate the beginning of the age to come.[17] The principal themes of Jewish eschatology were the day of the Lord – where Yahweh would return to judge the nations – the salvific vindication of Israel, the establishment of God's kingdom, and the overthrow of paganism and evil powers.[18] Paul maintains all aspects of Jewish eschatology but reinterprets these in the light of the coming of Christ and the outpouring of the Holy Spirit.[19] Therefore, Paul taught the churches he established that time was moving towards this final goal but with one dramatic difference – all of history was now understood in the light of the life and death of Jesus Christ.

This eschatology is Trinitarian. When the time had fully come, God the Father sent his Son to redeem humanity (Gal 4:4). The Father also sends the Spirit into the hearts of believers, and this outpouring incorporates them into the family of God (Gal 4:6). This universal outpouring of the Holy Spirit is a crucial aspect of Old Testament eschatology. According to the prophets, Yahweh would pour out his Spirit on all humanity (Acts 2:17, citing Joel 2:28), and he would remove their hearts of stone and put his Spirit within them to enable them to keep his laws (Ezek 36:25–27). Even though there is

---

16. Paul's use of Scripture has evoked various explanations from scholars. Bultmann, for instance, asserts that the Old Testament is not God's word in the true sense for Christians and can thus no longer serve as revelation. Bultmann, "Significance of the Old Testament," 32. Other scholars, like Gardner and Longenecker, affirm the importance of the Old Testament in Paul's letters but do not adequately emphasize Paul's sometimes drastic reinterpretations of Scripture. Gardner, *Religious Experience*; Longenecker, *Biblical Exegesis*. However, contemporary scholarship generally agrees that the Old Testament is indispensable to New Testament interpretation. Richard Hays affirms that Paul's proclamation of the gospel is grounded in the Hebrew Scriptures but suggests that an intertextual method would be more helpful to identify and interpret Paul's agreements with and deviations from the Hebrew Scriptures. See Hays, *Echoes of Scripture*; Hays, *Grain of Scripture*; Hays, "Conversion of the Imagination." Matthew Bates extends Hays's proposal by suggesting that while the Septuagint is important as a pre-text to interpret Paul's letters, co-texts, "subset of coeval texts," and post-text "subsequent texts" should not be neglected in intertextual endeavours. Bates, "Beyond Hays's," 263–291. See also Wagner, "Paul and Scripture," 154–171.

17. Wright, *Faithfulness of God*, 1045.
18. Wright, *Paul*, 132.
19. Wright, *Paul*, 135.

no developed Trinitarian doctrine, there is a "tripartite reality at the heart of this conception in Paul."[20]

This participatory eschatology is particularly evident in the epistle to the Corinthians, as evidenced in Paul's opening thanksgiving, which lays the foundation for the ethical issues he addresses later in the letter (1 Cor 1:4–9).[21] First, we see participation – the Corinthians received grace *in Christ* Jesus (1 Cor 1:4) and were called into κοινωνία with God's Son (1 Cor 1:9). Paul uses κοινωνία to point to believers' relationship with Christ, their sharing in Christian blessings, and their relationship with one another.[22] This union with Christ results from the believers' shared experience of the Holy Spirit:[23] "Fellowship with Christ also means living, suffering, dying, inheriting, and reigning with him (Rom 6:8; 8:17; 6:6; 2 Tim 2:12; cf. 2 Cor 7:3; Col 2:12–13; Eph 2:5–6)."[24]

Second, Paul's thanksgiving points to the believers' eschatological hope (1 Cor 1:7–8). The Corinthians eagerly wait for the revealing of Jesus Christ (1 Cor 1:7), who would keep them blameless till the day of the Lord Jesus Christ (1 Cor 1:8). This eschatological context affirms the liminal situation of the Corinthians. They were incorporated into Christ and had received spiritual blessings, but they still awaited the consummation of their salvation. Paul uses Old Testament tradition (Amos 5:18; Zeph 1:14) to remind them of the day of the Lord, which will be marked by judgement but will also be the time when the faithful God sets all things right.[25] These two themes are especially important for our discussion of ritual meals because Paul makes participation in demons and the future judgement his basis for discouraging participation in εἰδωλόθυτα (1 Cor 8:1–11:1). Likewise, Paul makes participation in Christ and the future hope of Christ's return the basis of his discussion about the proper way to participate in the Lord's Supper (1 Cor 11:17–34).

---

20. Campbell, *Quest for Paul's Gospel*, 41.
21. Horsley, *1 Corinthians*, 41.
22. Hauck, "κοινος, κοινωωος, κοινωεω, κοινωνια, συγκοινωνος, συγκοινωνεω, κοινωνικοσς, κοιωος," in the Theological Disctionary of the New Testament (TDNT), edited by Gerhard Kittel and translated by Geofferey W. Bromiley, 789–809.
23. Fee, *Corinthians*, 672.
24. Hauck, "κοινος," 806.
25. Thiselton, *Corinthians*, 101.

According to Horrell, the Spirit is the most vital sign of the commencement of the new age.[26] The Spirit is the principal manifestation of God among humans and stands opposed to the "present evil age" (Gal 1:4). The outpouring of the Holy Spirit also establishes the new covenant people of God: "The Spirit is one mark of the transfer of believers from one sphere to another: They are no longer 'in darkness' but are 'sons of light' (1 Thess 5:4)."[27] The new covenant people of God are supposed to live according to the Spirit – κατά πνεῦμα – as opposed to their unbelieving counterparts who live according to the flesh – κατά σάρκα (Rom 8:5).[28] The new covenant people must strive for holiness (2 Cor 7:1) and represent God to all his creation; they are Christ's ambassadors, actively calling humanity to be reconciled to their Creator (2 Cor 5:11–21).

This liminal period was a time for preparation. God was preparing a people set apart for his purposes. This mission includes restoring all creation to its Creator and preparing the cosmos for the *parousia* of Christ. In Romans 8:19–23, Paul declares that all of creation waits in eager expectation for the children of God to be revealed so that creation itself will be liberated from bondage and decay. Redemption thus includes the restoration of the created order. Believers are the first to experience this new creation through the power of the gospel, but all creation will be transformed at the *parousia*.[29]

Paul confirms this cosmological scope of the restoration in his correction of the Corinthians' negative attitude to his ministry: "Therefore, if anyone is in Christ, the new creation has come: The old has gone, the new is here!" (2 Cor 5:17). According to Paul, those whom the death and resurrection of Christ have transformed no longer live according to a worldly point of view (2 Cor 5:16) but according to that of the new creation. Fee asserts that the "new" and the "old" mentioned in verses 16–17 refer to the new and the old orders: "The old order has gone, the new 'creation' has come in its place – not just in the life of the individual, but in the total sense of what God is doing in the world through Christ and the Spirit."[30]

---

26. Horrell, *Social Ethos*, 79.
27. Horrell, 80.
28. Horrell, 79. See also Fee, *God's Empowering Presence*, 538–539; Bartlett, *Romans*, 74.
29. Wright, *Paul*, 147; Schweitzer, *Mysticism of Paul*, 54.
30. Fee, *God's Empowering Presence*, 331.

The *parousia* of Christ and the resurrection of believers will mark the end of this in-between age.³¹ The advent of Jesus at the end of this age is referred to by Paul as the *parousia* (1 Cor 15:23; 1 Thess 2:19), the *apocalypse* or revealing of Christ (1 Cor 1:7; 3:13; 2 Thess 1:7), and the day of the Lord (1 Cor 3:13; 1 Thess 5:4).³² According to Beker, the *parousia* is the climax of Paul's gospel.³³ Beker proposes that the resurrection of Christ should be viewed as anticipatory to the future resurrection of believers, just as the Spirit is the guarantee that the end time will happen (Rom 8:23; 2 Cor 1:22).³⁴ This view differs from Martyn, who focuses on the first advent and the cross as the core of Paul's gospel.³⁵ Irrespective of which view one adopts, the *parousia* is of central importance as it points to the consummation of God's promises for believers, while judgement and disaster await unbelievers.³⁶

The centrality of the *parousia* is evident in many of Paul's exhortations to the churches. For example, Mitchell argues that in 1 Corinthians 15, Paul depicts the resurrection at the *parousia* as the goal that governs the lives of believers.³⁷ According to Plevnik, the *parousia* functions as a referent in 1 Thessalonians.³⁸ In the context of ritual meals in Corinth, the *parousia* is central in Paul's reference to the wilderness generation as an example for the church, "on whom the culmination of the ages has come" (1 Cor 10:11). The liminality of the ἐκκλησία until the *parousia* plays an important role in shaping ethics and practice. Fee states, "This already/not yet perspective, in which they believed themselves to be living in the time of the end, is the eschatological framework that determines everything about them."³⁹

This liminal perspective permeates all of Paul's theology. Salvation is liminal because it has already been achieved for us through the death and resurrection of Christ, but its final fulfilment will only take place at his second

---

31. Fee, *Corinthians*, 17
32. Vos, *Pauline Eschatology*, 72–79.
33. Beker, *Paul's Apocalyptic Gospel*, 45.
34. Beker, 47.
35. Martyn, *Theological Issues*, 111–123.
36. Plevnik, *End Time*.
37. Mitchell, *Rhetoric of Reconciliation*, 283.
38. Plevnik, *End Time*, 72.
39. Fee, *Paul*, 51.

coming. The result is that the church becomes an end-time community that must live in the present while never losing sight of the end times.[40]

Christian Strecker, observing that Paul uses several metaphors to convey the liminal situation of the Pauline churches, cites the use of metaphors such as life, death, birth pangs, night to day, and light and darkness to explain the transitory nature of the believer's life here on earth.[41] Strecker points to Paul's comparison of the believer's present life to Israel's wilderness wandering (1 Cor 1:1–14), which suggests a liminal situation. Both situations are transitory and marked by pain and suffering, and life in this transitory state could influence an individuals final destiny.[42]

Paul interprets the nature of the community of believers in the light of the coming of Christ.[43] As Brower asserts, "The community of God's holy people is created through the death and resurrection of Christ, and its entire existence is shaped by it. All of the life of the believing community is transformed by the presence of the risen Christ."[44]

One of Paul's major focal points in addressing the problems in Corinth is the transitory nature of their earthly existence in the light of Christ's return. He tries to convince them that even though they had received salvation and the power of the Holy Spirit, they are still living between the times until "the day of our Lord Jesus Christ" (1 Cor 1:8).[45] Scholars suggest various possible root causes for the behavioural issues in Corinth, such as the Corinthians' views on eschatology, their emphasis on spiritual power, and even the influence of Graeco-Roman philosophy. A few examples will be discussed below.

The first suggestion is that eschatological expectations were the cause of contention between Paul and the Corinthians. Dale Martin holds that the Corinthians held a realized eschatology,[46] while Barclay suggests that the Corinthians did not have a sufficient eschatological mindset but, rather, a "non-apocalyptic perspective."[47] In Barclay's view, the main difference

---

40. Fee, 152.
41. Strecker, *Liminale Theologie*, 212–45.
42. Strecker, 223.
43. Fee, *Paul*, 65.
44. Brower, *God's Holy People*, 4.
45. Hays, *First Corinthians*, 10.
46. Martin, *Corinthian Body*, 165. See also Hays, "Conversion of the Imagination," 391.
47. Barclay, "Thessalonica and Corinth," 64.

between the Corinthian and the Thessalonian churches was in their reception and interpretation of the gospel they had received from Paul, and this in turn influenced the way they related to the surrounding society. The Thessalonians had a robust "apocalyptic framework,"[48] where they eagerly expected the *parousia* of Christ. This mindset encouraged strong boundaries with the surrounding cultural context. The Corinthians, however, appeared to have had no eschatological anticipation for the *parousia*, as evidenced in their integrated relationship with the surrounding culture. Barclay suggests that "unlike the Thessalonians, the Corinthians did not regard their Christian experience as eager anticipation of the glory to be revealed at the coming of Christ. Rather, their initiation in baptism and their receipt of the Spirit had signified the grant of a superior insight into divine truths."[49] The Corinthians' emphasis on the "already" aspects of their salvation to the neglect of the "not yet" aspects resulted in serious moral problems in the church.[50]

Matthew Malcolm, presenting a modified view of the realized eschatology theory, suggests that the behavioural problem manifested in the Corinthian church is "premature triumphalism."[51] His premise is that although it cannot be proven that the Corinthians had a realized eschatological doctrine, their behaviour did convey a premature triumphalism. According to Malcolm, their overemphasis on the Holy Spirit conveyed some form of eschatology. He suggests that "an emphasis on spiritual manifestation and perfection in an early Christian context constitutes an eschatological claim, whether or not the claimants offer sophisticated doctrinal articulation."[52]

Like Malcolm, Anthony Thiselton is unwilling to jettison the realized eschatology view entirely. According to Thiselton, "The eschatological approach pinpoints a single common factor which helps to explain an otherwise utterly diverse array of apparently independent problems at Corinth."[53] Thiselton argues that the realized eschatology view could have led to an "enthusiastic view of the Spirit" and that, therefore, the Corinthians believed they were immune to contamination by eating εἰδωλόθυτα: "The Corinthians'

---

48. Barclay, 51.
49. Barclay, 65.
50. Barclay, 73.
51. Hays, "Conversion of the Imagination," 394.
52. Malcolm, "Premature Triumphalism," 124.
53. Thiselton, "Realized Eschatology," 510.

position depended on two causally related axioms: first, that all had access to revealed knowledge because the last day had arrived; second, that an enthusiast, or spiritual man, is invulnerable to the pressures which bring about failure in the case of the ordinary man."[54] Thiselton is correct in asserting that Paul was attempting to demonstrate that they had not won yet the prize and that the present time was to be marked by "self-control and sustained effort."[55] Failure to adopt this attitude can lead to their falling away, as in the case of the Israelites (1 Cor 10:1–12).

The studies mentioned above suggest that the Corinthians did have a problem with their eschatological understanding, although scholars diverge on the source and the extent of this issue. The Corinthians showed little regard for the future implications of their behaviour, while Paul attempted to convince them of the liminal nature of their situation and the eternal consequences of their behaviour. This is why Paul admonishes the Corinthians to be careful: "So, if you think you are standing firm, be careful that you don't fall!" (1 Cor 10:12). The importance of eschatology in Paul's warning underscores the central role that liminality must play in the exegesis of these passages.

4.1.2 Liminality: Between the Realm of the Flesh and the Realm of the Spirit

The early Christians' situation was liminal because they lived between the times – that is, between the realms of the natural and spiritual worlds.[56] This concept is central to this research since it sheds light on Paul's comments about participating with either demons or Christ when eating food offered to idols (1 Cor 10:20–22). Believers live in a liminal space because they are inhabitants of both realms – the natural and the spiritual. They were

---

54. Thiselton, 519.

55. Thiselton, 519.

56. The liminality between flesh and spirit in Paul's writings reflects an apocalyptic dualism, where the cosmos is seen as under the influence of evil powers while God works through His Spirit to redeem it. This perspective aligns with Jewish apocalyptic thought, which views the created order as divided into heaven and earth, with humans having limited access to heavenly things unless revealed through divine means like dreams or visions. However, this division is not a vast separation but an interwoven reality where believers exist in anticipation of Christ's revelation. The first-century Jewish worldview, including Paul's, accepted supernatural powers' presence without explanation, as it was commonly understood. Paul's perspective in his letters, particularly in 2 Corinthians, is shaped by his belief in being "in Christ," which transforms how he perceives reality. "See discussion 7:2"

transferred into the realm of the Spirit when they were united with Christ, but they still inhabit fallen bodies in a fallen world as they await the return of Christ. The natural world is characterized by the influence and power of both demons and angels.[57]

Paul believed in the existence of angels, demons, and Satan.[58] However, he more frequently refers to sin, death, and the law as powers rather than as personal entities like demons or Satan. As Forbes says, "These existential realities are not seen as merely existential, but are precisely personified and/or hypostatised, and projected out onto the cosmic scene as opponents of Christ."[59] However, Paul does not depict evil as a present dominating reality; instead, he emphasizes that Christ overcame evil through the cross.[60]

Paul describes this victory over these powers as taking place in two stages. First, Christ has already overcome these powers through his resurrection and ascension (Phil 2:8–11). Second, the final victory will take place at his *parousia*: "Then the end will come, when he hands over the kingdom to God the Father after he has destroyed all dominion, authority and power" (1 Cor 15:24).[61] Paul's many warnings to believers show that he believed that these powers continue to be active, seeking to enter and harm the church. For example, Paul attributes his inability to visit the church in Thessalonica to the work of Satan (1 Thess 2:18); he commends married couples not to abstain from sexual relations for too long in order to avoid Satan's temptation (1 Cor 7:1–6); and Paul himself suffered under an " messenger of Satan," who was permitted to torment him (2 Cor 12:7).[62]

The new aeon is characterized by a mysticism where Christ has overcome all the evil powers in the world through his resurrection (Eph 1:20–22), and he will destroy all powers, of which the last will be death (1 Cor 15:24–26). Paul

---

57. See Schweitzer, *Mysticism of Paul*, 54; Beker, *Paul's Apocalyptic Gospel*, 39; wa Gatumu, *Supernatural Powers*, 128–159; Wright, *Paul*, 50–58.

58. See Caird, *Principalities and Powers*, x; Cullmann, *Christ and Time*, 37; Lincoln, *Paradise*, 174; Wright, *Faithfulness of God*, 451; Humphrey, "Apocalyptic as Theoria," 90; Forbes, "Paul's Principalities and Powers," 61.

59. Forbes, "Pauline Demonology," 57.

60. Witherington, End of the World, 19; de Boer, *Paul*, 32; Beker, *Paul's Apocalyptic Gospel*, 39.

61. See Lee, "Interpreting the Demonic Powers," 54–69; wa Gatumu, *Supernatural Powers*, 163–165; Wink, *Engaging the Powers*, 139–143.

62. Schweitzer, *Mysticism of Paul*, 65; Beker, *Paul's Apocalyptic Gospel*, 43.

admonishes that believers should stand firm against the powers opposed to Christ and submit to the power of the Holy Spirit to impact the cosmos and live in readiness for the return of Christ. In the meantime, Christians are to live in the Spirit to be able to overcome. Paul reminds believers that they do not belong to the realm of the flesh: "Those who are in the realm of the flesh cannot please God. You, however, are not in the realm of the flesh but are in the realm of the Spirit, if indeed the Spirit of God lives in you" (Rom 8:8–9). This life in the Spirit requires Christians to live by the Spirit (Gal 5:25), be renewed in their thinking (Rom 12:2, Col 3:1–2), and exhibit the fruit of the Spirit (Gal 5:22–23).

The Spirit initiated the new creation (2 Cor 5:17), but this process will be completed at the *parousia*. Paul sees evidence of this invasion of God's Spirit into the cosmos in the revelation of the divine redemptive plan (1 Cor 2:10), signs and wonders, and the outpouring of the gifts of the Spirit on the Gentiles. Paul also sees the unification of Jews and Gentiles as the new people of God as a significant aspect of this liminality. Now, all humanity can be filled with the Spirit and serve as God's representatives in the cosmos.

In view of this dual spiritual reality, Paul warns believers that what they do in the flesh matters. This includes matters such as their sexual conduct (1 Cor 6:15–17), the food they consume (1 Cor 10:18- 21), their worship (1 Cor 11:10), and their relationships with unbelievers: "Do not be unequally yoked with unbelievers. For what partnership has righteousness with lawlessness? Or what fellowship has light with darkness? What accord has Christ with Belial?" (2 Cor 6:14–15 ESV).

Similarly, the Lord's Supper should not be treated lightly but with an acknowledgement of its apocalyptic significance. Believers live in both realms, and "that is why, in the Lord's Supper traditions, believers proclaim Christ death until he comes (1 Cor 11:26). The Lord's Supper defines the context of Christian life, from the foundational sharing of Christ's death to its culmination in Christ's return at the end of history."[63]

---

63. Sampley, *Walking between the Times*, 10.

4.1.3 Liminality and Anti-structure in Paul

Anti-structure refers to conduct that is in opposition to the institutions, positions, and principles of the dominant culture.[64] Paul's theology of the Christ-event put him in contention with the axioms of both his Jewish heritage and the Graeco-Roman context. Moreover, according to Barclay, Paul's theology was "incongruous" with the prevailing ideologies of his time.[65] I propose that this incongruity set Paul and the churches he established in a necessary position of anti-structure with regard to the prevailing culture.

Paul's first disagreement was with his Jewish heritage. Paul was a Jew and a Pharisee (2 Cor 11:22; Phil 3:5), more advanced in Judaism than his fellow Jews and extremely diligent in keeping the law (Phil 3:6), and so zealous in protecting Jewish traditions that he even persecuted Christ-followers (Gal 1:13–14). In this chapter, I will limit the discussion to Paul's interpretations of Judaism, which was the major source of conflict.

Paul's first and most controversial claim was his insistence that Jesus Christ was the long-expected Messiah.[66] The Jews rejected this claim so strongly that they crucified Christ (1 Cor 2:8), and it was for this reason that Paul himself suffered persecution at the hands of the Jews on several occasions: "Five times I have received from the Jews the forty lashes minus one" (2 Cor 11:24).

Paul's interpretation of the Christ-event also put him at odds with Jewish believers because he insisted that observance of the Torah was not a prerequisite for salvation.[67] According to Barclay, the trajectory of the Christ-event represents God's promises to Abraham.[68] Unlike Wright, who suggests that Paul was trying to prove at every point that the "covenant God had done what scripture all along predicted,"[69] Barclay insists that "the Christ-event is a matter of discontinuity and reversal"[70] and states that "it represents not continuity, but interruption, transformation, caesura, and miracle."[71] Barclay

---

64. Turner, *Ritual Process*, 166.
65. Barclay, *Paul and the Gift*, 6.
66. Wright, *Faithfulness of God*, 1038.
67. Dunn, *Cambridge Companion*, 1.
68. Barclay, *Paul and the Gift*, 412.
69. Wright, *Faithfulness of God*, 1038.
70. Barclay, *Paul and the Gift*, 412.
71. Barclay, 413.

prefers "Martyn's emphasis on the invasive character of the Christ-event."[72] This invasive or incongruous stance fits Paul's anti-structural theology and ethics that is evident in his letters. In Galatians, Paul's call for freedom from Jewish rules and regulations and his disregard for the general criteria of honour and worth are evident.[73]

Second, Paul's reinterpretation of the people of God was contrary to the traditional Jewish understanding. According to Paul, God's people are not limited to ethnic or proselyte Jews but include all who believe in Jesus as the Christ: "For a person is not a Jew who is one outwardly, nor is true circumcision something external and physical. Rather, a person is a Jew who is one inwardly, and real circumcision is a matter of the heart – it is spiritual and not literal" (Rom 2:28–29 NRSV). Paul reinterprets the people of God in the light of the coming of Christ as the Messiah and the outpouring of the Holy Spirit. This new inclusive, universal expansion of the people of God would lead to various situations where believers had to relate to each other and the unbelieving community in an anti-structural way.[74]

Paul's stance on the law also caused significant conflict, which included persecution from the Jewish authorities and disagreement with Jewish believers in Christ.[75] This is because Paul believed that his mission was to preach

---

72. Barclay, *Paul and the Gift*, 413.

73. Barclay, 422.

74. Barclay, 423; See also Witherington, *Conflict and Community*, 80; Finney, *Honour and Conflict*, 3.

75. The subject of Paul and the law is a long-standing and complex discussion that is outside the scope of this thesis. Some considerations deemed relevant for this discussion are that Paul was a Jew and that he did not abandon *halakha* observance in his personal life (1 Cor 16:8; 2 Cor 11:24; Gal 2:3; Phil 3:5). Tomson, *Paul and the Jewish Law*, 260. Paul saw no harm in Jewish believers practising their culture unless it harmed the faith of fellow believers, as evident in his discussion in Romans 14. His primary concern was that law observance should not be viewed as a means for salvation since salvation was only possible through Christ, and Paul was adamant that the law should not be forced on fellow believers, especially not on Gentiles. Salvation happened apart from Torah observance, as evidenced in the case of Gentile believers. Barclay, *Paul and the Gift*, 390. Scholars have adopted a variety of positions concerning Paul's teaching on the law. Bultmann, for instance, emphasizes justification by faith alone and, therefore, classifies all legalism as works-righteousness. Bultmann, *Theology*, 259–269. To correct what he believes to be a misunderstanding of Paul's relationship to Judaism, Sanders suggests that Paul's negative comments on the law are not rooted in the negation of works-righteousness but, rather, in Paul's exclusivist soteriology: "Salvation is only by Christ." Sanders, *Paul and Palestinian Judaism*, 550–551. Hays suggest that in Romans, the law plays a key role in a three-act drama: first, the law defines the will of God and shapes the identity of the people; second, the law pronounces a sentence when it becomes clear that humans are unable to keep it; and,

the gospel to the Gentiles (Rom 15:15–16) and that Torah observance was not necessary for salvation.[76] These teachings sparked opposition from Jewish believers, as evident in the incident at Antioch (Gal 2:11–14). In his epistle to the Galatians, Paul passionately defends the gospel against those who tried to impose Torah observance on Gentile believers.

According to Paul, the law served as a παιδαγωγός (Gal 3:24), but Christ was the τέλος of the law (Rom 10:4). The law served as a temporary provision to teach humans about sin and the requirements of God (Rom 3:20), but it could not save them from the power of sin. It was only through faith in the resurrected Christ that humans could keep the law of God: "For God has done what the law, weakened by the flesh, could not do: by sending his own Son in the likeness of sinful flesh, and to deal with sin, he condemned sin in the flesh" (Rom 8:3 NRSV). The law belonged to the old age, but Christ inaugurated the new age – the age of the Spirit – where humans are enabled to please God because the law is now inscribed on their hearts. This divergence between Paul and some of his fellow Jews placed him and his churches on the margins of Judaism.

The second social context that required the believers to live anti-structurally was the Roman Empire. According to Gorman, Paul's narrative of salvation through Christ was a bold challenge to the narrative of the Roman Empire, where Caesar was hailed as Lord, as exemplified in the worship of the emperor.[77] Augustus was the emperor at the time of Christ's birth. As the son of Julius Caesar – who was hailed as a deity – Augustus was also deified. He was viewed as the bringer of good news (*euangelion/euangelia*).[78] Worship of the emperor was compulsory, and temples dedicated to this purpose were built across the Empire. Jews were permitted to worship their own God but were required to pray for the prosperity of Rome.[79] As a sect of Judaism, Christ-followers shared this privilege, but their refusal to engage in accepted

---

finally, the law acts as a witness to God's salvation through Jesus Christ. Hays, "Three Dramatic Roles," 151–164. See also Rosner, *Paul and the Law*; Martin, *Christ and the Law*.

76. Martyn, *Theological Issues*, 7; Barclay, *Paul and the Gift*, 388.
77. Gorman, *Apostle*, loc. 244, Kindle; Wright, *Faithfulness of God*, 279–347.
78. Gorman, *Apostle*, loc. 244, Kindle.
79. Bruce, *Paul*, 199.

social rituals and festivals was perceived as counter-imperial and anti-Roman, which brought them into conflict with both Jews and Gentiles.[80]

According to Peter Oakes, the relationship between Rome and early Christianity manifested in four possible ways: first, Roman and Christian discourses borrowing terminology from the same source; second, Christians following the same practices as Rome; third, Rome conflicting with Christianity; and fourth, Christianity conflicting with Rome.[81] Oakes states that the conflict between early Christianity and Roman Empire arose because

> the Roman Empire provided the basic structure and discourse of authority in the Mediterranean world; early Christians did not honor the Greco-Roman gods; early Christians saw Jesus as holding current authority; they expected an intervention by God, involving the return of Jesus, which would radically change the world's authority structures; some Christian practices cut against Greco-Roman social norm; Christians in both Thessalonica and Philippi had suffered at the hand of fellow townspeople.[82]

The above points of conflict reflect the sociohistorical situation of believers in the Roman Empire but do not necessarily convey Paul's mindset in his engagement with Roman authorities. Attempts to determine Paul's response to the Roman Empire has resulted in divergent views among scholars. Some scholars argue that Paul's rhetoric was extremely subversive and critical of the Roman Empire.[83] N. T. Wright, one of the strongest proponents of this view, argues that Paul's emphasis on the lordship of Christ serves as a powerful critique of the existing social powers of the Roman Empire. In addition, Paul adhered to a primarily Jewish narrative in relating to pagan empires, and this narrative allowed Paul to call Christians to live in peace with the existing social powers while simultaneously criticizing them.[84] According to Wright, the Jewish response to the Empire was twofold:

---

80. Gorman, *Apostle*, loc. 254, Kindle.
81. Oakes, *Empire*, 120–168.
82. Oakes, 127.
83. Horsley, *Paul and Politics*; Elliott, *Arrogance of Nations*; Kahl, *Galatians Re-Imagined*; Talbott, *Jesus, Paul, and Power*, 128–129.
84. Wright, *Faithfulness of God*, 1279.

Liminality, *Communitas*, and Holiness in Paul

On the one hand, Jews in exile and dispersion were to accept that the world's rulers were both appointed to their tasks by the one Creator God and accountable to that God for the way they carried them out. However, on the other hand, precisely because God would call the nations to account, there would come a time when the arrogant pagan rulers would finally be judged and when the people of the one God would themselves receive global sovereignty instead.[85]

According to Wright, a marked difference between Paul's view and the Jewish view described above is Paul's belief that the eschaton had already arrived in Christ, who, therefore, already rules as the world's Lord. However, there still exists a tension between the "already" and the "not yet" as the final victory is still to be won. Wright explains that it is because of this already/not yet tension that Paul gives apparently contradictory instructions concerning the proper relationship between the believer and the government.[86]

In Romans 13:1–7, Paul admonishes believers to be subject to the authorities because they are God's servants who work for the common good of the people. However, in 1 Corinthians 15:20–28, Paul assures believers that Christ already reigns as Lord and that the day is coming when "he hands over the kingdom to God the Father after he has destroyed all dominion, authority and power" (1 Cor 15:24). Wright suggests that by declaring Christ as Lord, Paul is showing that Caesar's claim to be the lord and bringer of peace and security was false.[87]

The second view, which is espoused by John Barclay, takes an apocalyptic approach to Paul's attitude to the Roman Empire. According to Barclay, Paul was not anti-empire; rather, his position can be described as theopolitical.[88] Barclay suggests that Paul viewed the world differently than ancient and modern politics, so he does not focus on politics and power plays in his theology but subsumes it under his apocalyptic world view.[89] According to Barclay, Paul's theology concerns the redemptive power of Christ,

---

85. Wright, 1279.
86. Wright, 1280.
87. Wright, 1283.
88. Barclay, *Pauline Churches*, 33.
89. Barclay, 33.

which creates and empowers new communities of social (and therefore broadly political) significance. These communities (inadequately) represent the advance of the gospel on a conflicted world stage, where the main players are what Paul calls "powers" (ἀρχαί and δυνάμεις, e.g. Rom 8:38): on the one side, the Spirit and grace, on the other, Sin, Death and the Flesh (and sometimes, Satan or δαιμόωια).[90]

Barclay suggests that Paul did not view the Roman Empire as one of the "powers" but focused on the more significant powers with which the Empire might have been aligned. Thus, for Barclay, "Paul's gospel is subversive of Roman imperial claims precisely by not opposing them within their own terms, but by reducing Rome's agency and historical significance to just one more entity in a much greater drama."[91]

These two positions are not mutually exclusive because there is evidence for both in Paul's letters. While Paul does have an apocalyptic world view, where he sees "powers" at work, the proposal that he might have been addressing Rome in a subversive manner is also compelling. For purposes of this study, it should be noted that both positions result in a situation where believing communities live anti-structurally towards the Roman Empire.

The lordship of Christ motivated believers to live anti-structurally in the Roman Empire. Paul's emphasis on the cross stands in stark contrast to the values of the Roman Empire. According to Peter Oakes – who cites Gordon Fee – Philippians 2:9–11 "places Christ in bold contrast with 'lord Nero.'"[92] Oakes suggest that Paul puts Christ above the emperor, who was the symbolic head of Graeco-Roman society,[93] to underscore that Christ's humility outweighs the values of the Roman Empire.

Since the Corinthians had forgotten the central trope of the gospel of Christ, Paul had to remind them that the gospel he preached was that of Christ crucified (1 Cor 2:2). This message of the crucified Christ was "a stumbling-block to Jews and foolishness to Gentiles" (1 Cor 1:23). This hostile reception of the gospel was due to the manner of Christ's death. Morna Hooker

---

90. Barclay, 383.
91. Barclay, 386.
92. Oakes, *Empire*, 123.
93. Oakes, 123.

aptly describes crucifixion as the most brutal, humiliating, and barbaric way form of execution in the first century, a punishment reserved for the lowest members of society.[94] She says, "The cross was a symbol weakness and total impotence."[95] The Corinthians only focused on the blessings and joy of being part of the new family of God.[96] They focused on the resurrection and the gift of the Holy Spirit, and this led to their unacceptable behaviour. Therefore, Paul holds himself up as an example of weakness because he identified with the crucified Christ, (1 Cor 2:3).

The symbol of the cross, with its connection to weakness, suffering, and death, thus stands in direct opposition to the axioms of the Graeco-Roman culture: "The apocalyptic gospel reveals the instability of the values assumed by the Graeco-Roman culture, replacing them with a mirror world in which top is bottom and bottom top."[97] Paul thus counters the imperialistic ideologies of Greece and Rome and advocates for an alternative, hidden, and more powerful kingdom. The structures of this world are only a shadow, and God will ultimately overthrow all human powers. Paul uses the image of Christ crucified as the central icon of the apocalyptic vision.[98]

Paul's admonition to the Corinthians is also reflected in his other epistles. He insists that their identity as the holy people of God requires them to live anti-structurally, differentiating themselves from the dominant culture by thinking and behaving differently. As "the saints" (1 Cor 2:1 NRSV; Phil 1:1 NRSV), their very nature is different because of their union with Christ, the Holy One. However, this does not mean that believers are to remove themselves from society; instead, they are to be agents of God's activity on the earth.[99] Christians must impact society positively while still maintaining their identity as heavenly citizens. In Philippians 3:20, Paul reminds the Philippians that, as people whose true citizenship is in heaven, they should live differently from those who have their minds set on earthly things. Paul's emphasis on the cross serves as a powerful critique of existing social powers.[100]

---

94. Hooker, *Not Ashamed*, 9.
95. Hooker, 9.
96. Hooker, 12.
97. Martin, *Corinthian Body*, 59.
98. Martin, 62.
99. Brower, *God's Holy People*, 29.
100. Brower, 96.

Paul's focus on believers as those called by God (Rom 1:7) and adopted into the family of God by the power of the Holy Spirit (Rom 8:14–17) underscores a need for boundaries with unbelievers. Through baptism, believers are included in Christ (Gal 3:27) and called to live in a manner that differentiates them from the surrounding society: "Do not conform to the pattern of this world, but be transformed by the renewing of your mind" (Rom 12:2).

The issue of boundaries is often controversial and complex because it raises questions about the extent to which Paul encouraged disconnection from the social structures of the Roman Empire and the implications of this for the church today. Annette Russell, whose doctoral thesis discusses liminality in early Christian communities, attempts to answer this question. According to Russell,

> Rather than strengthening insider/outsider boundaries as many sectarian groups did, they were to welcome all and transcend ingroup/outgroup boundaries. Within the community, they were to transcend the hierarchical and other structural statuses of Roman society and live in love and mutual submission within these statuses, thus transforming the fabric of Greco-Roman society.[101]

Russell argues that Paul does not encourage any form of anarchy but, rather, requires that believers follow the laws and regulations necessary for a governable society. But Paul also calls believers to relate differently to one another other and to society, with love and mutual submission guiding all their relationships.[102] According to Russell, Paul's declaration that in this "in Christ" community, "there is neither Jew nor Gentile, neither slave nor free, nor is there male and female" (Gal 3:28) is merely relational, and is not intended to dismantle existing social structures..

There appear to be two shortcomings in Russell's elaboration on boundaries. The first is the strong assumption that Paul does not challenge existing social structures.[103] The second is her neglect of the instances where Paul calls for firm boundaries, particularly with regard to situations where there could

---

101. Russell, "In the World," 242.
102. Russell, 243.
103. Malcolm, *World of 1 Corinthians*, 243.

be contamination (relating to holiness) of the church as the body of Christ. In contrast to Russell, Yung Suk Kim suggests an alternative interpretation. Kim postulates that Paul's "Body of Christ" metaphor is a forceful critique of the hegemonic ideology of the Roman Empire and suggests that instead of seeing the body of Christ as an organism or organization, it should be understood as a "cruciform reality."[104] Thus being "in Christ" means living as Christ lived or living Christ out.[105] According to Kim, "The image of Christ crucified may be seen as deconstructing powers and ideologies of wealth status, or belonging and reconstructing the community through sacrificial love."[106] For Kim, viewing Paul's instructions concerning social structures through the lens of the cross reveals that Paul was challenging the status quo in an utterly shocking manner.[107]

Kim is correct to emphasize that the church is a community that is shaped by the cross and the *kenotic* life of Christ, which refers to the way Jesus lived out His earthly ministry in a continual posture of self-giving, humility, and obedience to the Father. The instruction that believers should die to self and are mandated to be agents of justice to the marginalized in society – is well-supported by evidence. However, Kim's stance against boundaries seems exaggerated as there is definite evidence that Paul called for boundaries (1 Cor 5:8; 6:16; 10:21).

These two positions – Russell suggesting that Paul affirms existing social structures and Kim arguing that Paul opposes these through his use of the cross – reflect the confusion in the Corinthian ἐκκλησία regarding the appropriate relationship to the surrounding society. The Corinthians seems to have what Paul considered an inappropriate relationship to society (1 Cor 6:1–6; 8:10).[108] According to Barclay, Paul "detects a failure to comprehend the counter-cultural impact of the message of the cross (1:18–2:5)."[109] This failure also comes to the fore in their participation in ritual meals (1 Cor 8:1–11:1; 11:17–34) and helps to shed light on Paul's admonitions in this regard.

---

104. Kim, *Christ's Body in Corinth*, 31.
105. Kim, 65.
106. Kim, 31.
107. Kim, 31.
108. Barclay, "Thessalonica and Corinth," 58.
109. Barclay, 59.

4.2 *Communitas*

Communitas refers to a modality of egalitarian social relationships.[110] It is a state where social differentiations between gender, race, and status are dissolved, and it is marked by the gift of the Holy Spirit. *Communitas* means "living according to the principles of *communitas* established by the gift of the Spirit: egalitarianism, mutual upbuilding, the positive 'fruits of the Spirit' (Gal 5:22)."[111]

The ideal of *communitas* – true self-giving for the sake of the other – is impossible due to human fallenness. Brower describes the fall of humanity primarily in terms of marred relationships: "Because the primary human relationship with the creator God is marred, human relationships with each other and the created order are also damaged and distorted beyond human repair."[112] It is this fallenness that Paul describes as being in Adam (Rom 5:12–21) and being enemies of God (Rom 5:10). In this condition, humans are prone to violating relationships with others and with creation: "They have become filled with every kind of wickedness, evil, greed and depravity. They are full of envy, murder, strife, deceit, and malice. They are gossips" (Rom 1:29). Brower asserts that "at the root, the dysfunctional society in which the Gentiles live is a consequence of distorted relationships. Once the primal relationship with God is distorted, darkened minds, perverted desires and chaotic social relationships follow as night follows day."[113] For Paul, this lamentable situation makes *communitas* in unredeemed humanity an impossibility.

Salvation is also described in relational terms. Believers have "peace with God through our Lord Jesus Christ" (Rom 5:1), are reconciled to God through Christ (Rom 5:10), and are adopted into the family of God by the power of the Holy Spirit, all as a result of God's eternal love for humanity (Rom 5:8). This salvific action of God the Father, Son, and Holy Spirit enables humans to live in authentic *communitas*. Although Paul does not have a structured theology of the Trinity, the presence and activity of the three persons of the Trinity are always assumed. In Galatians 4:6, Paul says, "Because you are his sons, God sent the Spirit of his Son into our hearts, the Spirit who calls

---

110. Turner, *Ritual Process*, 96.
111. Johnson, *Religious Experience*, 101.
112. Brower, *God's Holy People*, 31.
113. Brower, 15.

out, '*Abba*, Father.'" Such texts lets us know that salvation is Trinitarian and implies the mutual relationship between the Father, Son, and Holy Spirit. This holy relationship is an example for believers of true *communitas*. Believers are empowered by the Holy Spirit to live in restored relationship with God, others, and creation.

4.2.1 *Communitas* as Participation in Christ

Communitas is possible for believers because they are united "in Christ." This theme of union or participation in and with Christ saturates all Paul's letters, and this research postulates that it reflects vertical and horizontal *communitas*.

Defining participation in Christ in Paul's writings and determining its role in Paul's soteriology has proven challenging. According to the "traditional" view, Paul's primary theme is justification by faith, and participation in Christ is a consequence of that faith.[114] However, current scholarship, influenced by the groundbreaking work of E. P. Sanders, generally advocates that participation in Christ is central to Paul's soteriology, with justification by faith being the outflow of such participation. This research concurs with the latter view and further proposes that participation in the Lord's Supper "discloses" and "activates"[115] the meaning of this participation in Christ. This will be elaborated on later in this chapter.

According to Sanders, Paul's soteriology can be defined as "participationist eschatology."[116] Sanders proposes that the gospel that Paul preached was that:

> Christ had died and that God had raised him, that Christ is Lord, that the Lord will return, that the *apistoi* will be destroyed (2 Cor 4:3f), that believers would be saved – if alive by having their bodies transformed and if dead by being raised in a "spiritual body" (1 Cor 15:44).[117]

Sanders, building on Schweitzer, proposes that Paul's central theme is participation in "the saving action of God in Jesus Christ" by "faith or believing."[118]

---

114. See Käsemann, *Perspectives on Paul*, 60–78; Conzelmann, *Theology of the New Testament*, 208–212; Bultmann, *Theology*, 270–285.
115. Grillo, "African Rituals," 114.
116. Sanders, *Paul and Palestinian Judaism*, 449.
117. Sanders, 445–446.
118. Sanders, 447.

Sanders proves that this theme permeates all of Paul's accepted epistles and is especially present when Paul addresses ethical issues.

We will now explore the nature of this participation in Paul's writing. Unfortunately, Sanders does not attempt to define participation because, as he admits, he did not have "a new category of perception" necessary for this task.[119] The difficulty in addressing this problem lies in the "mystical"[120] nature of participation in Christ, and modern scholars, for fear of a "magical" interpretation, have veered to the sad extreme of interpreting it more existentially.[121] Some attempts have been made to describe participation in Christ. While a comprehensive review of previous scholarship is beyond the scope of this research, I mention below a few key studies.[122]

Constantine Campbell's comprehensive exegetical study is particularly illumining as it endeavours to explore the concepts of this union with Christ.[123] Campbell asserts that this concept is so thick with meaning that it is impossible to limit it to one description. According to Campbell, to do justice to Paul's thought in this regard, union, participation, identification, and incorporation are all necessary terms as they convey various aspects of union with Christ.[124] Campbell affirms the spiritual reality of this union, stating that it is much more than a poignant metaphorical way to describe the relationship to Christ and one that always points to a concrete referent.[125] However, in reference to the sacraments, he advocates only for a metaphorical understanding and almost reluctantly admits that there seems to be some suggestion of union with Christ during the Lord's Supper.[126] This study will differ from Campbell as it suggests that the sacraments – both baptism and the Lord's Supper – are occasions where union with Christ is activated and re-enacted whenever the ritual is practised.

---

119. Sanders, 522.
120. Schweitzer, *Mysticism of Paul*, 3.
121. Bultmann, *Theology*, 259.
122. See Campbell's comprehensive study for a review of previous scholarship in Campbell, *Union with Christ*, 31–58; see also Gorman, *Inhabiting the Cruciform God*, loc. 48, Kindle; Gorman, *Cruciformity*; Campbell, *Quest for Paul's Gospel*, 39.
123. Campbell, *Union with Christ*, 29.
124. Campbell, 29.
125. Campbell, 412.
126. Campbell, 386.

Morna Hooker prefers the term "interchange in Christ" to describe participation in Christ.[127] According to Hooker, this does not mean that humans change places with Christ but, rather, that Christ, by his incarnation, crucifixion, and resurrection, transfers believers from one mode of existence to another. These modes, according to Hooker, are first "in Adam" and then "in Christ." Thus, Christ enters our experience by becoming human, allowing us to enter his experience.[128] This new mode is the perfect human, as intended at creation. Hooker states that

> the result is that in Christ men become what they were intended to be from the creation. In Christ there is a new creation, so that men now bear his image, as they have borne the image of Adam. They share his relationship with God by themselves becoming sons of God, and so finding blessing, righteousness, and glory. In other words, they become truly human.[129]

Hooker seems to allude to *Theosis* (the transformative process by which a human being becomes more like God, ultimately sharing in the divine nature through grace), in her delineation on this interchange with Christ. Since Christ is not just the perfect human but also the perfect image of God, believers who are being transformed into the image of Christ are also being restored to the image of God.[130] This interchange is indeed present in Paul's writings, as evidenced in the examples cited by Hooker.[131] It highlights an essential aspect of the true meaning of participation in Christ and points to the heart of Paul's gospel as described in 2 Corinthians 5:21. When incorporated into Christ, there is an interchange between the believer and Christ. Therefore, Christ becomes sin so that humans can become the righteousness of God "in Christ."[132]

Michael Gorman describes being "in Christ" as "participation in Christ, his crucifixion and resurrection, his story, and/or his present life."[133] He

---

127. Hooker, *Adam to Christ*, 5.
128. Hooker, 16.
129. Hooker, 22–23.
130. Hooker, 19.
131. Hooker, 13–25.
132. Hooker, 17.
133. Gorman, *Inhabiting the Cruciform God*, loc. 48, Kindle.

asserts that "the language of being 'in Christ' is characteristic of Paul's way of articulating the life of faith, it appears many times in his letters."[134] Paul describes this new condition of believers in various ways: being united with Christ (Rom 6:5), in Christ (2 Cor 5:17), and participation with Christ (1 Cor 10:16). Gorman explains it in this manner:

> Those who have believed the gospel and decided to make that faith known in the public act of baptism are baptised *into* him, *into* his death; they are buried *with* him *into* death in order to walk *in* newness of life; they have already been united with him in a death like his and will be united *with* him in a resurrection like his; their old self was crucified *with* him; they have died *with* him and will live *with* him.[135]

Gorman refers to this concept as "cruciformity," which is his "own term for a concept commonly believed to be central to Paul's theology and ethics: conformity to the crucified Christ."[136] However, Gorman suggests that rather than being mystical, "in Christ" is spatial:

to live within a "sphere" of influence. The precise meaning of the phrase varies from context to context, but to be "in Christ" principally means to be under the influence of Christ's power, especially the power to be conformed to him and his cross, by participation in the life of a community that acknowledges his lordship.[137]

Although I concur with this spatial view, I propose that the mystical should not be neglected in understanding and interpreting Paul's "in Christ" language. This is because believers die, are buried, and are resurrected with Christ in the spiritual realm, a process that is facilitated through ritual.

Gorman further affirms the transformational nature of Paul's "in Christ" language, which helps people to relate to God and other humans as they are supposed to.[138] In his comments on Philippians 2:6–11, Gorman asserts that this is Paul's "master story" that is present in all of his letters.[139] The *kenosis*

---

134. Gorman, *Becoming the Gospel*, 29.
135. Gorman, 26.
136. Gorman, *Cruciformity,* 4.
137. Gorman, 36.
138. Gorman, *Inhabiting the Cruciform God*, loc. 85, Kindle.
139. Gorman, loc. 122, Kindle.

of Christ is not just a model for Christian holiness but also the locale where believers are unified with Christ's death and resurrection and, therefore, share in Christ's glory and are transformed into his likeness. It is also the locale where believers are unified with one another. Believers are sanctified together in Christ, along with others who call on the name of the Lord Jesus Christ (1 Cor 1:2).

Douglas Campbell's emphasis on the transformational nature of participation is intriguing. According to Campbell, Paul's use of "in Christ" conveys ideas of "profound transformation" in the life of believers.[140] Campbell explains that "the very being of the sinful believer is taken into Christ's on the Cross, crucified, buried, then resurrected in a transformed state, and here free from sin, according to Paul."[141] Campbell asserts that this transformation is real and concrete for Paul, not just a mental identification.[142] This participation in Christ is a work and gift of the Holy Spirit that enables humans to relate to God and others in a new way. This process, according to Campbell, is thoroughly Trinitarian as this new new way of relating involves the Father, the Son, and the Holy Spirit.[143] This presupposition of transformation might be why Paul generally points back to union with Christ when addressing ethical issues. Believers are transformed into the likeness of Christ and are, therefore, enabled to live in holiness.

Richard Hays suggested four ways to understand "participation in Christ."[144] Focusing on metaphors used by Paul, he suggests that participation in Christ can be understood as belonging to a family, political or military solidarity with Christ, participation in the *ekklēsia*, and living within the story of Christ.[145] According to Hays, believers are "drawn into participation in a new narrative world, and their former ways of life are subjected to critical scrutiny in the light of the gospel."[146]

Although Hays's suggestion rightly describes various aspects of participation in Christ, his view seems to have more in common with Bultmann's

---

140. Campbell, *Quest for Paul's Gospel*, 39.
141. Campbell, 39.
142. Campbell, 40.
143. Campbell, 41.
144. Hays, "Real Participation in Christ," INSERT PAGE.
145. Hays, 339–347.
146. Hays, 346.

explanation of participation as a new self-understanding. According to Bultmann, Paul's use of "in Christ" should be understood primarily as an "ecclesiological formula"[147] that describes the state of being incorporated into the body of Christ and can also refer to being a Christian because the name was not yet coined in Paul's time.[148] For Bultmann, "in Christ" is an eschatological term because it refers to the new creation and being in the Spirit. However, Bultmann discourages any mystical understanding of "in Christ" and suggests that this term should be understood as belonging to Christ and a "willingness to let the cross determine one's self-understanding and one's conduct."[149] Bultmann, like Hays later does, seems to neglect Paul's apocalyptic world view.

Stowers's proposal, on the other hand, is interesting. He agrees with Schweitzer and Sanders that Paul belonged to a "milieu quite alien to modernity"[150] and, therefore, believed in *real* participation in Christ. Stowers affirms Schweitzer's insistence that "participation was a sharing in the corporeality (*leiblichkeit*) of Christ,"[151] but he also notes that Schweitzer lacked the ability to properly describe this concept. Stowers argues that a key aspect of modernity was to separate the natural realm from the supernatural, as in the theories of René Descartes. Ancient and medieval thinking, however, conceived of a "unified realm consisting of a hierarchy of being or substances, each of which had its own qualitative properties."[152] In this reality, anything, including God and God's activity, could be explained in physical terms."[153]

According to Stowers, Paul's concept of participation can, therefore, be explained physically. In Paul's cosmology, *pneuma* is seen as a substance – it was a more "refined, qualitatively higher substance with its own power of movement and intelligence"[154] then natural substances. So, when Paul says that believers participate in Christ because they have received his *pneuma*,

---

147. Bultmann, *Theology*, 311.
148. Bultmann, 311.
149. Bultmann, 312.
150. Stowers, "Pauline Participation," 354.
151. Stowers, 354.
152. Stowers, 355.
153. Stowers, 355.
154. Stowers, 356.

this is more than metaphorical and has a realistic meaning.[155] Stowers refers to 1 Corinthians 6:12–20 and 15:35–50 to explain that bodies are forms with different content – there is a distinction between the physical body and the body of the divine *pneuma*. Thus, those who have the Spirit of Christ are contiguous with him, in the same way that an arm is connected to the body.[156]

Stowers postulates that Paul drew from strains of Jewish thought related to "patrilineal lineage and physical relatedness"[157] to describe the human being in Christ.[158] He uses patrilineal lineage as a springboard to understanding participation in Christ. Stowers proposes that just as humans share "the same stuff" with one another and their descendants, so believers share the same substance (*pneuma*) with Christ. With reference to Romans 8:29, he says that Paul uses the language of ancient genetics and descent, where patrilineal thought held that "all the seed of all the descendants are in the ancestor."[159] Thus, Romans 8:29–30 is about God creating salvific participation that includes even the Gentiles.[160] According to Stowers, sharing in Abraham's faithfulness and the faithfulness of Christ has a corporeal implication. His explanation is worth quoting at length:

> The logic is this: Abraham and Jesus as blood relatives share the same stuff and the same characteristic of faithfulness to God's promises and are the crucial beginning and end of the God-chosen lineage bearing the promise of blessing. Paul takes the particular blessing promised to Gentiles as the gift of possessing God's pneuma. As Christ participated in Abraham and shared his stuff, Gentiles who come to share the pneuma of Christ in baptism share in this contiguity back to Abraham and are thus seed of Abraham and coheirs as they participate in the stuff of Christ.[161]

---

155. Stowers, 356.
156. Stowers, 358.
157. Stowers, 357.
158. Stowers, 357.
159. Stowers, 361.
160. Stowers, 361.
161. Stowers, 360.

Believers thus have their own human *pneuma* and that of Christ. The *pneuma* of Christ makes it possible for even the Gentiles to share in this pedigree that is received by faith. Stowers thus explains,

> The particular shape of God's pneuma that Jesus received in the resurrection is shared by believers; Christ can be said to be in them. But since they merely share what belongs first of all to Christ, they can also be said to be 'of him' or 'in him' just as Christ shared the stuff of Abraham and was in him.[162]

Christ's *pneuma*, however, does not replace the human spirit, but there is a communication between the two (1 Cor 2:11–15). Stowers is not clear on how the two intermix.[163] He suggests that, sometimes, Paul's writings make it appear like a type of possession; other times, the language of participation and sharing suggests a more "scientific" picture. He cites Aphrodisias's *De mixtione* (On the Mixture of Physical Bodies) and Philo's *De confusione linguarum* (on the Confusion of Tongues), (183–187) as examples of the use of the Stoic theory of the mixing of substances. Stowers explains, "It is not the mere juxtaposition of stuff. Nor is it fusion so that the pneuma and the other substance lose their identities, but the complete extension of active pneuma through passive matter so that each substance retains its identity."[164] In this way, the person shares in the life of Christ but retains their own identity. Stowers's proposition is particularly relevant to this research as it aligns with some aspects of vital participation in the African context.

The studies mentioned above all highlight important aspects of Paul's concept of being "in Christ" or participation in Christ. All these studies include aspects of participation, incorporation, and identification with Christ, as well as an interchange where Christ becomes what humans are in order to make them what he is. Gorman labels participation as "cruciformity," which is dying, rising, and living with Christ. Of cardinal importance is the transformative nature of being in Christ. Those who are in Christ experience the new creation and are themselves the prelude to the renewal of the cosmos. As Hays suggests, participation in Christ encapsulates metaphors such as being part of

---

162. Stowers, 362
163. Stowers, 362.
164. Stowers, *363*.

the family or political solidarity with Christ. Most important, participation in Christ is a real union with Christ. Believers receive the *pneuma* of Christ, are transferred into Christ, and are being transformed into the image of Christ.

Paul's concept of participation in Christ is multifaceted, and it is vital to consider Paul's world view when attempting to understand this concept.. While all the points mentioned are important, real union with Christ has often been neglected. Stowers's discussion proves helpful in unpacking this idea because it offers a way to interpret how this participation might take place. The suggestion that Paul believed that *pneuma* has substance and can be transferred to believers bears merit and correlates with the African concept of vital participation. Vital participation in the African context can aid us in our interpretation of participation in Paul, to which we now turn.

4.2.2 Analysing Participation "In Christ" through the Lens of African Vital Participation and Spirit Possession

This section will explore African vital participation and spirit possession to shed more light on the nature of participation in Christ. According to Adewuya, "When a text is read and heard from a particular cultural context, in this case African, [it] can inform, shape and enrich the understanding and interpretation of the text for the broader community."[165] Paul uses a similar approach when he draws a parallel between participation in Christ and participation with demons (1 Cor 10:20), isolating the aspects that are common to both these rituals. Perhaps African religious sensibility, communalism, and a spiritual world view may clarify the conceptual framework Paul uses here.[166]

Stowers's approach to participation is preferable because it privileges the world view of first-century believers, which has much in common with the African primal worldview. Stowers's suggestion and the African world view both emphasize the continuity between the spiritual and physical realms. African cosmology is divided into three tiers, where the borders between the realms are porous, which makes interaction with the divine possible. In addition, the concept of *pneuma* correlates with the African concept of *ntu* or life-force, which unites people from the same kinship group. This life-force is believed to have substance and can reside in and be transmitted through

---
165. Adewuya, "Revisiting 1 Corinthians 11:27–34," 96.
166. Grillo, "African Rituals," 113.

belongings and objects. These factors, along with the African concept of communalism, are helpful in our interpretation of participation in Paul's writings.

First, the spiritual world is the starting point for this discussion. As noted above, a wide cross-section of Africans share a sacramental world view that makes participation in the spiritual realm possible, thus offering a valid perspective for articulating Pauline spirituality.[167] Stowers affirms this world view, referencing Schweitzer as he states that "Paul's language did require a realistic conception of the supernatural existence that has entered the natural."[168] Paul also affirms this prerequisite: "Those who are unspiritual do not receive the gifts of God's Spirit, for they are foolishness to them, and they are unable to understand them because they are discerned spiritually" (1 Cor 2:14 NRSV). Thus, any attempt to understand participation must happen within a context where the supernatural is assumed.

Second, African vital participation is based on a belief in actual relatedness. Ways to determine this relatedness include the common origin of all humans in the creator God, common ancestors, and the sharing of blood – as seen when blood brothers consume each other's blood. This relatedness also includes the possibility of sharing in the same spirit or life-force.

Stowers's concept of patrilineal lineage and physical relatedness conveys the same ideas as vital participation. Expanding on Paul's discussion in Galatians 3:3, 7, and 18, Stowers demonstrates the ontological relatedness between Abraham – who was the ancestor of Jesus – and those who believe in Jesus (Gal 3:26). Even Gentiles share this relatedness because those who believe in Jesus receive his *pneuma* and are included in Abraham's lineage.

Stowers convincingly argues that Paul advances a concept of real relatedness, referring to the baptism of believers (Gal 3:27), where believers are baptized into Christ, clothed with Christ, and become the offspring of Abraham and heirs according to the promise.

Third, in Africa, vital participation includes sharing in the gifts and belongings of the ancestors through receiving their life-force. This vital life-force must be received continually, and it can increase or decrease. Stowers refers to this endowment by saying that believers receive everything that

---

167. Bediako, *Christianity in Africa*, 93.
168. Stowers, "Pauline Participation," 354.

belongs to Christ, which he terms the "stuff" of Christ.[169] Paul also connects participation with access to the gifts of Christ. Gardner, commenting on 1 Corinthians 1:9, says, "There Paul outlined how the Corinthians shared together in the 'enrichment' in Christ (v. 5), the spiritual gifts (v. 7), and the benefits accruing to those in Christ Jesus."[170] Paul elaborates further on this in his discussions on the gifts of the Spirit – which are the birthright of all believers (1 Corinthians 12; Rom 12:4–8) – and the fruit of the Spirit (Gal 5:22–23).

The other African manifestation of vital participation that may enhance our understanding of Pauline participation is spirit possession. Stowers states that Paul describes participation in various ways, noting that sometimes it seems that "Paul's language makes it sound as if the divine *pneuma* inhabits the person by a kind of possession so that the natural human *pneuma* and the divine *pneuma* are distinct *homunculi* inside the person."[171] This is the way spirit possession is generally understood in Africa. In African spirituality, spirit possession is seen as "the condition of being affected by forces or entities that are normally invisible and external to humans."[172] These forces can be the spirits of ancestors, culture heroes, or various spirit forms that are familiar to a particular society.[173] Since spirit possession is a complex, multi-layered condition that cannot be fully explored within this research,[174] the discussion here will focus on exploring the relationship between the possessing spirits and the human bodies they occupy.

According to Rasmussen, in African spirituality, "spirits enter human bodies via organic and non-organic illnesses, dreams, sudden allergies or aversions, depressions, and dissociation. Hosts often resist or resent possession when first occurs."[175] Spirit possession also serves various community functions, including "therapeutic, religious, aesthetic, ludic, pedagogical [and] political."[176] Rasmussen explains that a spirit may be exorcised or appeased

---

169. Stowers, 360.
170. Gardner, *Gifts of God*, 162.
171. Stowers, "Pauline Participation," 363.
172. Rasmussen, "Spirit Possession in Africa," 185.
173. Rasmussen, 185.
174. For more information on spirit possession see Rasmussen, "Spirit Possession in Africa," 184–197; Zuesse, *Ritual Cosmos*, 183–205.
175. Rasmussen, 186.
176. Rasmussen, 189.

and permanently accommodated.[177] The relationship between the host and the spirit can play out in various ways: the host may perform rituals to get rid of the spirit or enter into a "therapeutic contractual relationship with the spirit, thereby becoming healthy again, and sometimes themselves practicing mediumistic or divinatory healing."[178] According to Laura Grillo, possession trance is not always indicative of evil, "but is beneficent and ritually invoked. It is a spectacle of revelation."[179] Grillo observes that since hosts can intentionally invoke or invite spirits through ritual postures and movements, this implies the host's conscious participation. However, paradoxically, possession trance can also lead to a host losing or surrendering their role as a "self-conscious agent directing ritual action."[180] Thus, there are many occasions when the spirit takes over. Hosts choosing to accommodate the spirit are conferred with embodied knowledge and unique healing abilities, powers of divination, or other extraordinary capabilities[181]

To what extent can this outline of African spirit possession shed light on participation in Paul? First, the body is the locus for the Spirit to become embodied in believers.[182] This idea is present in 1 Corinthians 6:18–20, where Paul warns the Corinthians that their bodies are temples of the Spirit and, therefore, should not be joined with a prostitute because this will make the believer one with the prostitute. Such a union with a prostitute may cancel the union with Christ "see 4.3.3". According to Stowers, Paul's warning is based on Genesis 2:24 and has physical implications, as Adam's union with Eve had.[183] Paul suggests the image of the *pneuma* inhabiting humans when he says that God makes his appeal through believers (2 Cor 5:20). He also states, "If the Spirit of him who raised Jesus from the dead dwells in you, he who raised Christ from the dead will give life to your mortal bodies also through his Spirit that dwells in you" (Rom 8:9 NRSV). Thus, the Spirit takes up habitation within the believer.

---

177. Rasmussen, 186.
178. Rasmussen, 186.
179. Grillo, "African Rituals," 119.
180. Grillo, 119.
181. Grillo, 119.
182. Grillo, 119.
183. Stowers, "Pauline Participation," 357.

Second, a spirit's presence is made known in tangible ways that the host and those around can perceive. In other words, it takes up space and manifests perceivable behaviours and powers. This is reflected in Paul, where he cautions the Corinthians that participation with demons will cancel out participation with Christ (1 Cor 10:21). Demons and the Spirit of Christ cannot inhabit the same space. The Spirit of Christ gives life to the body (Rom 8:11), leads believers (8:13), testifies with believers (8:16), and intercedes on their behalf (8:27).

Third, in African spirituality, participation involves sharing the power of the spirit while maintaining the host's identity. According to Paul, believers also share in all of Christ, but they live their lives in the power of Christ (Gal 2:19–20). In contrast to pagan spiritual trances, Paul encourages believers to pray, speak, and sing with understanding for the edification of the body of Christ (1 Cor 14:15–16). Paul also says, "The spirits of prophets are subject to the prophets, for God is a God not of disorder but of peace" (1 Cor 14:32–33 NRSV). In stark contrast to some instances of spirit possession in Africa – where hosts go into a trance and are totally under the control of the spirit, losing their ability to act as a "self-conscience agent"[184] – participation in Christ requires continual consent and cooperation with the Spirit.

Participation involves a mutuality between the believer and the Spirit, as in the case of prophecy or healing empowered by the Spirit. This kind of mutuality is also implied in 1 Corinthians 2:11–16. The Spirit of Christ reveals the things of God, grants wisdom, and gives believers the ability to make judgements that supersede human judgement. The Spirit also bestows various gifts and abilities (1 Cor 12:4–11), which serve as tangible manifestations of the Spirit's presence (1 Cor 12:7). The Spirit's nature is also evident in the fruit he produces within the believer (Gal 5:22–23).

This comparison between participation in Christ in Paul's writings and spirit possession in Africa underscores the corporal experience of participation. This union is so real that believers become the body of Christ, belong to Christ, and are raised with Christ (1 Cor 6:13–14). The believer's body becomes a member or body part of Christ's body, and is intended to glorify God rather than be used for sinful gratification (1 Cor 6:20). Participation is holistic, involving bodily union, spiritual communion (Rom 8:16), and the renewal of the mind (Rom 12:2).

---

184. Rasmussen, "Spirit Possession in Africa," 190.

4.2.3 Horizontal *Communitas*

What then does such participation in Christ signify for relationship among believers? According to Stowers, believers are together the seed of Abraham and Christ. Just as Abraham and Christ share the same *pneuma*, so believers together share the *pneuma* of Christ. From a patrilineal viewpoint, believers are not related because they share the same belief system or are a part of the same association but, rather, because they share the same *pneuma* and are, therefore, real kin. Gentiles are adopted into this kinship by faith (Gal 3:8) and reception of the promised *pneuma* (3:14). In interpreting Galatians 3:28, Stowers says, "Gal 3:28 is first of all a denial of a set of ontological differences and an affirmation of an ontological unity, those in Christ are literally of the same stuff. All share the very same pneuma – Christ's."[185]

Meeks also emphasizes the unification of humanity in Christ. According to Meeks, the existing awareness of reunification philosophies evidenced in the first century, along with the baptism ritual context of Gal 3:28, would have reinforced the plausibility of a unified humanity for the first Christians.[186] Therefore, Meeks states, "A factual claim is being made, about an 'objective' change in reality that fundamentally modifies social roles. New attitudes and altered behaviour would follow – but only if the group succeeds in clothing the novel declaration with 'an aura of factuality.'"[187] However, Meeks does not suggest that gender distinctions are done aways with in the new faith communities: "Women remain women and men remain men and dress accordingly, even though 'the end of the ages has come upon them.'"[188]

Meeks suggests that there is an "equality of role of men and women in this community which is formed already by the Spirit that belongs to the end of days."[189] This egalitarian relationship includes all areas where people would traditionally be divided: Jews and Gentiles, slaves or free people. However, this does not signify that believers lose their identity. As Bruce rightly asserts, "It is not their distinctiveness, but their inequality of religious role, that is abolished in Christ."[190]

---

185. Stowers, "Pauline Participation," 360.
186. Meeks, "Image of the Androgyne," 166.
187. Meeks, 12.
188. Meeks, 26.
189. Meeks, 27.
190. Bruce, *Galatians*, 190.

This ontological likeness[191] has specific implications for how believers should relate to one another. Paul's kinship language is more than a rhetorical device to encourage reconciliation or coherence. He truly believed in the kinship of all who participate in Christ. His teaching on love in 1 Corinthians 13 is thus a logical foundation for his admonitions, in the context of a family unit. Seen in the light of the real relatedness of believers, Paul's warning not to sin against a brother or sister (1 Cor 8:11–12) takes on a new meaning, calling to mind the relationship between blood relatives and how one should relate to them.[192]

Paul's use of the body metaphor also underscores the union of the church. Believers are all included in the body of Christ by the Holy Spirit (1 Cor 12:13), and all members of the body are dependent on one another for the proper functioning of the body (12:15–18). In addition, "If one member suffers, all suffer together with it; if one member is honoured, all rejoice together with it" (12:26).

The Holy Spirit, who is the life-giving force of this new community, takes the community to a higher level because their relatedness is grounded in their union with the divine. This shared experience of the Spirit breaks down common barriers that separate believers and creates an environment of spiritual unity. Fee explains it like this:

> How did many of them all become one body? by their common, lavish experience of the Spirit. To emphasise that the many ("we all") have become one through the Spirit, Paul adds parenthetically, "whether Jews or Gentiles, slave or free." So, in effect, their common life in the Spirit had eliminated the significance of the old distinctions, hence they had become one body.[193]

The African kinship culture, with its communal nature, offers valuable insights because it shares many similarities with the Second Temple period and Graeco-Roman culture. We mentioned earlier that communal morals

---

191. Ontological likeness refers to the fact that believers share in the *pneuma* of Christ, and since the *pneuma* changes their being, they share similar characteristics that are wrought by the *pneuma*.

192. See Ok, *Constructing Ethnic Identity*, and Glanville and Glanville, *Refuge Reimagined*, for further discussion on early Christian identify as ethnic identity.

193. Fee, *Corinthians*, 672.

dictate the moral code, and neglecting or diminishing community members may result in calamity for the community. This community ethic is also evident in Paul's writings. In 1 Corinthians 11:27–34, Paul suggests that the illness and death experienced within the community at Corinth resulted from dishonouring the poor or less privileged.

Love is the central characteristic of the believing community.[194] The source of this love is the Holy Spirit (Rom 5:5; Gal 5:22), and this love is exemplified in the crucifixion of Jesus Christ on behalf of sinners (Rom 5:8). Therefore, life in the Spirit is expressed through love, which forms the foundation of the Christian community.[195] Love is the core value that stood in opposition to the surrounding context, thus acting anti-structurally. Commenting on Galatians 5:13–14, Barclay asserts that "Paul lived in a face-to-face society where self-advertisement, rivalry, and public competition were a perpetual cause of tension in everyday life."[196] Love was the means to target "habits of intra-communal rivalry that were characteristic of ancient Mediterranean society."[197] This is evident in the Corinthian correspondence, where Paul addresses various problematic situations by calling for love towards fellow believers (1 Cor 10:23–24), sometimes specifically mentioning love (1 Cor 8:1) but other times advocating for an ethic that privileges others. Thiselton's comments on 1 Corinthians 13, the love chapter, ring true: "Every word in the chapter has been chosen with this particular situation at Corinth in mind."[198]

This call to loving relationships is evident in Paul's directives to the churches. He advises Philemon to treat his slave Onesimus as a "dear brother" (Phlm 16). The Corinthians are called to live in a manner that would distinguish them from the prevailing culture: the strong should give up their rights for the sake of the weak (1 Corinthians 8:1–12), leaders should seek to please God as faithful servants and give up their rights for the sake of those they serve (1 Corinthians 9:15), and spiritual gifts should be used to build up the community of believers rather than for personal gain (1 Corinthians 12:1–31).

---

194. Russell, "In the World," 231.
195. Barclay, *Paul and the Gift*, 430.
196. Barclay, 433.
197. Barclay, 432.
198. Thiselton, *Corinthians*, 1027.

Paul advocates that the community, as an alternative society, should be governed by the law of love (Gal 5:14–15).

Love is also tied to the vocation of the community. According to Paul, love should be extended to all humans, not just those who are part of the believing community (Gal 6:10; 1 Thess 3:12). Gorman suggests that love, along with faith and hope, are the "missional marks" of the community: "It is a kind of participation in God that means participation in the world in a radically new and different way."[199] The love of Christ is the driving motivation behind Paul's apostolic work (2 Cor 5:14) and prompts the Corinthians' generosity towards the poor (2 Cor 8:8). Love should thus be the identity marker that distinguishes believers and welcomes unbelievers into the fellowship.

The deeply spiritual and loving nature – the *communitas* – of the believing community guides the way believers should relate to one another. If the heart of Paul's gospel is participation in Jesus Christ, the Son of God, through the power of the Holy Spirit, then the essential nature of the community is that of a spiritual community who share the very *pneuma* of Christ. As a community that has its origin and existence in Christ, they all share in the one loaf (1 Cor 10:17) and are governed by a communal ethos of love.

4.3 Holiness

This section examines the theme of holiness in Paul's writings. The hypothesis here is that holiness is at the heart of Paul's discussion of ritual meals in 1 Corinthians 8:1–11 and 11:17–34. Therefore, it is necessary to begin by addressing Paul's understanding of holiness.

The holiness of the community was a central concern for Paul.[200] This conviction was rooted in his Jewish background. Paul believed that the coming of Jesus Christ was the fulfilment of the Old Testament covenant: "The key point is that Paul does not convert from Judaism to Christianity so much as re-shape his whole perspective on his ancestral faith in the light of Christ."[201] This continuity with the Old Covenant necessitated the same call to holiness that is present in the Old Testament. Paul answers these pivotal questions

---

199. Gorman, *Becoming the Gospel*, 65.
200. Brower, *God's Holy People*, 2.
201. Brower, 3.

in all his letters: What does it mean to live as God's holy people during this "between/betwixt" time? How must the church prepare itself for the return of Christ at the *parousia*? Thus, Paul urgently desired the holiness of believers, and his prayer was that Christ would find them "blameless" at his second coming (1 Cor 1:8; 1 Thess 5:23). Blamelessness at the *parousia* results from living as God's holy people during this liminal phase.

Holiness is primarily communal or community oriented,[202] and it must be understood in terms of a covenant relationship with the holy God and the resulting relationship with others.[203] It is a result of participation in Christ.[204] Paul's understanding of holiness is rooted in his conviction that Jesus Christ is the revelation of the holiness of God and that humans are made holy as they become one with Christ.[205] His understanding of holiness is also Trinitarian. In 1 Thessalonians, Paul states that the sanctification of believers is the will of God (1 Thess 4:3, 6), who gives his Spirit to accomplish this purpose (4:8), and the Son judges wrongdoing (4:6). According to Gorman, "Human holiness is participation in divine holiness. Holiness is, therefore, both the property and the activity of the Father, the Son, and the Spirit."[206]

Holiness is a result of κοινόνια with Christ and this, in turn, allows for fellowship with the Father: "Therefore, since we are justified by faith, we have peace with God through our Lord Jesus Christ" (Rom 5:1 NRSV). Thus, holiness is a result of *communitas* with the Triune God. *Communitas*, in this context, does not signify equality with God, but it does point to the believer's ability to share in God through the work of Christ and the power of the Holy Spirit (Rom 8:15–17).

Holiness is the focus of 1 Corinthians.[207] According to Deasley, holiness in Corinthians has three different aspects: "commitment, character, and conduct."[208] The believers are sanctified because of their faith in Christ, but they must also grow into this holy identity in their character and conduct.[209]

---

202. Adewuya, *Holiness and Community*, 2.
203. Adewuya, "Paul's Understanding of Holiness," 108.
204. Winter, "Carnal Conduct," 67.
205. Gorman, *Inhabiting the Cruciform God*, loc. 2058, Kindle.
206. Gorman, loc. 1100, Kindle.
207. Brower and Johnson, *Holiness and Ecclesiology*, 149.
208. Deasley, *1 Corinthians*, 41.
209. Deasley, 41.

This holy identity is characterized by love[210] and unity.[211] According to Theissen, love was the first fundamental value of the early believing communities.[212] He suggests that this mutual love encourages at egalitarian relationships, where the superior renounce their status and the inferior are elevated.[213] Such a radical ethic of love requires crossing boundaries, and as outsiders are welcomed into the community and boundaries of social class are transcended, a disposition of humility is cultivated among believers.[214] The community is guided by the law of love (Gal 5:14), and a communal ethic of sacrificial love is evident in all relationships.

Such holy relationships are countercultural to the self-centred orientation of the surrounding culture, which is marked by sin. Therefore, a brief discussion of Paul's view of the problem of sin is necessary to better understand holiness. This study assumes that, for Paul, idolatry is the primal manifestation of humanity's sinful condition. This is evident in his introduction to the problem of fallen humanity in Romans 1. This discourse on humanity's guilt and their hopeless condition suggests, as Lints affirms, that "idolatry is a large conceptual framework by which Paul describes the moral transformation of humans."[215]

In Romans 1, Paul portrays the pervasive nature of sin in humanity. According to Wright, Paul does this by alluding to the account of the fall in Genesis and the episode of the golden calf in Exodus 32.[216] God revealed himself to humans in the created universe, but humans embraced sin by suppressing God's revealed truth, becoming futile in their thinking and turning to worship created things instead of the Creator. Paul's use of ἀνθρώπων (1:18) and his later reference to Jews (2:1–11) demonstrate that all humans – Jews and Gentiles alike – are guilty of sin.[217]

---

210. Deasley, 41.
211. Barton, "Sanctification and Oneness," 39.
212. Theissen, *Earliest Churches*, 64.
213. Theissen, 69.
214. Theissen, 70–71.
215. Lints, *Identity and Idolatry*, 110.
216. Wright, *Faithfulness of God*, 769; see also Hooker, *Adam to Christ*, 73–84; Adams, "Abraham's Faith," 47–66.
217. Greathouse and Lyons, *Romans 1–8*, 68.

Morna Hooker suggests that Adam's primal sin was idolatry. She acknowledges that this is not obvious from the Genesis narrative but explains,

> It may perhaps be objected that there is nothing in the narrative in Genesis to suggest that Adam ever offered worship to idols. He can however, as we have seen, be justly accused of serving the creature rather than the creator, and it is from this confusion between God and the thing which he has made that idolatry springs.[218]

Hooker suggests that humans also placed themselves in subservience to creatures over whom they were intended to have dominion, which opened the way for idolatry.[219] Witherington sees this subversion of the created order as sparking the fall of humans. He states, "Idolatry is by definition the worshiping or obeying of something as God that is in fact less than God."[220] By attempting to be like God, humans plunged all of creation into a downward spiral, and, as Paul so vividly explains, all kinds of wickedness and immorality followed. In Romans 5, Paul describes in detail how sin was introduced to the world through Adam, who was humanity's representative. In solidarity with Adam, all humans inherit the sinful condition and its consequence of death.[221] However, in Jesus Christ, humans are set free from the power of sin and death (Rom 8:2).

The problem of human sinfulness is exacerbated by the operation of non-human or supernatural powers, who tempt humans to commit idolatry and other evils.[222] Paul assures the believers that these powers also work against the good purposes of God through idols and earthly human rulers.[223] In the present liminal circumstances of believers – where the final defeat of the powers awaits the *parousia* – a hostile environment is created, in which believers are vulnerable to temptation.

---

218. Hooker, *Adam to Christ*, 78.
219. Hooker, 78.
220. Witherington, *Paul's Narrative Thought World*, 12.
221. Brower, *God's Holy People*, 16.
222. Witherington, *Paul's Narrative Thought World*, 15. See also Romans 5–7, where Paul refers to sin as a power, and Romans 8:38, where Paul assures believers that no angels, rulers, or powers can separate them from the love of God in Christ Jesus.
223. Wright, *Paul*, 771.

The good news is that God's faithfulness, revealed in Jesus Christ, who defeated sin by taking on human nature (Romans 5–6), will ultimately destroy these evil powers.

The downward spiral presented in Romans 1:18–32 is also evident in 1 Corinthians 10:1–14. God revealed himself to the wilderness generation by providing spiritual food and drink. However, the people became idolaters, worshipped the golden calf, and indulged in sexual immorality. As a result, God rejected them, and they all died in the desert. The disastrous impact of idolatry runs like a scarlet thread through these examples: it was present the Genesis account, among the wilderness generation, and now threatens the holiness of the Corinthian community. Just as in Romans 1, Paul points to the good news of the crucified Christ, who is present in the celebration of the Lord's Supper (1 Cor 10:16–17), as the means by which to appropriate reconciliation with God.

4.3.1 Holiness and Liminality

Paul's concept of holiness is in continuity with Israel's story,[224] with one radical difference: holiness is now possible because of the universal outpouring of the Holy Spirit. This continuity with the Old Covenant necessitates the same call to holiness found in the Old Testament, where holiness resulted from being in a relationship with the holy God (Lev 11:44–45). However, in the new age, God enables his people to live holy lives by changing their hearts by the power of his Holy Spirit (Ezek 36:25–27; Joel 2:28). For Paul, holiness is the primary identity marker of believers, and this is reflected in his use of the term ἁγίοις – the holy ones to address believers (Rom 1:7; 1 Cor 1:2; 2 Cor 1:1).

The relationship between holiness and liminality is evident in Paul's Thessalonian correspondence: "May he strengthen your hearts so that you will be blameless and holy in the presence of our God and Father when our Lord Jesus comes with all his holy ones" (1 Thess 3:13). Here, Paul advises the believers to continue in holiness during the in-between time as they await the return of the Messiah. Like Israel, they are called to avoid defiling practices, including sexual immorality, in anticipation of Christ's return. Therefore, he admonishes them, "It is God's will that you should be sanctified: that you should avoid sexual immorality" (1 Thess 4:3).

---

224. Gorman, "You Shall Be Cruciform," loc. 2053, Kindle.

Paul's call to live anti-structurally is a call to holiness. Believers must live in a manner that is discernibly different from the surrounding pagan culture, "not in passionate lust like the pagans, who do not know God" (1 Thess 4:5). They are also to live in *communitas*, not taking advantage of their fellow believers (4:6) because this is unholy behaviour. Instead, they should continue to live in love for all of God's family, a lesson taught to them by God himself (4:10). All this is a testimony to outsiders to the community of faith, "that your daily life may win the respect of outsiders" (4:12). This discourse is followed by a lengthy description of the resurrection and the day of the Lord. The correlation between holiness and liminality is undeniable: believers are to live holy lives as they await Christ's return.

4.3.2 Holiness and *Communitas*

Holiness is also revealed as *communitas* with fellow believers. As the called-out people of God, believers share a common identity as the ἁγίοις – the holy ones – of God (Rom 1:7; 1 Cor 1:2; Phil 1:1). As the holy ones, they are united with Christ and also with one another. They were all baptized into one body, the body of Christ, and were all made to drink of the same Spirit (1 Cor 12:13). This unity in Christ breaks down all forms of division and allows believers to stand on equal footing before God: "There is no longer Jew or Greek, there is no longer slave or free, there is no longer male and female; for all of you are one in Christ" (Gal 3:28 NRSV). Together, the believers are the temple of God (1 Cor 3:16–17) and the body of Christ (1 Cor 12:13).

This is exemplified in the church in Corinth. Believers are incorporated into the body of Christ through the baptism of the Holy Spirit (1 Cor 12:13), and their life together expresses this holiness: "The Church is not a collection of individuals but the corporate body of Christ from which persons take their identity."[225] Sin acts as a contagion that defiles, while divisions damages the wholeness of the body of Christ.[226] It is for this reason that they must be careful of sexual misconduct (1 Corinthians 5–7), avoid eating food offered to idols (1 Cor 8:1–11:1), avoid marriage to unbelievers (1 Cor 7:12–16), and expel the incestuous man (1 Cor 5:1–11). Paul's primary objective is to teach that the church is not intended to be mixture of those who persist in sin and

---

225. Brower, *God's Holy People*, 74.
226. Neyrey, "Body Language," 140.

those who do not, but, rather, that they should not tolerate any sin in their midst because this could affect their union with Christ.

4.3.3 Holiness and Anti-structure

This section will explore anti-structure as it relates to holiness. The church's status as God's holy people was the principal motivation for the early believers to live anti-structurally. Paul emphasizes this status by reminding believers that they are the ἅγιος – the "holy ones." They had gained this status because of their relationship to the holy God, who chose them and set them apart for his holy purposes (Rom 1:7). Thus, their holiness is accomplished by their union with Christ. This is evident in how Paul addresses the Corinthians: "Those who are sanctified in Christ Jesus, called to be saints, together with all those who in every place call on the name of our Lord Jesus Christ" (1 Cor 1:2 NRSV).

The power of the Holy Spirit also accomplishes this holiness: believers were "sanctified by the Holy Spirit" (Rom 15:15–16). This election and sanctification transferred believers from the ordinary to the "sphere of the holy."[227] These believers were extraordinary because they were chosen by God and made holy by the Holy Spirit; therefore, they and were required to live in a manner that distinguished them from unbelievers.

Different laws now governed them, the law of the Spirit (Rom 8:2). Paul also points to their separateness by reminding them that they were children of God by the same power of the Spirit and, therefore, heirs of God and co-heirs with Jesus Christ (Rom 8:17). According to Oakes, "Identity with the divine is the peak of holiness. Therefore, Paul ties the Christians very emphatically into existence as God's sons or children."[228] This identification with the holy God sets a boundary between believers and unbelievers, and firm boundaries are also required to maintain this status.

Paul advocates for boundaries to avoid contamination, as seen in his admonition to the Corinthians: "Therefore come out from them, and be separate from them, says the Lord, and touch nothing unclean; then I will welcome you, and I will be your father, and you shall be my sons and daughters, says the Lord Almighty" (2 Cor 6:17–18 NRSV). Sarah Whittle points out

---

227. Oakes, "Made Holy," loc. 2286, Kindle.
228. Oakes, loc. 2436, Kindle.

that "Gentile converts should put away evil deeds since they are 'called . . . not to impurity (*akatharisa*) but to holiness (*hagiasmos*)' (1 Thess 4:7). Thus, Paul exhorts the Corinthians 'let us cleanse ourselves (*katharizō*) from defilement (*molysmos*), making holiness (*hagiōsynē*) perfect' (2 Cor 7:1)."[229]

This leads to the question of the significance of purity as it relates to holiness.[230] Just as in the history of Israel, people who desired proximity to the holy God had to be purified. For Paul, this purification was a result of Christ's sacrifice. According to Mary Douglas, rules of pollution and purity are vital for maintaining the order and identity of a particular society – an idea that is evident in Paul's writings.[231] Paul's use of the temple metaphor (1 Cor 3:16) is an example of this and should be understood in the light of Jewish temple worship. Paul stresses the importance of purity because they, as the new community of faith, were now the temple of the Holy Spirit.[232] This was true for them as a community as well as the individual. This purity included physical purity as well as ethical and moral purity. They had to make sure that they kept their bodies pure, which included care in how they conducted themselves sexually (1 Cor 6:12–20), and what they ate (1 Cor 10:21). However, their purity was not dependent on observing cleansing rituals and animal sacrifices but on their new position in Christ: "But you were washed, you were sanctified, you were justified in the name of the Lord Jesus Christ and in the Spirit of our God" (1 Cor 6:11 NRSV).

Believers were to avoid sin because of their unity with Jesus Christ, the Messiah. Ginsburskaya suggests that Paul had the purity rules of Leviticus 18 in mind when he wrote 1 Corinthians 6.[233] This is plausible because of the

---

229. Whittle, "Purity in Paul," loc. 4420, Kindle.

230. In the past, the relationship between holiness and purity has often proved unclear because the terms have been used interchangeably. However, holiness and purity have distinct meanings. According to Theissen, "holiness is primarily a quality of God which can be transferred secondarily to human beings, objects, and rites," while purity is a quality of humans and objects, which relates to their being qualified to approach the divine. Theissen, *Earliest Churches*, 108. Purity is thus essential for understanding or approaching God. Latz and Ermakov, *Purity*, loc. 178, Kindle. According to Ginsburskaya, purity prepares the way for holiness and includes both physical and moral aspects. Ginsburskaya, "Purity and Impurity," loc. 642, Kindle. For further discussion on holiness and purity, see Milgrom, *Leviticus*; Horrell, *Solidarity and Difference*, 146–167; Newton, *Purity at Qumran*; Blidstein, *Purity, Community, and Ritual*.

231. Douglas, *Purity and Danger*, 2–3.

232. Newton, *Purity at Qumran*, 9.

233. Ginsburskaya, "Purity and Impurity," 3–29.

similarity of phrases used and the types of impurities mentioned in both texts. Paul's reminder that believers are temples of the Holy Spirit also emphasizes this connection (1 Cor 6:19–20). According to Jacob Milgrom, the Levitical priests believed that defiling or immoral behaviour – such as that described in Leviticus 18 – could drive God out of the temple and that regular purging was needed to atone for the wrongs of the people.[234] In 1 Corinthians 6:17, Paul says that believers are united with the Lord and must, therefore, shun fornication. This suggests that Paul feared that their union with Christ was at risk because of their defiling behaviour. Moreover, just as in Leviticus, believers must be holy because of the Lord their God (Lev 18:2; 1 Cor 6:19–20).

4.3.4 Holiness and Aggregation

Aggregation refers to the last stage in the ritual process, where neophytes are incorporated into their final state. In Paul's view, this is an eschatological state where believers will be perfected in holiness at the second coming of Jesus Christ.

To address the aggregation of believers, we return to 1 Thessalonians 5:23 (NRSV): "May the God of peace himself sanctify you entirely; and may your spirit and soul and body be kept sound and blameless at the coming of our Lord Jesus Christ." It is evident that God is the one who sanctifies, and he does a complete work. However, believers also have a responsibility to remain pure and blameless. Their ongoing maintenance of purity is critical, and it is in this sense that both purity and holiness have an eschatological goal. Paul emphasizes that the Thessalonians must be blameless at the coming of the Lord (1 Thess 5:23). He took this call to purity very seriously, seeing it as vital to preventing believers from falling away. His reference to Israel's idolatry serves as a severe warning to the Corinthians, who believed that they had already attained complete salvation. This is why Paul admonishes the Corinthians to be careful: "So, if you think you are standing firm, be careful that you don't fall" (1 Cor 10:12). Paul warns against the dominant forms of defilement prevalent in Corinth: eating, drinking, and sexual misconduct. This liminal time was a time of testing and preparation, and failure to live in holiness would present the real possibility of falling away.[235]

---

234. Milgrom, *Leviticus*, 9.
235. Oropeza, "Apostasy in the Wilderness," 73.

The final state of believers will also involve physical change. Those who have passed away will be raised, and the living will be changed and receive new glorified bodies. This is another result of *communitas* in Christ. As believers share in Christ's death, they will also share in his resurrection: "But in fact Christ has been raised from the dead, the first fruits of those who have died" (1 Cor 15:20 NRSV). Believers will be resurrected because God first raised Christ from the dead. By using the term "first fruits," Paul stresses the connection between Christ's resurrection and that of believers; Christ's resurrection assures the Corinthians that they will also be resurrected.[236] Their new bodies will be "heavenly" (1 Cor 15:40 NRSV), "imperishable" (15:42), raised in "glory" and "power" (15:43), clothed with "immortality" (15:54), and will "bear the image" of the resurrected Christ, the "man of heaven" (15:49). The final enemies that Christ will overcome are sin and death, representing the final stage in the sanctification of believers: "In v. 56, Paul connects sin, death, and Law. Jesus, through his death and resurrection, forgives sin, overcomes death, and annuls the condemning power of the Law."[237]

4.4 Conclusion

This chapter explored the concept of liminality in Paul. Liminality in the Pauline Epistles has been identified in three ways. First, believers live between the times: salvation begins with the incarnation, death, and resurrection of Christ but will be completed at the *parousia*. Second, believers live between the flesh and the Spirit. Although transferred to the realm of the Spirit when they were united with Christ, believers still live in a fallen body, in a fallen world. Evil powers are still operative in this world; however, Christ has defeated these powers through his resurrection and will complete their defeat at his second coming. Third, believers are called to live anti-structurally in relation to the institutions, positions, and axioms of the surrounding cultures.

Next, this chapter discussed the concept of *communitas*. In Paul's thinking, *communitas* is an egalitarian and sacred relationship. This *communitas* is vertical, as believers participate in the life of the Triune God through Christ Jesus, and this is exemplified in the African philosophy of vital participation.

---

236. Witherington, *Conflict and Community*, 304.
237. Witherington, 311.

Baptism is the initiation rite where believers are united with Christ. Paul presents baptism as the ritual space where believers are transformed into Christ's likeness and filled with the Holy Spirit. *Communitas* is also horizontal, as believers are united because they share the *pneuma* of Christ and are heirs together to all the blessings of Christ.

Finally, this chapter discussed holiness. Paul's presentation of the human condition in Romans 1:18–32 reveals that the primary manifestation of sin is idolatry, leading to social disintegration. Holiness, therefore, is defined as living in a reconciled and faithful relationship with God and one's neighbours through Jesus Christ. Holiness is cardinal as it is the primary identity marker of believers during this in-between time and a prerequisite for the completion of their salvation at Christ's second coming. Holiness is thus encapsulated in *communitas* with God and fellow believers. Holiness is embodied in the community's life and in their mission and vocation to spread the good news to the lost. Holiness will be perfected at the coming of Christ, when believers who have fallen asleep will be resurrected and those who are still alive will be changed and receive glorious bodies like that of Jesus, the risen Messiah.

CHAPTER 5

Sociohistorical Context for Ritual Meals in 1 Corinthians 8:1–11:1 and 1 Corinthians 11:17–34

5.0 Introduction

The previous chapter examined liminality and *communitas* in the Pauline Epistles. We determined that liminality in Paul includes both the temporal – life in the new age or the age of the Spirit – and the spatial/cosmological (between heaven and earth) axes. This "between and betwixt" situation required that believers live as the holy people of God – thus living anti-structurally – as they awaited their aggregation in Christ at the *parousia*.

We also found that this liminal state is characterized by *communitas*. Believers enter *communitas* with Christ and fellow believers in baptism by the agency of the Holy Spirit. We defined holiness as being in *communitas* with a holy God and fellow believers while living anti-structurally with regard to the surrounding culture. Failure to live in this manner could lead to judgement and even exclusion from the promises of Christ.

This chapter discusses the sociohistorical context for ritual meals in 1 Corinthians 8:1–11:1 and 1 Corinthians 11:17–34. First, it will examine background information pertaining to the church in Corinth and the motivation behind defining the Lord's Supper as a ritual rather than a ceremony. It will then define what we understand by "strong" and "weak" members in the Corinthian church and construct an overview of the meal culture in

Corinth. This sociohistorical background will enhance our understanding of ritual meals in Corinth.

5.1 The Use of Ritual or Ceremony

In this research, the use of "ritual" rather than "ceremony" to refer to the Lord's Supper is deliberate. According to Victor Turner,

> The term "ritual" is to be more fittingly applied to forms of religious behaviour associated with social transitions, while the term "ceremony" has a closer bearing on religious behaviour associated with social states, where politico-legal institutions also have greater importance. Ritual is transformative, ceremony confirmatory.[1]

This definition by Turner has persuaded several scholars to label baptism as an initiation ritual, while seeing the Lord's Supper as a ceremony. According to Horrell, the Lord's Supper is a "ceremony to maintain and to shape the community,"[2] and Margaret McDonald terms it a ceremony that "served essentially to confirm roles and status."[3] Concepts of maintenance and integration are present in Paul's discussion of the Lord's Supper. Notwithstanding the description of the meal as a "ceremony," many suggest that this diminishes the power of the Lord's Supper to transform and shape the believing community.

This research prefers to describe the Lord's Supper as a ritual. According to Strecker, there was a difference of opinion between Paul and the Corinthian congregation concerning the nature of the Lord's Supper.[4] Paul expected the meal to reflect egalitarian relationships where social differences were dissolved, but the opposite was taking place in Corinth, with the love feast and celebration of the Lord's Supper replicating the social conditions and fixed status positions within Graeco-Roman society at that time. This was reflected in the explicit trophic, temporal, and spatial differences during the meals.[5]

---

1. Turner, "Betwixt and Between," 235.
2. Horrell, *Solidarity and Difference*, 117–118.
3. MacDonald, "Ritual," 234.
4. Strecker, *Liminale Theologie*, 324–326.
5. Strecker, 321.

First, the trophic considers the quantity and quality of food that was served during the communal meals. It appears that there was an unequal distribution of food since some went hungry while others overate. The second factor concerns the timing of the meals. Theissen postulates that the poor people in the community would probably have arrived later than the rich did and would thus have been served leftovers. Third, spatial differences could also have been an issue. Strecker explains that the wealthy members would eat in the triclinium – that is, the dining room – while the poor, arriving later, would be seated in the atrium.[6] These stark differences would not only have undermined *communitas* among believers but, as we shall see later, would also have rendered the Lord's Supper ineffective in the community.

The Corinthians viewed the Lord's Supper as a ceremony that affirmed the social hierarchy rather than reflecting the *kenotic* life of Christ. Strecker postulates that Paul tried to "re-ritualize" the Lord's Supper by emphasizing the ritual qualities in 1 Corinthians 11:17–34.[7] Paul thus counters the problem by advising the Corinthians to eat at home if they were hungry and instructing them to wait for one another to partake in the Lord's Supper. In this way, Paul was restoring the ritual nature of the meal.[8]

I agree with Strecker concerning the re-ritualization of the meal. However, Strecker does not go far enough in his exploration of the impact of the Lord's Supper on the community. More can be done in conversation with African spirituality to explore how the meal transforms the community, the repercussions of εἰδωλόθυτα, and the allegorical significance as well as actual changes that the Lord's Supper creates for an ideal community.

Ritual meals are believed to have spiritual significance and mediate spiritual transformation through their material consumption.[9] This cultic nature may be in relation to the history of the meal or its present cultic context.[10] Treating the meal as a ritual will serve to answer the question presented by this research: How do ritual meals affect the holiness of the believing community? We propose that, for Paul, ritual meals are occasions with

---

6. Strecker, 321.
7. Strecker, 324.
8. Strecker, 324.
9. Schweitzer, *Mysticism of Paul*, 229.
10. Gooch, *Dangerous Food*, 55.

spiritual significance, influence, and transformation. Indeed, all the meals in 1 Corinthians 8:1–11:1, 11:17–34 are rituals that transform the community – whether they are the table of demons or the table of the Lord.

5.2 Liminality and *Communitas* in 1 Corinthians 8:1–11:1 and 1 Corinthians 11:17–34

The dominant culture in Corinth – which was one of the great and thriving cities of the Roman Empire during the first century – was Graeco-Roman. Corinth was colonized by Roman veterans, freed slaves, and urban plebians, *cives*, as well as some Greek inhabitants, the *incolae*, who had no civic rights.[11] According to Horrell, Corinth's social and administrative structures functioned within the broader political system of the Roman Empire:[12] "The social structure of the empire as a whole is probably best visualised as a large pyramid; a representation of a system in which power, wealth and status are concentrated heavily within a tiny population."[13]

This hierarchy was also present in the household run by the *paterfamilias*, who had power over all people in the family, including household slaves.[14] The Corinthians "lived within an honour-shame cultural orientation, where public recognition was often more important than facts and where the worst thing that could happen was for one's reputation to be publicly tarnished."[15]

The influence of this honour-shame culture is evident in the Corinthian ἐκκλησία (church), as reflected in several of the issues Paul addresses. The members' social levels were diverse. While the majority were from the lower social classes (1 Cor 1:26–28), there is enough evidence to suggest that several were from higher social levels. According to Witherington, two members might even have been government officials.[16] Gerd Theissen argues that the Corinthian church was marked by "internal social stratification" and suggests that a few of the Corinthians named probably enjoyed a high social status.[17]

---

11. Witherington, *Conflict and Community*, 6–7.
12. Horrell, *Social Ethos*, 65.
13. Horrell, 65.
14. Horrell, 65.
15. Witherington, *Conflict and Community*, 8.
16. Witherington, 32.
17. Theissen, "Social Stratification," 105.

It appears that social status was a factor in both situations – εἰδωλοθύτων and the Lord's Supper – where discord was manifested. This will be discussed further in section 5.3.

In both cases, the Corinthians seemed to have insisted on maintaining their social contacts and status within the surrounding social context.[18] Paul attempts to resolve this conflict by reminding the Corinthians that they belong to the kingdom of Christ and should, therefore, be governed by the ethos of this kingdom. He does this by contrasting the value system of the Roman Empire or the present age with that of the kingdom of Christ.

1 Corinthians 8:1–11:1 and 11:17–34 deal with the overarching question of how followers of Christ should relate to God and one another while living amid a pagan culture. In 1 Corinthians 8:1–11:1, Paul addresses the issue of εἰδωλόθυτα – that is, eating food offered to idols – and in 11:17–34, he deals with the abuse of the Lord's Supper. In both situations, the "strong" in the community pursue their rights and self-interest to the detriment of the "weak." In the context of εἰδωλόθυτα, the strong insist on their right to eat food offered to idols, and they showed no empathy with their weaker fellow believers. In the context of the Lord's Supper, some believers overate and got drunk, not caring that their family in Christ were going hungry. In both situations, Paul uses the Lord's Supper both to discuss the desired nature of the community of believers and to correct negative behaviour.

Paul locates his discussion of ritual meals within the liminal context. The believers were the people "on whom the ends of the ages have come" (1 Cor 10:11 NRSV); and by eating the Lord's Supper, they "proclaim the Lord's death until he comes" (11:26). Paul's objective is to warn the Corinthians that they, like the Israelites in the wilderness, are in a liminal situation (10:1–13) and that their conduct during this period may lead to them being excluded from the kingdom at the coming of Christ. He reminds them of a new cosmology, where their new identity in Christ influences and determines their behaviour. This new creation, accessed through Christ, allows Paul to redraw believers' ethical map and lay a new foundation for the practise of their freedom.[19]

Paul calls the "strong" to live according to the values of *communitas* as defined in the previous chapter. As the ἅγιος (1 Cor 1:2), they are united with

---

18. Horrell, *Social Ethos*, 109.
19. Leese, *Cosmic Goal of Redemption*, 79.

Christ and with one another and are to live anti-structurally with regard to the surrounding pagan culture (2 Cor 6:17). In his discussion of εἰδωλόθυτα in 1 Corinthians 8 and 9, Paul encourages the Corinthians to be guided by love rather than knowledge (8:1–3), surrendering their rights and freedoms to their fellow believers. He sets himself up as an example of self-denial (9:19–23) and self-discipline (9:24–27), giving up the right to monetary benefit and the right to travel with a spouse for the sake of the gospel and becoming "a slave to everyone" he ministers to (9:19). In 1 Corinthians 10, Paul moves to the example of the exodus generation to demonstrate the fate of those who failed due to idolatry. He uses the Lord's Supper as a metaphor to explain the true nature of εἰδωλόθυτα. In 1 Corinthians 11:17–34, Paul returns to the Lord's Supper, rebuking the Corinthians for their thoughtless behaviour towards the disadvantaged in the community and, once again, using the Lord's Supper as a metaphor for true *communitas* among believers.

In all these examples, Christ is the common denominator or "mediator," as McDonough puts it.[20] Paul notes the presence of Christ at creation (1 Cor 8:6), in the desert (10:4–9), in Paul's own calling (9:1), and, most significantly, in the ritual meal (10:16). In 1 Corinthians 11:17–34, Paul warns that the Lord's Supper should be κυριανκὸν δεῖπον (the Lord's Supper) and not their own meals. *Communitas* with Christ is, thus, central to Paul's discussion of ritual meals. It prohibits participation with idols, facilitates *communitas* among believers, and is a means to proclaim Christ to the surrounding culture.

5.3 Defining the "Strong" and the "Weak" in Corinth

The topic of the "strong" and the "weak" in Paul is a comprehensive discussion that includes 1 Corinthians 8:1–11:1; 11:17–34 and Romans 14:1–23 and cannot be dealt with extensively in this study.[21] Therefore, this section

---

20. McDonough, *Christ as Creator*, 150.

21. For an overview of previous discussions, see Gäckle, *who* defines the "strong" and the "weak" considering popular Stoic thought. According to Gäckle, the "strong" refers to the self-assured, elite intellectual and educated group and the "weak" to those with inadequate intellectual understanding, who are of low status. Gäckle, *Die Starken*, 216–218. Mark Reasoner also approaches the subject in the light of the first-century Roman context. He describes the "strong" as prominently Gentile, while also including some Jews who identified with Roman

will focus on how this issue pertains to the "strong" and the "weak" in relation to two passages dealing with ritual meals – 1 Corinthians 8:1–11 and 1 Corinthians 11:17–34.

In 1 Corinthians 8, Paul uses the term "weak" to refer to those Corinthians with weak consciences, who should avoid eating food offered to idols so that their conscience would not be defiled (8:9–10). Although Paul does not use the word "strong" in 1 Corinthians 8, this is inferred from his references to the "weak" and the "strong" elsewhere (1 Cor 1:25, 27; 2:3; 4:10). In this study, these terms will be used more inclusively since we are considering two passages: 1 Corinthians 8:1–11:1 and 1 Corinthians 11:17–34.

In 1 Corinthians 11:17–34, Paul rebukes the wealthier members of the church for humiliating "those who have nothing" (11:22). In this study, the terms "strong" and "weak" are based on two factors: the nature of the believer's knowledge and their socio-economic situation. This does not imply that both conditions must necessarily coexist for a person to be classified as "weak." Socio-economic status *or* insecurity in conscience or faith may result in a believer being classified as "weak."

First, "strong" and "weak" may be related to the believer's socio-economic situation. The socio-economic background of the Corinthian congregation has been discussed comprehensively by scholars.[22] According to Thiselton,[23] Reasoner,[24] and Yeo,[25] "weak" can refer to those who are either secure or insecure in terms of their social-economic status. The Corinthian church consisted of a "cross-section of urban society."[26] This probably included some wealthy people and some impoverished people.[27] Although Paul's comment in 1 Corinthians 1:26–30 might create the impression that the congregation were primarily from the lower classes, enough evidence exists to show that the congregation included wealthy members. According to Theissen, the Corinthian

---

culture. The "weak" consist of some Jews, as well as Gentiles, of low status. They might have been vegetarian because of their Roman beliefs. Reasoner, *Strong and the Weak*, 218–219.

22. See Meeks, *First Urban Christians*, 51–73; Witherington, *Conflict and Community*; Martin, *Corinthian Body*; Yeo, *Rhetorical Interaction*, 84–94; Finney, *Honour and Conflict*, 49–63; Theissen, *Social Setting*; Engels, *Roman Corinth*; Murphy-O'Connor, *St. Paul's Corinth*.

23. Thiselton, *Corinthians*, 604.
24. Reasoner, *Strong and the Weak*, 200–220.
25. Yeo, *Rhetorical Interaction*, 90–91.
26. Meeks, *First Urban Christians*, 73.
27. Witherington, *Conflict and Community*, 22.

congregation was marked by social stratification, where the "strong" refers to the small group of wealthy members who opposed the majority who were from lower social classes.[28] Theissen suggests that "the 'powerful' would be influential people; the 'wise,' those who belong the educated classes (that is, 'wise' according to worldly standards) for whom wisdom is also a sign of social status."[29]

On the other hand, the "weak" would have included the poor, those with no connections to Rome, and those of low cultural sophistication.[30] These differences seem most evident during the celebration of the Lord's Supper. Some members arrived early and ate their private meals, while others went hungry (1 Cor 11:21). Some scholars suggest that this indicates an economic disparity, with higher-ranking members – who probably had more freedom to arrive early – overeating and getting drunk, while those of lower status might have arrived late and gone hungry.[31] Paul's comment about "humiliating those who have nothing" (1 Cor 11:22) emphasizes economic and social divide.[32] Yeo describes the "weak" as "those of low social standing', the 'poor,' or 'the mass of undifferentiated citizens who have no social standing."[33]

Second, "strong" and "weak" may refer to differences in terms of knowledge. The "weak" were those who did not possess the knowledge that "an idol is nothing at all in the world" and that "there is no God but one" (1 Cor 8:4). Since these believers' συνείδησις (consciences) are weak (8:7), they could be destroyed by eating food offered to idols (8:11). This is because they had were so accustomed to idols that they believed that idols were real representations of deities and thought of the food as food offered to these deities (8:7).

There are many interpretations of what Paul might have meant when referring to believers' consciences as "weak."[34] For Ciampa and Rosner, this weakness refers to the inability to resist social pressure to participate in eating food

---

28. Theissen, "Social Stratification," 69–120.

29. Theissen, 98. See also Oakes, *Empire*, 63–119; Chow, *Patronage and Power*.

30. Witherington, *Conflict and Community*, 22; Lampe, "Eucharist," 38–39; Yeo, *Rhetorical Interaction*, 90.

31. Strecker, *Liminale Theologie*, 322; Oakes, *Empire*, 63–119; Lampe, "Eucharist," 39.

32. Theissen, *Social Setting*, 97.

33. Yeo, *Rhetorical Interaction*, 90.

34. Pierce, *Conscience*; Witherington, *Conflict and Community*, 190; Horrell, *Social Ethos*, 10–109; Willis, *Idol Meat in Corinth*, 92–96; Yeo, *Rhetorical Interaction*, 90; Smit, *About the Idol Offerings*, 86; Murphy-O'Connor, *Keys to First Corinthians*, 94.

offered to idols even though they perceived this as sin.³⁵ They arrive at this conclusion based on the Roman concept of weakness, which was associated with the inability to make sound, independent judgements, as well as the Old Testament context, where idolatry is often depicted as resulting from social pressure.³⁶ Believers might succumb to this pressure because "the strength of their own convictions is not sufficient to resist the social pressure (*if their conscience is weak*), they defile themselves."³⁷ This view is questionable since the point of this passage is that the "weak" are not eating εἰδωλόθυτα, but the idea of social pressure is relevant in the Corinthian church.³⁸

According to Joop Smit, Paul's use of "weak" in 1 Corinthians 8:7 may refer to new believers, who were still immature in their knowledge.³⁹ Similarly, Pierce makes an interesting point by comparing the weak to the "little ones" found in the Jesus tradition (Matt 18:6; Mark 9:42; Luke 17:2).⁴⁰ He suggests that those believers who have not yet reached maturity or gained enough knowledge are vulnerable and require extra consideration from their more mature brothers and sisters. For Fee, "weaknesses refer to a lack of experiential knowledge."⁴¹ Their former experience of idols continues to inform their thinking, and so they cannot eat without believing that they had done something wrong. The general idea is that the "weak" might have been less mature in their knowledge and faith than the "strong." Smit's and Fee's observations are valid; however, this research suggests that there is more to this discussion than the internal struggles of the "weak" believers. We must also consider the nature of idols and the spiritual forces behind them, which can make participation in food offered to idols dangerous for believers. This will be discussed further in chapter 6.

This leads to our next question: What is the meaning of συνείδησις in this context? Gooch advocates that συνείδησις, as used in 1 Corinthians 8 and 10, should be translated as "bad feelings."⁴² He comes to this conclusion

---

35. Ciampa and Rosner, *Corinthians*.
36. Ciampa and Rosner, 385.
37. Ciampa and Rosner, 385.
38. Gardner, *Gifts of God*, 44.
39. Smit, *About the Idol Offerings*, 86.
40. Pierce, *Conscience*, 78.
41. Fee, *Corinthians*, 417.
42. Gooch, "Conscience," 244–254.

because he does not find any evidence that Paul might be referring to moral conscience in these passages. However, this view seems limited in light of Paul's stern warning that eating idol-food could lead to the destruction of fellow believers and is a sin against Christ (1 Cor 8:11–12). Could "bad feelings" have such dire consequences?

Willis,[43] Horsley,[44] and Gardner[45] prefer self-awareness or self-reflection as the most appropriate definition of συνείδησις. Horsley argues that συνείδησις should be translated as "inner consciousness or awareness."[46] In this sense, συνείδησις functions to prevent the soul from wrong or to accuse and convict when a person has acted in an unjust manner.[47] Horsley postulates that Hellenistic Judaism, which in turn was influenced by Stoicism, can help to illuminate Paul's use of συνείδησις in conjunction with γνῶσις (knowledge) (1 Cor 8:1–3). According to this view, the possession of divine γνῶσις or σοφία (wisdom) "convicts one's consciousness (or mind) with such strength that one enjoys almost absolute spiritual freedom and authority."[48] This invincible attitude and arrogance is evident in the insistence of the "strong" on eating idol-food and even assuming that it is harmless to participate meals in idol temples (1 Cor 10:14–17). This is also implied in Paul's warnings concerning the use of their ἐξουσία (authority) (10:23).

Horsley thus suggests that the "strong conscience" is not a positive thing, as perceived by the "strong" in Corinth, but, rather, part of the problem.[49] The self-assured abuse of freedom practised by the "strong" damages the community's well-being by harming the "weak" believers. This inverted stance is congruent with Paul's use of "strong" and "weak" in this epistle (1 Cor 1:25, 27; 2:3; 4:10). It also aligns with Paul's understanding of the true source of wisdom. Instead of pointing to the Graeco-Roman culture or the Torah as the source of true wisdom, Paul points to Christ as the true wisdom of God (1 Cor 1:22–24), revealed by the Spirit (2:9–10).[50] True wisdom is far more

---

43. Willis, *Idol Meat in Corinth*, 94.
44. Horsley, "Consciousness and Freedom," 578–589.
45. Gardner, *Gifts of God*, 46.
46. Horsley, "Consciousness and Freedom," 578–589.
47. Horsley, 582.
48. Horsley, 577.
49. Horsley, 586.
50. Davis, "Individual Ethical Conscience," 1–18.

than reciting slogans; it is the wisdom of God revealed and embodied in the self-sacrificial life of Jesus Christ, who is God's wisdom (1:30).

Although it initially appears that Paul agrees with the Corinthian slogans (1 Cor 8: 4, 8), a closer look at this passage reveals that he is more intent on guiding the "strong" Corinthians to discover that they "do not yet know as they ought to know" (1 Cor 8:2). Paul does not seem to have felt any need to correct the "weak," and the "strong" remain his target audience for correction. The problem is not the "over-sensitive conscience" of the "weak"; rather, it is the "under-sensitivity" of the "strong" that requires transformation.[51] The "strong" have a responsibility to their fellow believers to build them up in love (1 Cor 8:1-3), rather than scarring their consciences by the arrogant pursuit of self-gratification.[52]

Based on this discussion, the "strong" and the "weak" may be described as being secure or insecure in social and economic terms, as well in their level of self-awareness.[53] The experiential knowledge of the "weak" did not allow them to eat meat offered to idols without defiling themselves, while their socio-economic circumstances made them vulnerable to abuse during the Lord's Supper. The "strong," on the other hand, are those who believed that their knowledge allowed them the freedom to participate in the consumption of εἰδωλόθυτα without regard for the "weak." They might also have been members who enjoyed higher status within the community, who were also able to influence how the Lord's Supper was celebrated.

5.4 Meals in Corinth

Since scholars have paid great attention to the possible historical background of the Corinthian meals,[54] this research only provides a brief overview of some of the key findings.

---

51. Pierce, *Conscience*, 81.
52. Söding, "Starke und Schwache," 69-92.
53. Thiselton, *Corinthians*, 644.
54. See Jamir, *Exclusion and Judgment*, 1-113; Gooch, *Dangerous Food*, 40-42; Cheung, *Idol Food in Corinth*, 27-36; Smith and Taussig, *Many Tables*, 21-35; Philip, *Paul and Common Meal*, 1-36; Willis, *Idol Meat in Corinth*, 47-62; Finney, *Honour and Conflict*, 151-155; Marshall, *Last Supper*, 13-29; Coutsoumpos, *Lord's Supper*, 9-22; Last, *Pauline Church*.

While meals in ancient times served various functions, they were first and foremost communal. Eating together was a foundational aspect of the Mediterranean communal culture.[55] Meals were used to form new affiliations and to strengthen existing ones.[56] According to Jamir, one indication of the importance of fellowship meals is the fact that so many Greek and Roman authors wrote about them, offering important insights into these meal practices.[57] The general format of dinner parties included dinner or the first course, this was called first tables, followed by a break. This was followed by "second tables", better known as the "symposium." The symposium was an occasion on which the gods might be invoked or honoured, and it included drinking and entertainment. Philosophical schools used the symposium as an opportunity for discourses and discussions.[58] According to Jamir, these meals were often "under the patronage of poets, philosophers and other thinkers."[59]

Meals were also utilized to shape society in diverse ways. Different types of meals served a range of functions, and regulations concerning food, seating, and procedures contributed to their transformative impact. According to Smith and Taussig, social stratification during meals and the ranking of guests was evident in the seating arrangements, the type and quantity of food served, and the order in which guests were served.[60] On the other hand, social equality was pursued by intentionally disregarding these accepted distinctions in certain circles.[61]

According to James Walters, meals were effective tools for transforming social status, and people used meal invitations for social advancement.[62] Walters's research demonstrates that these meal practices were not only

---

55. Jamir, *Exclusion and Judgment*, 1.
56. Jamir, 62.
57. Jamir, 3.
58. Some examples include Plato's famous *Symposium* that describes philosophical banquets in honour of Socrates; Plato, *Symposium*; Plutarch's discussion on the appropriateness components of philosophical banquets; Plutarch, *Moralia, Table Talk*; Xenophon, *Symposium*; Lucian's comical portrayal of the Greek Symposium; Lucian, *Carousal*; and Dio Chrysostom's discourse on how the foolishness of humans is revealed during the Symposium; Dio Chrysostom, *Discourse 27*.
59. Jamir, *Exclusion and Judgment*, 9.
60. Smith and Taussig, *Many Tables*, 33.
61. Smith and Taussig, 33.
62. Gooch, *Dangerous Food*, 41–42.

effective for making friends, gaining allies, and affirming animosities[63] but were also an essential tool in the politician's arsenal.[64] Walters examined various political documents from this period and found that meals were used to persuade voters to support their hosts. According to Walters, there are several points of overlap between these political documents and the situation surrounding the Lord's Supper in Corinth:

> Paul's regulations for the community meal in Corinth sought to accomplish something quite similar to what the colonial charter from Urso sought to accomplish: individual candidates – or their supporters – would not be able to use their status as meal hosts to tilt 'voters' towards their aspirations of leadership in the colony.[65]

Walters's findings suggest that some Corinthians might have used the communal meal as an opportunity to grab positions of leadership in the church. This attempt to create desired change supports our proposition that meals were used as a tool for social transformation.

Meal fellowship was not just horizontal but also vertical in function. Graeco-Roman society offered a variety of opportunities to partake in ritual meals, including cults to deities, state festivals, and private banquets that generally included some religious element, irrespective of the intended purpose of the gathering.[66] Since there was no strict compartmentalization between the sacred and the secular in the Graeco-Roman era, it is difficult to differentiate between the sacred and secular nature of meals during this period.[67] Ancient literature has many examples of fellowship meals eaten in the presence of gods or goddesses – either to honour them or to avert their displeasure.[68]

While Gooch says that sacrificial meals were generally held to mark and facilitate transitions in society – for example, birthdays and funerals[69] – he also notes instances where sacrificial meals were held without there being any

---

63. Gooch, *Dangerous Food*, 43.
64. Walters, "Politics of Meals," 351.
65. Walters, 363.
66. Willis, *Idol Meat in Corinth*, 13.
67. Willis, 17–20; Gooch, *Dangerous Food*, 31; Cheung, *Idol Food in Corinth*, 33.
68. Coutsoumpos, *Lord's Supper*, 9–12.
69. Gooch, *Dangerous Food*, 31–36.

special occasion.[70] This demonstrates the pervasiveness of ritual meals; and, as Gooch suggests, the Corinthians would probably have been confronted with food that had some cultic associations even while visiting private homes.[71]

In the Hebrew culture, meals were central to building and shaping community and relating to Yahweh. According to Jamir, ritual meals occurred at pivotal points in salvation history; they were an integral part of the ratification of covenants and the setting where the close relationship between Yahweh and his people was enacted.[72] The promise of food was thus a central part of the covenant God made with Israel. Throughout history, God's relationship with Israel was linked with the food motif.[73]

Sharing fellowship meals was thus a crucial act that represented both the relationship between Yahweh and his people and the relationship among God's people.[74] This sacred function is reflected in the celebrations and festivals commemorating key events in Israel's history,[75] with the Passover meal being the most significant since this meal was probably the forerunner to the Lord's Supper.[76]

While some elements that are common to both Graeco-Roman and Jewish meal cultures, Hal Taussig suggests that the differences are minor because meals in both cultures followed a similar format and shared similar interpretations and functions.[77] The ritual context of sacrificial meals will be elaborated on in chapters 6 and 7.

5.5 Conclusion

This chapter offered a brief overview of the sociohistorical context of the Corinthian congregation. It provided a summary of ritual meals in the Corinthian ἐκκλησία and suggested that Paul uses the Lord's Supper in

---

70. Gooch, 36–7.
71. Gooch, 38.
72. Jamir, *Exclusion and Judgment*, 25.
73. Jamir, 27.
74. Philip, *Paul and Common Meal*, 3.
75. Jamir, *Exclusion and Judgment*, 38.
76. Wright, *Faithfulness of God*, 1347; Jeremias, "This Is My Body," 196; Jamir, *Exclusion and Judgment*, 29; Gardner, *1 Corinthians*, 506.
77. Taussig, *In the Beginning*, 23.

both 1 Corinthians 8:1–11:1 and 11:17–34, to encourage *communitas* among believers.

Second, it was suggested that the term "ritual" – rather than "ceremony" – be used to refer to the meals in 1 Corinthians 8:1–11:1 and 11:17–34 because rituals are transformative, while ceremonies maintain social structures. The overview of meals in the Graeco-Roman context suggested that sacrificial meals were pervasive in the first-century context and were utilized to effect change in society.

Third, the "strong" believers were defined as those who were socio-economically strong and boasted about their knowledge. The "weak," on the other hand, could refer to either the poor in the community – those marginalized in terms of resources – or those whose consciences were too sensitive to permit participation in εἰδωλόθυτα. Both these conditions could also be present in a single "weak" individual, and a broad definition was chosen to be inclusive for both definitions.

Finally, the ubiquity of sacrificial meals was discussed in the light of the role they play in facilitating social change and connection with deities. It was noted that ritual meals in Graeco-Roman culture were used to accomplish social transformations, achieve political gains, and influence the behaviour of deities – either to atone for wrongdoing or petition for well-being.

This chapter provides the sociohistorical background for interpreting ritual meals in Corinth. It also clarifies some key terms used in this study and lays the groundwork for interpreting 1 Corinthians 8:1–11:1 and 11:17–34.

Part 3

Ritual Meals in 1 Corinthians 8:1–11:1 and 1 Corinthians 11:17–34

This section brings together Victor Turner's theory of liminality and *communitas*, our discussion on African Traditional Religion, and a consideration of Paul's context in order to analyze ritual meals in 1 Corinthians 8:1–11:1 and 11:17–34. This section aims to highlight the sacramental nature of ritual meals, explore their capacity for transformation, and discuss the ethical changes that participation in such meals brings about. The answers to these questions are essential to this study because they will help us to address the primary questions of this research: Does the continued practice of ritual meals to ancestors constitute idolatry? Can evangelical churches use the Lord's Supper more effectively to facilitate transformation to holiness of the believing community.

Chapter 6 discusses participation in εἰδωλόθυτα in 1 Corinthians 8:1–11:1. This chapter endeavours to answer the following questions: Does participation in εἰδωλόθυτα constitute idolatry, and how does such participation impact the holiness of the community? This section suggests that Paul discourages participation in εἰδωλόθυτα because it destroys *communitas* with Christ and, consequently, fellow believers.

Chapter 7 explores the celebration of the Lord's Supper in 1 Corinthians 11:17–34. Paul rebukes the wrongful treatment of the "weak" in relation to their deficient participation in the Lord's Supper. Does this signify that Paul believed that participation in a worthy manner could serve as a means of transforming the community to live in Christlike love?

Chapters 6 and 7 explore the suggestion that ritual meals – whether to pagan deities, demons, or Christ – may hold transformative power and may, therefore, affect the holiness of the ἐκκλησία (church).

CHAPTER 6

Feasting with Demons in 1 Corinthians 8:1–11:1

6.0 Introduction

This section discusses the consumption of εἰδωλόθυτα in 1 Corinthians 8:1–11:1 in the light of African cultural concepts of spirituality and communalism. Such a reading privileges the sacramental and communal nature of the discussion. First, we will discuss the ritual context of 1 Corinthians 8:1–11:1. DeMaris, referencing Strecker, suggests that a text should be read from a ritual perspective when "a text concerns itself with the meaning, function, or implementation of a rite."[1] Prioritizing rituals may thus highlight crucial information concerning the text. Ritual references and echoes permeate the text; the theme of εἰδωλόθυτα already alerts us to the ritual nature of this discussion. In 1 Corinthians 9:13, Paul compares his ministry to that of a priest serving at the altar, and 1 Corinthians 10 is replete with ritual references (10:2–4, 7, 14, 16–21, 28). Ritual must take precedence in the discussion of εἰδωλόθυτα.

Next, I will define idolatry to ascertain if participation in εἰδωλόθυτα constitutes idolatry. In 1 Corinthians 8:1–11:1, Paul addresses this question: Should believers participate in eating εἰδωλόθυτα, and if so, under what circumstances should this be allowed? The concern about idolatry is evident in Paul's introductory remark "Now concerning food sacrificed to idols," his earnest warning "Therefore, my dear friends, flee from the worship of idols"

---

1. DeMaris, *New Testament*, 6.

(1 Cor 10:14 NRSV), his examples of idolatry in Israel (10:1–14, 18–22), and his use of εἰδωλόθυτα instead of ἱερόθυτον (meat sacrificed for sacred use).[2] Εἰδωλόθυτα (1 Cor 8:1) is translated as "food offered to idols" (RSV) and "food sacrificed to idols" (NRSV, NIV).[3] Since the word "idols" in this phrase implies a negative view of the practices it describes, it is clear that, right from the outset, Paul was negatively disposed towards the consumption of εἰδωλόθυτα and wanted to discourage participation in it.

Thereafter, I will examine the exodus narrative and the Old Testament covenant – reinterpreted in the light of the sacrificial life and death of Christ – as the underlying myths[4] for ritual meals in Corinth. Paul grounds his argument in God's larger salvation story by alluding to the Genesis account (1 Cor 8:6), referencing the covenant between God and Israel (1 Cor 10:1–13), and considering all this within the framework of the salvation accomplished by the life, death, and resurrection of Jesus Christ. This broader scheme of things results in a situation where what appears to be innocent participation in their cultural context might have spiritual and cosmological implications for the believing community.

Next, I will consider *communitas* as participation "in Christ," which transform believers into greater Christlikeness. Paul's principal concern in this passage is the holiness of the community, which, he believed, was being undermined by idolatry. This is in line with Paul's broader concerns for holiness in the letter to the Corinthians (1 Cor 1:2; 3:17; 6:11, 19).[5] Paul's intentions go beyond simply correcting the Corinthians' behaviour; his deeper concern is their purity and holiness.[6]

Finally, I will consider the ritual outcomes of participating in εἰδωλόθυτα, examining a possible impact this practice can have on the community.

---

2. It seems likely that εἰδωλόθυτα is a word of early Christian origin that "expresses Christian abhorrence of pagan sacrifices." Thiselton, *Corinthians*, 617–718. This is because there seems to be little evidence of the word in Hellenistic Judaism, except in 4 Maccabees 5:2. Witherington, *Conflict and Community*, 189; see also Gardner, *Gifts of God*, 15.

3. Thiselton, *Corinthians*, 617.

4. Myths refer to the beliefs behind rituals. They are the religious narratives believed to be true by the ritual practitioners. Horrell, *Solidarity and Difference*, 99; Theissen, *Earliest Churches*, 23.

5. DeMaris, *New Testament*, 80.

6. Brower, *God's Holy People*, 59.

6.1 The Ritual Context of 1 Corinthians 8:1–11:1

This section will focus on the ritual background of meals in the Mediterranean context, based on the assumption that context is crucial to interpreting rituals.[7] Religion was pervasive in Corinthian culture and foundational to how Corinthian society functioned.

First, Corinth was marked by religious pluralism, as revealed by archaeological evidence of numerous temples and shrines dedicated to various gods and heroes in the city's public spaces.[8] This array of temples points to the pantheon of gods worshipped in the Graeco-Roman world, including Greek and Roman gods, as well as deities from Egypt and the Far East. According to Larry Hurtado, religion impacted every sphere of life in the Roman world:[9] "Birth, death, marriage, the domestic sphere, civil and wider political life, work, the military socialising, entertainment, arts music- all were imbued with religious significance and associations."[10] Gods were thus acknowledged and included in daily life through various devotional practices.

Second, the religious world view required a "rich variety of ritual actions for various occasions and for various deities."[11] Sacrifices, especially animal sacrifices, were a common element of rituals and vital to the well-being and prosperity of both the city and the Empire.[12] Temple priests performed sacrifices on behalf of the city or families on various occasions for purposes such as thanksgiving, petitions, and other seasonal observances.[13] Most of these sacrifices were coupled with a feast where the sacrificial animal was the main course.[14]

According to William Barclay, sacrificial victims were very seldom burned up entirely; instead, the priest and the worshippers usually consumed them.[15] Barclay describes various ritual meals from the mystery religions:

---

7. DeMaris, *New Testament*, 7.
8. Winter, "Religious Pluralism," 210.
9. Hurtado, *Origins of Christian Worship*, 9.
10. Hurtado, 9.
11. Hurtado, 23.
12. Finney, *Honour and Conflict*, 147.
13. Finney, 148.
14. Hurtado, *Origins of Christian Worship*, 24.
15. Barclay, *Lord's Supper*, 98.

> At Eleusis the sacrifice to Demeter and Korē was followed by a banquet in which the flesh of the victims was eaten. In the Mysteries of Mithra, bread and a cup of water were offered to the initiate. In the Samothracian Mysteries it was said that "the priest shall break and offer the food, and pour out the cup to the initiates. In the Dionysus-Zagreus cult the communicants rushed madly upon the sacrificial animal, tore it to pieces, and ate it raw, believing that the god was resident in the offering."[16]

Barclay suggests that initiates participated in these rituals as a means of enjoying communion with the gods and nourishing their own lives.[17]

Barclay's suggestions are affirmed in a study by Peter Gooch.[18] Gooch discusses the dining rooms of Lerna, which were connected to the Asklepios in the city of Corinth, the sacred precinct where cultic activities and petitions for healing took place.[19] According to Gooch, the dining rooms at Lerna would have been used for family celebrations, but their proximity to the Asklepios suggests that most of these meals were probably connected to the ritual activities of the precinct.[20] However, there might have been occasions when the dining halls were used for celebrations that were not connected to religious rituals.[21] Gooch suggests that food was used in three ways in the cult of Asklepios:

> First sacred food was used in the rites of the cultus. Second, sacred food was eaten by priests and worshippers inside the sanctuary and taken outside the sanctuary for consumption elsewhere. Finally, there is attested the use of ordinary food (that is, food not sacrificed) either prescribed or prohibited by the god to effect a cure.[22]

Gooch's study underscores the diverse circumstances and practices in which εἰδωλόθυτα might have been consumed and the questions this might

---

16. Barclay, 99.
17. Barclay, 99.
18. Gooch, *Dangerous Food*, 15.
19. Gooch, 19.
20. Gooch, 20–21.
21. Gooch, 15.
22. Gooch, 21.

have raised for the believing community. Gooch suggests that the location of Lerna and the diverse ways in which food was used could have created some ambiguity for the Corinthians and that those defending their involvement in such practices might have played on this ambiguity to suit their own purposes.[23] This ambiguity is a consequence of the pervasive influence of religion in all spheres of Roman life and culture.

Next, we consider the elaborate ritual procedures involved in sacrificial meals. According to George Philip, people decorated the temples and had processions accompanied by singing, dancing, and feasting.[24]

> The sacrificial ceremony typically involved the following elements: a procession of the victims to the altar, prayer of the officiant, pouring of the wine over the animal's head by the officiant, killing of the animal by the slaves, examination of the entrails for omens, burning parts of the animal on the altar, followed by a banquet with the rest of the meat.[25]

Philip explains that worshippers consumed portions of the meat while the leftover meat was sold in the marketplace.[26] He also explains that these civic rituals were not the only occasion when animals were slaughtered. Ritual slaughter also took place during domestic celebrations such as birthdays, weddings, and funerals.[27] Philip notes that during ritual meals, not only was food sacrificed and offered to the deity, but entertainment and discussion also revolved around the deity as the central focus.[28]

The sequence of ritual procedures and symbols, the sacred space, and the prescribed behaviours and words all combined to create favourable conditions for effective rituals, while failure to comply with these regulations could lead to ritual failure.[29] Laura Grillo asserts, "Ritual is not just 'symbolic.' It transforms practitioners, by eliciting direct bodily ways of knowing."[30]

---

23. Gooch, 26.
24. Philip, *Paul and Common Meal*, 27.
25. Philip, 27
26. Philip, 28.
27. Philip, 149.
28. Gooch, *Dangerous Food*, 55.
29. Gruenwald, *Rituals and Ritual Theory*, 245.
30. Grillo, "African Rituals," 114.

The principal purpose of these rituals was to cross the boundary between humans and the gods.[31] This is evident in the cult of Asklepios, where the god was petitioned for healing. The sacrifices to the gods and the request for omens and good fortune all point to the religious nature of meal rituals in the Graeco-Roman context.

The situations that Paul addresses in 1 Corinthians 8:1–11:1 include occasions where food offered to idols (εἰδωλόθυτα) could have been consumed in private homes, bought at the market, or even consumed during sacrificial occasions in the temple precincts. However, as Gooch states, "it would be a mistake to think of the social context under discussion in categories of 'sacred' and 'secular'"[32] since most social meals included an offering of libation and thanksgiving to the gods.[33]

The obscure ritual context of εἰδωλόθυτα could be a possible reason why Paul appears to give contradictory advice to the Corinthians. In 1 Corinthians 8, Paul seems to permit eating food offered to idols if it does not hurt another believer or cause a weaker believer to stumble (8:7, 9). In 1 Corinthians 9, he affirms the right of the "strong" to eat but uses himself as an example to encourage the Corinthians to give up their right to eat for the sake of the weaker believers (9:1–27). However, in 1 Corinthians 10, he equates eating in pagan temples with idolatry and participation with demons, and he forbids this altogether (10:20–22). Scholars have struggled with Paul's seemingly contradictory instructions concerning food offered to idols and have attempted to explain this in various ways.

Scholars such as Wendell Lee Willis,[34] Derek Newton,[35] Joop Smit,[36] and Coye Still[37] suggest that Paul consistently opposes the consumption of εἰδωλόθυτα throughout 1 Corinthians 8–10. Other scholars argue that Paul addresses different issues. Fee, for instance, argues that 1 Corinthians 8:10 and 10:1–22 pertain to participating in cultic meals – which is prohibited – while eating food from the market and in private homes (1 Cor 10:23–11:1)

---

31. Patterson, *Keeping the Feast*, 38.
32. Gooch, *Dangerous Food*, 31.
33. Taussig, *In the Beginning*, 32.
34. Willis, *Idol Meat in Corinth*, 184–188.
35. Newton, *Deity and Diet*, 23.
36. Smit, *About the Idol Offerings*, 72.
37. Still, "Paul's Aims regarding εἰδωλόθυτα," 333–342.

is allowed unless someone at the table draws attention to the cultic history of the meal.[38] Gooch[39] and Stowers,[40] on the other hand, advocate for maintaining the tension between Paul's seemingly contradictory counsel. According to Gooch, Paul's discussion "retains a strong tension between a view of idol-food as infectious and idol-food as itself harmless."[41]

Paul's admonitions should be understood in the light of the liminal situation of the believers, which sheds light on the apparent gravity of εἰδωλόθυτα in the life of the church. According to Barrett, "The basic answer [to Paul's response] is to be found in the new eschatological circumstances in which Paul believed himself to be living."[42] These eschatological circumstances refer to Paul's belief that believers were living in the new age that was inaugurated by the coming of Christ and the outpouring of the Holy Spirit but will only come to completion at the second coming of Christ. This liminality is reflected in 1 Corinthians 10:11–13, where Paul states that the wilderness generation serves as an example for those "on whom the ends of the ages have come" (10:11 NRSV). This liminality gave a sense of urgency to Paul's response because the final salvation and judgement were drawing near.[43] The Corinthians' participation in εἰδωλόθυτα posed a real danger for them because it could lead to them falling away (1 Cor 9:27; 10:11–12). However, Paul assures them that God, in his faithfulness, would help them to overcome testing (10:13).

It is in the light of the already/not yet nature of their salvation that Paul can say that eating food sold at the market and eating at an unbeliever's home is neutral because Christ has redeemed the cosmos through his resurrection and ascension (Phil 2:8–11; Col 2:15). However, participating in temple meals is idolatry and participating with demons (1 Corinthians 10) because Christ will gain complete victory over the powers only at the *parousia* (1 Cor 15:24), as discussed in chapter 4. This "betwixt and between" situation of the believers calls for "God's wisdom" (1 Cor 2:7) in dealing with life in the surrounding pagan culture.

---

38. Fee, *Corinthians*, 396.
39. Gooch, *Dangerous Food*, 59.
40. Stowers, "Elusive Coherence."
41. Gooch, *Dangerous Food*, 59.
42. Barrett, "Things Sacrificed to Idols," 148.
43. Ciampa and Rosner, *Corinthians*, 465.

The Corinthians should thus approach what might have been for them an obscure dilemma of εἰδωλόθυτα with their liminal situation at the forefront of their minds. They were to keep the eschatological expectation of Christ's imminent return in mind as they navigated life in their cultural context. This meant living anti-structurally, not governed by the concerns and demands of the surrounding society. They were to maintain their identity as the ἁγίοις, empowered by the Holy Spirit.

Paul sees participation in εἰδωλόθυτα in the temple as idolatrous. These meals are transformative and progressive, with the process starting with idolatrous practices and leading to immorality and wickedness. This progression is evident in 1 Corinthians 10:1–10, which describes how the Israelites committed idolatry and indulged in revelry (1 Cor 10:7). Witherington states that "Paul's reason for associating idol food, temples and πορνεία (sexual immorality, primarily prostitution in 6:13) is that on some occasions in the temple precincts part of the entertainment was likely sexual."[44] Thus, Paul probably viewed some of the other moral problems in Corinth in the light of idolatrous behaviour.

According to Ciampa and Rosner, the testing Paul refers to in 1 Corinthians 10:13 is idolatry, which they describe as "the most common and fundamental temptation of humanity,"[45] with sexual immorality and greed as related temptations.[46] Fee suggests that temptation refers to ordinary trials but contrasts these ordinary trials with idolatry (1 Cor 10:14), for which there is no help from God because it is putting Christ to the test.[47] Although these two positions differ in their interpretation of the kind of temptation in view, both underscore the gravity of idolatry because it can lead to the loss of their salvation.[48]

Paul's frequent references and allusions to idolatry in his discussion of εἰδωλόθυτα highlights the centrality of idolatry in this discussion. He refers to the cult to the golden calf in the wilderness as found in Exodus 32 (1 Cor 10:7). This incident is a classic example of idolatry in Israel,[49] and the worship

---

44. Witherington, *Conflict and Community*, 190.
45. Ciampa and Rosner, *Corinthians*, 467.
46. Ciampa and Rosner, 467.
47. Fee, *Corinthians*, 508.
48. Fee, 508.
49. Meeks, "Rose Up to Play," 69.

of the golden calf is the quintessential demonstration of the people turning away from Yahweh to idols, as described in Exodus: "They have been quick to turn aside from the way that I commanded them; they have cast for themselves an image of a calf and have worshipped it and sacrificed to it" (Exod 32:8 NRSV). The implication is that the Corinthians are facing the same temptation as the wilderness generation – idolatry. Therefore, they are called to learn from the failure of the wilderness generation and flee from idolatry (1 Cor 10:14).

Paul draws a parallel between the Lord's Table, the people of Israel who partake in the sacrifices at the altar, and pagan sacrifices (1 Cor 10:16–20). One important conclusion that can be drawn from this comparison is that Paul believed that all rituals have transformative effects, irrespective of the deity involved. There are at least three effects evident in this passage: first, rituals affect participation with the deity (10:21); second, rituals shape people's morality and third, rituals impact how members relate to one another.

6.2 Defining Idolatry in 1 Corinthians 8:1–11:1

Idolatry is a notoriously complex concept to define, but the discussion is critical because it addresses the issue of whether participation in εἰδωλόθυτα constitutes idolatry. Most scholars prefer to focus on defining idol-food rather than idolatry, and rightly so since the issue at hand in 1 Corinthians 8:1–11:1 is εἰδωλόθυτα. However, those interested in the intercultural significance of the passage offer some suggestions for defining idolatry. This points back to the importance of inculturation because it highlights that people from diverse cultural contexts ask different questions concerning the text. The nature of idolatry is crucial in a cultural context where ancestral veneration is still prevalent. This question is a burning issue in Africa because it addresses how to remain faithful to the African identity while worshipping God wholeheartedly.

We begin by examining the nature of idols. Paul states that "an idol is nothing at all in the world" and that "there is no God but one" (1 Cor 8:4).[50] At first glance, this appears to be a straightforward monotheistic statement

---

50. Scholars generally accept that these were slogans coined by the Corinthian church. See Gardner, *1 Corinthians*, 367; Rogers, *God and the Idols*, 171.

with which Paul agrees. However, the argument becomes confusing when Paul says, "For even if there are so-called gods, whether in heaven or on earth (as indeed there are many 'gods' and many 'lords')" (1 Cor 8:5). The confusion is compounded when Paul later argues, "The sacrifices of pagans are offered to demons, not to God, and I do not want you to be participants with demons" (1 Cor 10:20).

To resolve this apparent contradiction, scholars like Moses,[51] McDonough,[52] and Yeo[53] cite two traditions found in Hebrew Scripture and Second Temple Judaism. The first tradition states that idols are nothing – futile and the mere work of humans. This is exemplified in the Hebrew Scriptures in passages such as Isaiah 40:19–20, Jeremiah 51:17–18, and Psalm 115:5–7. It is also present in Second Temple writings such as the Letter of Jeremiah, the Wisdom of Solomon, and the Apocalypse of Abraham.[54] As Moses notes,

> The depiction of idols and the absurdity of their worship in these works aims to show that the idols of the nations are 'nothing in the world' (1 Cor 8:4); they are weak and helpless. The weakness and impotence of the idols are contrasted with the God of Israel; this God dwells in the heavens (Ps 115:3, 135:5–6).[55]

This tradition is in line with Paul's apparent agreement with the Corinthians.

However, a second tradition is also evident in Paul's response. This view holds that even though idols are made by human hands, they are the work of demonic forces. Evidence for this view is found in the Septuagint (Deut 32:16–17; Pss 95:4–5; 105:37; Isa 65:11) and in literature of the Second Temple period (Jub. 22:17; 1 En. 99:7; T. Sol. 26:7).[56] Thus, even though Paul establishes common ground with the Corinthians by affirming their slogan, he reminds them that this is only half the truth: while idols are not gods, there is a demonic power behind them (1 Cor 10:20–21). This suggests that although idols are merely objects of stone or wood made by human hands, they become a "means" for demonic powers when their makers welcome

---

51. Moses, "Love Overflowing," 28.
52. McDonough, *Christ as Creator*, 155.
53. Yeo, *Rhetorical Interaction*, 100.
54. Moses, "Love Overflowing," 23.
55. Moses, 24.
56. Moses, 26.

demons by dedicating objects through rituals. Although participating in idol feasts may appear innocent, in doing so, participants open themselves to participating with demons. As an apocalyptic thinker, Paul believed in the power of evil and idolatry, but he also believeds in idols' ultimate demise because of God's cosmic triumph over evil.[57]

Paul's view is thus congruent with the traditions mentioned above: there is no god but God and all other "gods" and "lords" are nothing when compared to the majesty of the true God. Therefore, worshipping idols is foolish (Rom 1:22). However, behind these idols are demonic powers that continue to infiltrate the church. These powers are opposed to Christ and can cause spiritual harm to believers.

The Corinthian believers had diverse beliefs about what constitutes idolatry, but Paul had a clear stance on the matter, as evidenced by his exhortations in 1 Cor 10:14 and 1 Cor 10:1–10. Although Paul does not define idolatry; much can be inferred about his understanding of idolatry from the examples he cites from the Old Testament.

First, idolatry can be described as unfaithfulness to God. According to Richard Phua,

> The "strong" could be considered idolatrous for being "unfaithful" to God through their participation in the ritual eating in a pagan temple. The category of "unfaithfulness" shows they disregarded ancestral tradition/customs. In light of the tradition that Paul had passed on to them (the Lord's Supper), their behaviour is considered contrary to the gospel.[58]

The theme of unfaithfulness to God is in continuity with the Old Testament prophets' charge that the people of Israel had betrayed the one true God and turned to idols instead.[59] Paul describes himself as an apostle of the new covenant in Christ, following in the tradition of the Old Testament prophets.[60] According to William Lane, "His pastoral ministry is an expression of

---

57. Yeo, *Rhetorical Interaction*, 100.

58. Phua, *Idolatry and Authority*, 137.

59. Fowl, *Idolatry*, 10.

60. This assertion of Paul's prophetic call is more evident in Paul's discussion of his apostolic role in 2 Corinthians (see 2:17; 3:6; 4:1, 7, 16). It is also evident in Galatians 1:12, 15 and 1 Corinthians 15:8. See also Barclay, *Paul and the Gift*, 358; Conzelmann, Ciampa and Rosner, *Corinthians*, 416–417; Gardner, *1 Corinthians*, 401.

covenant administration."⁶¹ Lane suggests that the Corinthians exhibited blatant disregard for the new covenant and that Paul was mandated to call them back to the covenant stipulations.⁶² This prophetic call also is also evident in Paul's discussion of the correct use of ἐξουσία in 1 Corinthians 9.

According to Nasuti, Paul's reference to the commission entrusted to him in 1 Corinthians 9:17 is reminiscent of the Old Testament prophets.⁶³ Nasuti also points to Paul's "self-directed woe formula" in 1 Corinthians 9:16, which echoes Isaiah 6:5 and Jeremiah 45:3. Paul experiences distress because of his calling, yet he rejoices in his suffering because he views it through the lens of the cross of Christ.⁶⁴ Recognizing these prophetic echoes strengthens the place of 1 Corinthians 9 in Paul's discussion of εἰδωλόθυτα. Paul is not just holding himself up as an example of one who had renounced his ἐξουσία but as a prophet of the new covenant, speaking on behalf of Christ, calling for a return to *communitas*, and exhorting the Corinthians to live in such a way that they might not be disqualified (1 Cor 9:27). Thus, Paul reminds the Corinthians of their identity as God's holy people and warns them against unfaithfulness by referencing the exodus narrative and the Old Testament covenant.

Second, idolatry takes place when God is approached through the wrong medium. According to Sean McDonough, "The central issue is not only who is to be worshipped but, even more pressingly, how God is to be worshipped. Who or what provides the nexus between heaven and earth?"⁶⁵ He explains that Paul lays the foundation for this argument in 1 Corinthians 8:6:

> Paul takes pains in 8:6 not only to unite God and the Messiah as the only objects of veneration, but also to distinguish their respective roles vis-à-vis the world. God is the source and goal of all things, Christ is the one through whom God brings all things to pass.⁶⁶

Thus, there are two aspects involved in idolatry: the object of worship and the mediator. Getting either of these aspects wrong can lead to idolatry.

---

61. Lane, "Covenant," 8.
62. Lane, 10.
63. Nasuti, "Woes of the Prophets," 246–264.
64. Nasuti, 257.
65. McDonough, *Through Whom?*, 160.
66. McDonough, *Through Whom?*, 158.

Phua also alludes to the issue of mediation. He states that idolatry involves practising the wrong kind of worship, which involves wrong intentions and actions, confusing God with the created world, and failing to recognize the sovereignty of God.[67] Forms of worship that involve making anything other than Christ the means to approaching God can lead to idolatry. The διά (through) language in 1 Corinthians 8:6 stresses that Christ is the only mediator between God and humans,[68] the only one through whom believers live and worship.[69]

Third, idolatry includes misrepresenting God or using objects to represent him. Paul cites the example of the golden calf in Exodus 32. According to J. Gerald Janzen, the wilderness generation intended the golden calf to represent God's might as the Divine Warrior.[70] Aaron's words – "Tomorrow shall be a festival to the Lord" (Exod 32:5 NRSV) – indicate that the calf was intended to be a representation of God. According to Fowl, "The Israelites' idolatry in this instance is not so much a turning away from the Lord as a fabrication of an illegitimate image of the Lord."[71] Fowl suggests that the Israelites resorted to idolatry because of the prolonged absence of Moses, God's representative to the people. The calf was thus an "illegitimate attempt to make YHWH present."[72] Therefore, it can be said that while the Israelites' motivation in creating the idol was positive, but they committed wrong acts of worship by making an illegitimate image of God.

The attitude of the "strong" in Corinth may be construed as idolatrous because, even though they held a monotheistic view of God and might not have intended idolatry, their attitudes and actions misrepresented God.[73] Their motivation might not have been to commit idolatry, but their insistence on conforming to the dominant culture suggests that they were attempting to create a god who would fit their own agendas.

Fourth, idolatry shapes worshippers into the image of the idol. According to Menghun Goh, "Paul's critique is practical in addressing the power of

---

67. Phua, *Idolatry and Authority*, 34.
68. Goh, "Issue of Eidōlothyta," 92.
69. Gardner, *1 Corinthians*, 373.
70. Janzen, "Character of the Calf," 599.
71. Fowl, *Idolatry*, 14.
72. Fowl, 15.
73. Phua, *Idolatry and Authority*, 137.

the idol that forms one's habitus."⁷⁴ Goh says that instead of giving a direct answer to the Corinthians' questions concerning εἰδωλόθυτα, Paul focuses on the idol's power to influence world view and behaviour. In the case of the Corinthian "strong," their negative self-oriented *habitus* revealed the power of the idol.⁷⁵ Therefore, Paul points the Corinthians to Christ: in all they do, believers should orient themselves towards God through Christ (1 Cor 8:6).⁷⁶ Paul counters the idol's power by emphasizing the work of God through Christ.

Fowl also defines idolatry as "a process that slowly, incrementally misdirects believer's attention and love away from the one true God towards other things or people."⁷⁷ He suggests that the best way to understand idolatry is "primarily in terms of acquisition of habits, practices and dispositions that ease and even accelerate this process of directing love and attention away from God."⁷⁸ Therefore, the Corinthians had to avoid practices that could "stain" them.⁷⁹

Idolatry can lead believers to participate in the pagan practices and attitudes of their fellow worshippers. Joel Marcus argues that Paul sees idolatry as the root of other transgressions, such as fornication and greed.⁸⁰ Marcus offers this explanation:

> Idolatry is thus the primal sin, which leads ineluctably to all others, including, prominently, fornication – a connection that is especially close because both transgressions involve mistaking the creature for the Creator and bestowing upon the former the reverence and servitude that belong to the latter (see Rom 1:25).⁸¹

Our discussion of Paul's view of sin in section 4.3 supports Marcus's suggestion. Could it be that Paul saw a connection between the Corinthians' idolatry and their other sins? Marcus argues that the desire to indulge in

---

74. Goh, "Issue of Eidōlothyta," 80.
75. Goh, 90.
76. Goh, 90.
77. Fowl, *Idolatry*, 31.
78. Fowl, 31.
79. Fowl, 19.
80. Marcus, "Idolatry," 114.
81. Marcus, 114.

fornication often led to indulgence in idolatry, and vice versa, because there was such a strong connection between the two.[82] This relationship between idolatry and other vices is also evident elsewhere in this letter (1 Cor 5:11; 6:9–11; 12:2). This certainly seems to be the case in 1 Corinthians 10:7, where Paul associates idolatry with eating, drinking, and what was probably sexual playing.[83] Karl Sandnes terms this behaviour "belly-worship," which points to an enslavement to the flesh that is contrary to their identity as God's holy people.[84] This suggests that idolatry may have a more significant impact on the holiness of the ἐκκλησία than the Corinthians realized and also demonstrates the importance of 1 Corinthians 8:1–11:1 for the message of the whole epistle.

In light of the above discussion, idolatry can be defined as unfaithfulness to God by worshipping created things, approaching God through the wrong medium – that is, anything other than Jesus Christ – or misrepresenting God through wrong intentions or wrong actions that can lead to a *habitus* that is contrary to the cross of Christ.

6.3 The Exodus Narrative and Old Testament Covenant as Ritual Myth in Light of Christ's Sacrifice

This section explores Paul's references to the Old Testament covenant and the exodus narrative in 1 Corinthians 8:1–11:1. It advances the discussion by exploring the myth that underlies Paul's discussion of ritual meals. The Exodus narrative and the Old Testament covenant, reinterpreted in the light of the coming of Christ, seek to establish the Corinthians' identity as the new people of God. The reference to covenant also points to *communitas* with God and others in 1 Corinthians 8:1–11:1. Therefore, a discussion of the Old Testament covenant and the exodus narrative is foundational for interpreting Paul's argument in 1 Corinthians 8:1–11:1.

---

82. Marcus, 112.

83. Sandnes, *Belly and Body*, 199; See also Meeks, "'Rose Up to Play,'" 69; Collier, "Not Crave Evil," 74.

84. Sandnes, 181–215.

6.3.1 The Exodus Narrative to explain the believing communities new identity.

First, Paul uses the exodus narrative to establish identity (1 Cor 10:1–12), which, as Linda Stargel aptly demonstrates, is in line with traditional interpretations in the Hebrew Scriptures.[85] Stargel says, "Israel's first sense of solidarity or 'us-ness' is portrayed in the primary exodus story with images of collective suffering and crying out (Exod 2:23, cf. 6:8–9)."[86] She proposes that the memory of their previous status as slaves helps to clarify their current identity and that the retold exodus narratives in the Old Testament call them to live as God's holy people.[87] In Joshua 24, Israel's prior identity as slaves and as the people delivered by Yahweh forbids them to take on the identity of idolaters.[88] They are commanded to put away the foreign gods among them and incline their hearts to the Lord, the God of Israel (Josh 24:23). In Deuteronomy 11, the Exodus narrative is followed by instructions to love the Lord with their whole hearts, keep his commandments, and refrain from following the gods of the people around them. Likewise the exodus narrative in Jeremiah 32:20–23 is followed by is an assurance of their "future, illogical exodus-like hope, independent of behavioural qualifications (Jer 32:36–44)."[89] As Stargel demonstrates, these retold exodus narratives contain the foundations for Israel's identity as the delivered people of God and give directives for acceptable behaviour congruent with their new identity.

In a similar vein, Paul makes the connection between the identity of God's holy ones and their ethical behaviour. By referring to the Jewish ancestors as "our ancestors" (1 Cor 10:1), he assumes that the Corinthian believers are heirs of the same covenantal promises given to the Jews (Rom 2:26–29; 4:1; 9:8).[90] They are the eschatological people of God, created in Christ (1 Cor 1:3–6) and sanctified by the Holy Spirit (1 Cor 6:11). This inclusion took place when they believed in the Messiah (Gal 3:6–9), and were baptized into one body by the same Spirit, regardless of whether they were Jews or Greeks, slaves or free (1 Cor 12:13).

---

85. Stargel, *Exodus Identity*, 139.
86. Stargel, 139.
87. Stargel, 143.
88. Stargel, 139.
89. Stargel, 143.
90. Oropeza, *Paul and Apostasy*, 72.

Paul's use of the phrases "cloud," "passed through the sea," and being "baptised into Moses" (1 Cor 10:1–2) prefigures the believer's baptism.[91] Baptism, as an initiation rite into the believing community,[92] not only affirms their identity as the delivered people of God but also hints at the holiness of the community. As the new people of God, they were "washed," "sanctified," and "justified in the name of the Lord Jesus Christ and by the Spirit of God" (1 Cor 6:11). This reference to passing through the water recalls their washing and symbolizes their new identity as God's holy people. It also alludes to the prophetic promises of personal and covenant renewal,[93] especially those found in Ezekiel 36:25–27. Paul begins his discussion in 1 Corinthians 10 by reminding the Corinthians of their baptism into Christ and their new identity as the covenant people of God, an identity they received through participation in the body and blood of Christ.

Second, Paul uses the narrative of Christ crucified as the new Exodus story that shapes the believer's identity. This is evident in his references to the blood and body of Christ in his warning against participation in idol ritual meals in 1 Corinthians 10, and his charge to celebrate the Lord's Supper in "remembrance" of Christ (1 Cor 11:25) also emphasizes this idea in 1 Corinthians 11. This remembrance is more than merely recalling Christ; according to Thiselton, this remembrance means recalling with gratitude, being united with the crucified Christ, and also "self-transforming retrieval of the founding event of the personal identity of the believer (as the believer) and the corporate identity of the church (as the Christian church of God)."[94] According to Stargel, such a collective memory necessitates three dimensions to shape collective identity: cognitive, temporal, and behavioural.[95] During the Lord's Supper, reflection is encouraged by the ritual's actions, elements, and words. The temporal aspect is reflected in looking back to the crucifixion and forward to the return of Christ while also appropriating the blessings of Christ's provision in the present. The required behaviour is the call to proclaim the Lord's death until his return (1 Cor 11:23–26).

---

91. Fee, *Corinthians*, 488.
92. Theissen, *Earliest Churches*, 123; Meeks, "Rose Up to Play," 65.
93. Wright, *Faithfulness of God*, 1337.
94. Thiselton, *Corinthians*, 880.
95. Stargel, *Exodus Identity*, 46.

Paul uses both the exodus narratives and the cross of Christ as the underlying myth for the Lord's Supper. His purpose is to create a communal identity where their shared experience of deliverance provides the basis for their life together. These narratives also provide the lens through which to interpret the symbols used during the Lord's Supper, and this idea will be discussed below. According to Paul, the narrative of Christ crucified must provide the "sacred postulates"[96] that will guide the ethical life of the community.

6.3.2 References to the covenant in 1 Corinthians 8:11–11:1

We turn now to Paul's references to the covenant in 1 Corinthians 8:1–11:1. The proposal is that *communitas* is the overarching theme of the passage in covenantal terms because it points to both the relationship between people and God and the relationships among people.

God gave the covenant to establish the relationship between himself and his people; according to the prophets, however, this divine-human relationship did not always fare so well.[97] Therefore, in his prophetic promise in Jeremiah 31:31–33, Yahweh promises to make a new covenant with Israel, in which he would write his law on their hearts. The fulfilment of this promise in Jesus Christ created a new covenant (1 Cor 11:25). In referring to the Old Testament generation as a *topos,* Paul shows that the difference between the Corinthians and the wilderness generation is that now, in the new covenant, believers can remain faithful to the covenant because God, in his faithfulness (1 Cor 10:13), has provided a way in Jesus Christ, the Messiah.[98]

According to Michael Gorman, any attempt to understand Paul should begin with a recognition that Paul believed that the purpose of the Christ-event was to restore covenantal relations between God and humanity.[99] God has always initiated this covenant and called for a response of love, for both God and neighbour, from the people.[100] N. T. Wright agrees that Paul believed that the Christ-event was the divine fulfilment of God's covenant promises

---

96. Turner, "Betwixt and Between," 239.

97. See Isaiah 1:2–20; 3:13–15; Jeremiah 2:2–37; Hosea 2:4–17; 12:13–15; Micah 6:1–5; Malachi 3:5.

98. In Galatians 3:15–19, Paul declares that Jesus is the "seed" of Abraham in whom the covenant was fulfilled.

99. Gorman, *Apostle*, loc. 1449, Kindle.

100. Gorman, loc. 1449, Kindle.

to Abraham, resulting in a "re-formation" of a holy people of God.[101] This covenant was the new covenant promised by the prophets (Jer 24:7; 31:33; Ezek 18:31; 36:26).

6.3.2.1 Paul's use of the shema

In this passage, Paul reinterprets this covenant relationship in the light of Christ in various ways. First, the reference to the *shema* in 1 Corinthians 8:6 sets the discussion within the context of the *communitas* with God through Jesus Christ. Using the *shema* to teach about the believers new identity suggest that, like Israel, believers are monotheists, it expands the scope of the gospel's impact on creation, and gives a possible framework of what it might look like to live as the holy people of God.

In 1 Corinthians 8:6, Paul expands the well-known *shema* to include Jesus Christ as Lord, thus ascribing to Jesus a mediating role in creating the cosmos. According to Wright, this monotheism is both creational and cultic.[102] By including Christ in the covenant relationship, Paul radically restates the *shema*. For Paul, God the Father is the source and goal of everything, while Jesus Christ is the means through which everything came into existence.[103] This does not signify acceptance of polytheism; rather, Jesus Christ is viewed as the revelation of the one God who is mentioned in 1 Corinthians 8:4.[104]

Not all scholars agree with this high Christology. Gaston and Perry, for instance, are not convinced that Paul is rewriting the *shema* here or equating Christ with God the Father. They suggest that Paul "assigns the Father and Jesus to different classes."[105] Thus, according to Perry and Gaston, Paul puts the Father in the class of "god" and Jesus in the class of "lord," a term they interpret as meaning master.

On the other hand, Murphy-O'Connor argues that 1 Corinthians 8:6 "has an exclusively soteriological meaning and that the cosmological interpretation

---

101. Wright, *Faithfulness of God*, 782. See also Hays, "Conversion of the Imagination," 395. Hays, Gorman, and Wright all emphasize that accepting that Paul's theology was rooted in the Jewish Scriptures does not signify an acceptance of a "linear *Heilsgeschichte*"; rather, it points to the radically "reconfigured" people of God through the cross of Christ.

102. Wright, *Faithfulness of God*, 661.

103. Wright, 666. See also McDonough, *Christ as Creator*, 150; Rogers, *God and the Idols*, 178–179; Leese, *Cosmic Goal of Redemption*, 75.

104. Wright, *Faithfulness of God*, 666.

105. Gaston and Perry, "Christological Monotheism," 193.

is unfounded."[106] He proposes that 1 Corinthians 8:6 is just an acclamation that celebrates the "salvific action of God in Christ."[107] The creational and cosmological questions are important to this discussion because they pertain to the nature of εἰδωλόθυτα and Paul's apparently contradictory advice. If we see Paul as referring to the creation narrative in his argument, this would explain why he concludes that food is neutral (1 Cor 8:8). The creational aspect supports the idea that food is part of God's good creation and is, therefore, harmless when divorced from a ritual context, as suggested in 1 Corinthians 10:25–26.

Gaston and Perry disregard the context of 1 Corinthians 8:6, a passage that is saturated with direct quotes from and allusions to the Torah. Paul intention is to affirm the monotheistic Corinthian slogan of "but one God," as opposed to the "many 'gods' and many 'lords'" of the surrounding society (1 Cor 8:5). It is unlikely that Paul would have placed God the Father and Jesus Christ in separate categories since doing so would imply that Christianity was just another polytheistic religion with many gods and many lords as in paganism. Taken in its entirety, 1 Corinthians 8:1–11:1 uses the exodus narrative and the Old Testament covenant as a foundation for Paul's ethics, and the *shema*, as Wright suggests, "sustains both the unity and the holiness of the community."[108]

In 1 Corinthians 8:1–11:1, Paul grounds his discussion in the eschatological work of Jesus Christ (1 Cor 10:11) and includes "all things" in the salvation provided by Christ: "Yet for us there is but one God, the Father, from whom all things came and for whom we live; and there is but one Lord, Jesus Christ, through whom all things came and through whom we live" (1 Cor 8:6).

The use of τὰ πάντα (all things) suggests the need for a broader application, as Johnson Leese persuasively argues that "all things" should include all of creation because the semantic field supports a reading that views Christ's salvific role as extending beyond humans to the cosmos. According to Leese, "The use of such key terms as κόσμος, αἰών (10:11), ὁ οὐρανός and ἡ γῆ and τὰ πάντα alongside the terse use of ἐκ and διά collectively suggests that a cosmological sphere is intended."[109]

---

106. Murphy-O'Connor, *Keys to First Corinthians*, 59.
107. Murphy-O'Connor, 63.
108. Wright, *Faithfulness of God*, 666
109. Leese, *Cosmic Goal of Redemption*, 74.

Leese is right; Paul is preaching an eschatological gospel where God has put all things under the dominion of Christ (1 Cor 15:27–28). Paul, in quoting the *shema*, begins his discussion by affirming Jesus Christ as one with the covenant-faithful God. This has implications for the Corinthians because Paul, by affirming that faith in Christ is monotheistic, precludes any continuation of polytheistic practices. In addition, Paul emphasizes that Jesus Christ is the only means for the believer's existence. This challenges practices that the Corinthians might have believed were necessary for their existence in the Roman cultural context and also points to their identity as followers of Christ. Paul calls the Corinthians to be marked by the love of God in their response to the question of εἰδωλόθυτα. Their faith and allegiance to God the Father, revealed and represented in Jesus Christ, should be the foundation of their behaviour as God's covenant people living within a pagan community.[110]

6.3.2.2 Paul's use of the wilderness generation as a reference to covenant relationship.

The allusion to the wilderness generation points to the covenant relationship between God and the Israelites. According to Joop Smit, Paul compares the situation of the Corinthians to that of Israel.[111] By using kinship language, Paul includes the Corinthians in the covenant people, and by referring to "our ancestors" (1 Cor 10:1), he includes them in the heritage of God's people.[112]

Paul also uses ritual language[113] to include the Corinthians in Israel's salvation narrative. His references to "the cloud," passing "through the sea," "baptised into Moses," "spiritual food," and "spiritual drink" (1 Cor 10:1–4) recall the narrative of God's eschatological salvation of Israel and serve as analogies

---

110. Wright, *Faithfulness of God*, 663.

111. Smit, "Do Not Be Idolaters," 40–53.

112. Rogers, *God and the Idols*, 188; Fee, *Corinthians*, 490; Gardner, *1 Corinthians*, 426; Wright, *Faithfulness of God*, 668.

113. There is much discussion about the extent to which these references in 1 Corinthians 10:1–4 should be understood as sacramental. Gardner, Fee, and Ciampa and Rosner propose that rather than emphasizing the sacramental aspect, this should merely be viewed as Paul's way of establishing the Corinthians' identity as the people of God, in the same way that the exodus event established Israel's identity. Gardener, *1 Corinthians*, 427; Fee, *Corinthians*, 493; Ciampa and Rosner, *Corinthians*, 448. However, it cannot be denied that these are ritual terms used in a ritual context, which implies that the sacramental implications should not be ignored. This will be discussed in section 6.5.

of the believer's experience of being baptized into Christ.[114] The Corinthians were all included in the people of God, and they all experienced the blessing of God's faithful presence and provision. However, as Paul explains in 1 Corinthians 10:5, this did not exempt them from the risk of falling away. The wilderness generation thus serves as an example to the Corinthians: they must be careful lest they fall in the same way (1 Cor 10:12).

The *topos* (rhetorical device denoting a common theme, motif or pattern) Paul uses from the wilderness generation also recalls instances when Israel broke their covenant with God and incurred his wrath. In Exodus 32, they violated the covenant relationship – and thus their *communitas* – with God by eating in honour of the golden calf. Paul cites this incident where the people, in the absence of Moses, demanded that Aaron make "gods" for them (Exod 32:1–6). Aaron made a golden calf from their jewellery, and the people then sacrificed to the calf – feasting, drinking, and engaging in orgies. The result of their apostasy was that "God was not pleased with most of them, and they were struck down in the wilderness" (1 Cor 10:5 NRSV). Similarly, Numbers 11 records how their evil desires led them to reject the food God provided because they craved the meat of Egypt, thereby violating their *communitas* with God and rejecting Yahweh. This troubled relationship between God and Israel served as a warning to the Corinthians.

Third, Paul concludes his argument on εἰδωλόθυτα by quoting Psalm 24 (1 Cor 10:26), another allusion to the covenant because this psalm is deeply associated with covenant fidelity among the Jews. By quoting Psalm 24, Paul reinforces the idea that God's people must remain exclusively devoted to him. The emphasis on purity of hands and heart in Psalm 24 aligns with Paul's argument that worship is not merely about external actions but about faithfulness to the covenant.[115] This reference to Psalm 24 contains echoes of creation, covenant, and eschatology,[116] which are all themes that run through Paul's discussion on idol-food. The psalm's declaration that "the earth is the Lord's and everything in it" asserts God's absolute sovereignty, contrasting with the false claims of idols. The reference to Psalm 24 strengthens Paul's

---

114. Gardner, *1 Corinthians*, 426.

115. Wright, *Paul*, 669–670.

116. For a discussion on Psalm 24, see Cooper, "Mythology and Exegesis," 37–60; Smart, "Psalm 24," 175–180.

exhortation against idolatry and extends the significance of participating in idol-food beyond actions to heart purity.[117] According to Leese, the placement of 1 Corinthians 8:6 and 1 Corinthians 10:26 are "weighty" because they convey Paul's earliest redrawing of monotheism.[118] I would also add that these two verses – 1 Corinthians 8:6 and 1 Corinthians 10:26 – serve as bookends that place the discussion of εἰδωλόθυτα firmly within the context of the covenant relationship. It is within the bounds of this covenant relationship that the ethics of the community should be established.

Paul also refers to the *communitas* with God in Christ as the basis for discouraging participation in pagan cultic meals. According to Rogers, "Paul's argument is based in part upon the intimate care and provision of God for the wilderness generation."[119] The cosmological scope of Paul's discussion is vital because it shows that the redemption won by Christ affects both human beings and the created order. Therefore, this has ethical implications for how believers should relate to one another and to creation.[120] The simple question of whether or not to eat εἰδωλόθυτα (1 Cor 8:1–11:1) or how the community should celebrate the Lord's Supper (1 Cor 11:17–34) can have eschatological implications for the believing community. The way believers choose to act in these matters may constitute a violation of their relationship with Christ and their fellow believers.

Paul's use of the exodus narrative and the covenant serves to establish the identity of the Corinthians as the ἅγιος of God and point to the desired relationships within the believing community. In addition, the exodus narrative and the covenant functions as the central myth for his discussion of ritual meals and underscores the possible cosmic implications of the behaviour of the Corinthian believers.

6.4 *Communitas* in 1 Corinthians 8:1–11:1

In chapter 4, we discussed the concept of *communitas*, describing it as a sacred, egalitarian relationship. If, as shown earlier, this *communitas* is both

---

117. Rosner, *Paul and the Law*, 168.
118. Leese, *Cosmic Goal of Redemption*, 79.
119. Rogers, *God and the Idols*, 190.
120. Leese, *Cosmic Goal of Redemption*, 42.

vertical – relating to the divine – and horizontal – referring to interpersonal relationships – it can be argued that Paul's concept of participation "in Christ" reflects both vertical and horizontal *communitas*. According to Campbell, this "in Christ" language can be described as an ontology of being that transforms believers and make them fully relational beings, enabling them to relate correctly to God and others.[121] This participation "in Christ" should be the basis on which to interpret 1 Corinthians 10:16–17.

Participation in the Lord's Supper facilitates *communitas* that is conducive to transformation. *Communitas* is reflected in Paul's use of the κοινωνία/κοινωνός word groups, his use of kinship and sibling language (1 Cor 8:12), his call for humility and the renunciation of rights and status (1 Corinthians 9), and his emphasis on the centrality of love (1 Cor 8:1; 13:13; 14:1).[122] *Communitas* is an effective means of transformation because the believer is united with Christ, learns about self and the "other," and can relate to others in the light of Christ's sacrifice.

Christian Strecker identifies two forms of *communitas* in 1 Corinthians 10:16–17.[123] He suggests that Paul refers to vertical *communitas* with Christ when he speaks about "participation in the blood of Christ" (1 Cor 10:16) and to horizontal *communitas* when he says that believers "all share the one loaf" (1 Cor 10:17).[124] However, not all scholars agree that this is the case. Hollander, for instance, suggests that "it is the unity of the Corinthian Christians with each other that Paul wants to emphasise in these verses, and not so much the 'fellowship-establishing event between Christ and the believers.'"[125] Hollander's view is based on his analysis of κοινωνία and its cognates with the genitive. However, for a comprehensive understanding of κοινωνία as used in this context, it is necessary to consider both Paul's use of this concept and the ritual context of the passage.

The ritual context of the discussion of εἰδωλόθυτα implies a sacramental dimension to κοινωνία. The context of worship – whether it be of idols or Christ – presupposes a relationship with the deity.[126] Various clues in the

---

121. Campbell, *Quest for Paul's Gospel*, 41.
122. Russell, "In the World," 224–334.
123. Strecker, *Liminale Theologie*, 320.
124. Strecker, 321.
125. Hollander, "Idea of Fellowship," 457.
126. Rogers, *God and the Idols*, 197.

passage point to the sacramental nature of Paul's discussion. For instance, Paul uses an Old Testament text where idolatrous sacrifices were performed as a *topos* to discourage participation in pagan cults (1 Cor 10:7). In addition, Paul references to the Lord's Supper (1 Cor 10:16–17) and Israel's relationship to the altar (1 Cor 10:18) underscore the sacramental aspects of the discussion. The vertical *communitas* is also evident in Paul's comment that "God was not pleased with most of them" (1 Cor 10:5). All this points to the importance of a relationship with the deity in the context of worship.

Communitas with Christ is affirmed and activated every time believers partake in the Lord's Supper. Turley suggests that the Lord's Supper is more than just a ritual for remembering Christ and that the life of Christ is reproduced in believers as they participate in this ritual. This life is characterized by self-giving love rather than entitlement and a need for self-elevation: "Paul was thus convinced that the Lord's Supper was the ritualised space that facilitated the fulfilment of the ethical transformation foreseen by Jeremiah where God would 'write his law on the hearts of his people' and deal decisively with the perennial problem of disobedience."[127] This transformation takes place as believers participate in the blood and body of Christ. Paul envisions a dynamic change when participating in Christ in this manner and explains this transformation in Romans: "For if we have been united with him in a death like his, we will certainly be united with him in a resurrection like his. We know that our old self was crucified with him so that the body of sin might be destroyed, and we might no longer be enslaved to sin" (Rom 6:5–6 NRSV). Participating with Christ means sharing in his *kenotic* death and resurrection, which, in turn, produces a new person.

In 1 Corinthians 10:17 (NRSV), Paul shifts the discussion from *communitas* with Christ to *communitas* among believers. He says, "Because there is one bread, we who are many are one body, for we all partake of the one bread." Here, κοινωνία refers to the corporate fellowship of the believers, which is a result of their shared participation in Christ. The "one loaf" (1 Cor 10:17 NIV) refers to the body of Christ, and their participation in Christ shapes them together as "the body of Christ," the church (1 Cor 10:16). This extraordinary unity with Christ and fellow believers forbids κοινωνία with demons. Strecker suggests that when Paul refers to the πολλοί, he must have

---

127. Turley, *Ritualized Revelation*, 169.

had in mind a diverse, multi-layered community.[128] Strecker thus emphasizes the remarkable transformational power of the Lord's Supper, where participating together makes it possible to overcome divisions resulting from socio-economic, gender, or ideological differences and create a truly equal and loving community in the context of ritual *communitas*.[129]

6.5 Ritual Outcomes of Εἰδολωθυτα

Paul's concern about the Corinthian believers' participation in εἰδωλόθυτα is based on three adverse outcomes: violation of *communitas* with Christ, violation of *communitas* with fellow believers, and the possibility of falling away completely.

Paul's concern for the believers' *communitas* with Christ is also evident from his warning: "You cannot drink the cup of the Lord and the cup of demons. You cannot partake of the table of the Lord and the table of demons" (1 Cor 10:21 NRSV). The relationship between the participants and their God is at the forefront of Paul's mind.[130] His strong "you cannot" sit at the table of demons and the Lord functions as both a warning and a prohibition.[131] Paul warns that participation in pagan cults would provoke the Lord to jealousy, and he prohibits it because the two actions are incompatible.[132]

The reference to provoking the Lord to jealousy alludes to the Song of Moses (Deut 32:21) and is rooted in God's self-revelation in Exodus 20:4–5. In the Old Testament, God's jealousy is associated with idol worship and the resulting judgement.[133] This points back to the example of the wilderness generation who provoked the Lord to jealousy (1 Cor 10:1–13). Gardner observes that the word παραζηλόω is derived from ζῆλος, which refers to the "zeal" of the Lord.[134] In Ezekiel, this zeal is compared to jealousy in a marriage and results in wrath and judgement (Ezek 16:38).[135] This relational imagery

---

128. Strecker, *Liminale Theologie*, 317.
129. Strecker, 318.
130. Gardner, *Gifts of God*, 162.
131. Fee, *Corinthians*, 521.
132. Fee, 521.
133. Collins, *First Corinthians*, 381.
134. Gardner, *1 Corinthians*, 456.
135. Gardner, 456.

emphasizes that the Lord demands exclusive worship and that participating with demons will have dire consequences for believers. This note of warning is also evident in Paul's rhetorical question concerning the strength of the Lord (1 Cor 10:22). The Corinthian "strong" had a high opinion of themselves, but they were foolish to challenge the strength of the Lord.[136]

Participation in idolatry leads to a breach in the covenant relationship between God and believers.[137] As mentioned earlier, God established the covenant to create *communitas* with humanity, and ritual meals were an important aspect of confirming and maintaining this relationship. Participating in rituals to idols – or to the demons behind them – constituted unfaithfulness (Deut 32:18, 20) and signified rejecting covenantal allegiance to Christ in favour of allegiance to demons.[138]

Idolatry leads to the violation of *communitas* with fellow believers. By comparing the Lord's Supper, the Israelite altar, and pagan sacrifices (1 Cor 10:18), Paul demonstrates that both the Lord's Supper and pagan rituals involve vertical and horizontal fellowship.[139] Just as the Lord's Supper is a participation with Christ[140] and other believers, so participation in pagan rituals creates allegiances with other participants. Therefore, Paul calls for unity among believers and exclusion of outside cultic associations.[141] This stance against associating with unbelievers in the context of pagan worship is reinforced elsewhere. For example, in 2 Corinthians 6:14, Paul warns the Corinthians not to be "yoked together with unbelievers" because they have nothing in common. Associating with idol temples and pagan worshippers can contaminate God's holy people, who are his temple (2 Cor 6:16–17).

Participation in the "table of demons" (1 Cor 10:21) orients believers away from God and towards the world of demons. This orientation is demonstrated in the arguments and behaviour of the "strong" and reflects the individualistic and status-hungry culture of the city of Corinth.[142] The Corinthians boasted about their knowledge and enlightenment, and Paul had to remind them

---

136. Fee, *Corinthians*, 523.
137. Gardner, *Gifts of God*, 156.
138. Gardner, 167.
139. Rogers, *God and the Idols*, 197.
140. Rogers, 197.
141. Mitchell, *Rhetoric of Reconciliation*, 255.
142. Turley, *Ritualized Revelation*, 144.

that "knowledge puffs up while love builds up" (1 Cor 8:1). Their callous attitudes towards "weak" believers prompted Paul to warn them that they are sinning against Christ when they disregard the family members in Christ. Paul's example of his own relinquishing of rights (1 Cor 9:19–23) and his call for the Corinthians to follow his example as he followed the example of Christ (1 Cor 11:1) suggest that the Corinthians' orientation was not towards the cross of Christ.

Paul warns that participation in pagan temples may lead to falling away. This is because the "strong" believers were arrogant and felt secure in their salvation.[143] Paul's use of ὥστε "therefore" in 1 Corinthians 10:12 after his discussion of the wilderness generation (1 Cor 10: 1–11), shows Paul's point in recounting the story; "So if you think you are standing, watch out that you do not fall" (1 Cor 10:12). He warns the Corinthian believers that God could reject them just as he had rejected the wilderness generation because of their idolatry.[144] Although the Corinthian believers had been delivered from the present evil age and the coming wrath, they were still in a liminal situation until the *parousia*. Paul's metaphor of the race in 1 Corinthians 9:24–27 underscores this warning and exhorts believers not to be foolish – like a runner running aimlessly or a boxer beating the air – and risk losing the prize.

These verses not only underscore the importance of a disciplined life but also warn, once again, of the possibility of falling away. In 1 Corinthians 10:13, Paul affirms that the believers are indeed in an in-between place of testing; however, he assures them that God is faithful to his covenant and will always provide a means of escape. The urgency of Paul's exhortation is reinforced in 1 Corinthians 10:14, the use of διόπερ "therefore,"[145] once again demonstrates Paul's purpose in recounting the wilderness story, he was giving an urgent warning against any form of idolatry Believers must flee from idolatry because it puts them in danger of being cut off from God's promises; however, God in his faithfulness will provide the strength necessary to resist the temptation to idolatry.

---

143. Gardner, *1 Corinthians*, 438.
144. Oropeza, "Apostasy in the Wilderness," 80.
145. Trail, *Exegetical Summary*, 30.

6.6 Conclusion

This chapter has examined the subject of ritual meals in 1 Corinthians 8:1–11:1, resulting in several important insights. Paul's primary concern in this passage is the holiness of the community, which was being threatened by idolatry (1 Cor 10:13–14). In his discussion, Paul gives central place to the covenantal relationship with God through Christ – this is clear in his extensive references to the Israelites and their wilderness journey. Covenant violation through idol worship, which was the sin of the wilderness generation, was also the threat facing the Corinthian believers.

The ritual context of the discussion is vital for a proper interpretation of the passage. The context shows that the relationship with God is central to this discussion because the purpose of rituals is to establish a connection with the deity, whether this deity be God or demons. While idols are not real, the power behind them is demonic, and participation in ritual meals to idols leads to participation in demons (1 Cor 10:20–21).

Idolatry, which is unfaithfulness to God, may take the form of worshipping created things, approaching God through any medium other than Jesus Christ, or misrepresenting God through wrong intentions and wrong actions that may lead to a *habitus* that is contrary to the cross of Christ. The exodus narrative and the Old Testament covenant – interpreted in the light of the Christ-event – form the foundational myth that underlies Paul's discussion of εἰδωλόθυτα. By asking the Corinthian believers to change their meal practices, Paul "required them to dissociate themselves from core aspects of their former self-understanding, which was intertwined with religious, social, civic and ethnic aspects."[146] Paul calls for a new identity that transcends both their Graeco-Roman and Jewish cultures, as well as any other categories of self-definition. As the people of God, delivered from the power of sin, believers are called to avoid idolatry at all costs.

For Paul, participation in pagan temples violates believers' *communitas* with Christ and their fellow believers. Idolatry creates fellowship with unbelievers and orients believers towards the individualistic and status-seeking culture of the surrounding society, rather than with the self-giving life of Christ. This misdirected orientation was also evident in the inconsiderate ways in which the Corinthians treated their brothers and sisters in Christ.

---

146. Ehrensperger, "Eat or Not to Eat," 130.

In chapter 3, we discussed the importance of taking political and narrative power into account when addressing people in liminality. Narrative power refers to the capacity of the "strong" – that is, those who are socially and economically privileged – to control the narratives that shape communities. Paul empowers the "weak" by being their voice and telling their side of the story.

The insistence of the "strong" Corinthians on participating in εἰδωλόθυτα was based on a limited narrative that privileged them but marginalized the "weak," thereby created a community shaped by the narrative of the surrounding pagan culture. Therefore, Paul speaks on behalf of both the weak and Christ, who died for them.

Paul's discussion centres around three key slogans that were influencing the attitudes and behaviour of the Corinthians. The first slogan that Paul challenges claims that "all of us possess knowledge" (1 Cor 8:1 NRSV). The second slogan declares that "no idol in the world really exists" and that "there is no God but one" (1 Cor 8:4 NRSV). The third slogan says, "Food will not bring us close to God. We are no worse off if we do not eat, and no better off if we do" (1 Cor 8:8 NRSV).

Paul first challenges the assumption that one person's knowledge is necessarily the same as another's. He emphasizes that not everyone has the same knowledge (1 Cor 8:7), explaining that knowledge is a result of experiences. The experiences of the "weak" in Corinth had led them to believe that idols were representations of real deities; therefore, participating in εἰδωλόθυτα while believing this could damage or destroy their faith. The past experience of the "weak" believers, and their lack of experience in walking with Jesus, are all factors that must be considered when relating to them. Paul also explains that clinging blindly to what is assumed to be common knowledge is dangerous for both the "weak" and the "strong" and can threaten the general well-being of the believing community: the "strong" might become puffed up (8:1), the "weak" might be destroyed (1 Cor 8:11), and the believing community will be defiled by idolatry (10:1–22).

The second slogan – "no idol in the world really exists" and "there is no God but one" (1 Cor 8:4 NRSV) – was addressed in sections 6.2 and 6.3. The Corinthians misrepresented God by focusing only on truths that supported their position. Paul, by his reinterpretation of the *shema*, shows that believers always come to God through Christ and that this relationship impacts their nature and behaviour. Since the identity of believers is rooted in the self-sacrificial life of Christ, they must live by the ethic of renouncing their rights for the sake of their "weak" brothers and sisters in Christ (1 Cor 9:11–12). Paul also corrects their misrepresentation of the spiritual realm – while there is only one God, idols are empowered by demons and, therefore, pose a real threat to the church.

Paul also counters the third misconception: "Food will not bring us close to God. We are no worse off if we do not eat, and no better off if we do" (1 Cor 8:8). As explained in section 6.3, the whole of creation should be included in the interpretation of the reinterpreted *shema* (1 Cor 8:6), which implies that food is not neutral as the Corinthians believed. Paul's warning makes it clear that food can either build up the church or destroy it (1 Cor 10:23–24). All things can be a means either to glorify God or to sin against him (1 Cor 10:31). Through Paul's engagement with the one-sided story of the "strong" in Corinth, he cautions them to use their privilege to build up the church in love.

CHAPTER 7

Feasting with Christ in 1 Corinthians 11:17–34

7.0 Introduction

This section will consider Paul's discussion of the Lord's Supper in 1 Corinthians 11:17–34. First, we will establish the ritual context of 1 Corinthians 11:17–34. Next, we will examine vertical and horizontal *communitas* in this passage. Finally, we will consider the ritual outcomes of participation in the Lord's Supper. The hypothesis is that Paul's intention in 1 Corinthians 11:17–34 was to correct the abuses of the Lord's Supper because this could destroy the faith of fellow believers and lead to God's judgement on the community. The mistreatment of the "weak" and the humiliation of those who had nothing (1 Cor 11:22) demonstrates the Corinthians' disregard for the Lord's Supper. The "strong" were using the table of the Lord for their own pleasure – gorging themselves and becoming drunk (1 Cor 11:21) – and to affirm status distinctions.[1] Such conduct was a misappropriation of the meal. Therefore, Paul admonishes the Corinthians and instructs them to participate appropriately in the Lord's Supper because he believed that correct participation in the meal could transform the community and lead to relationship that were more cruciform.

That the Lord's Supper is Paul's primary concern is evident from several factors in the passage. First, this section is part of the larger context where Paul

---

1. Walters, "Politics of Meals," 356.

addresses problems in the congregation's worship practices (1 Corinthians 11–14).² In 1 Corinthians 11:2–16, he addresses the issue of head coverings during prayers and prophecies; in 1 Corinthians 11:17–34, he deals with abuses of the Lord's Supper; in 1 Corinthians 12, he addresses spiritual gifts and the role of each member of the body during worship; in 1 Corinthians 13, he teaches that love should be the motivation behind the use of the spiritual gifts; and in 1 Corinthians 14, he deals with prophecy and the use of tongues during meetings. The placement of 1 Corinthians 11:17–34 within this structure suggests that it should be read in the light of worship practices. In her outline of 1 Corinthians, Margaret Mitchell rightly places 1 Corinthians 11:17–34 alongside other worship issues, under a section titled "Manifestation of Corinthian Factionalism When 'Coming Together.'"³

Second, the ritual focus of Paul's discussion is clear as he summarizes the problem in 1 Corinthians 11:20: they were not eating the Lord's Supper (κυριανκὸν δεῖπον); instead, they were eating their own dinners (ἴδιον δεῖπον). Paul's reference to the tradition he received from the Lord (1 Cor 11:23–25) and the judgement resulting from wrongful participation (1 Cor 11:27–30) indicate the ritual nature of the meal, and the division and mistreatment of fellow believers are, outcomes of misdirected worship. Therefore, correct participation in the Lord's Supper may create a community that is shaped by the cross of Christ, where members die to self and build up their fellow believers. Grillo affirms that "ritual is not just 'symbolic.' It transforms practitioners, by eliciting direct bodily ways of knowing."⁴

Paul's concern is for the holiness of the community. Holiness is a relational term; it refers to being made holy through a covenantal relationship with the holy God and loving God and neighbour. This relationship is made possible through participation in Christ and exemplified in restored relationships between human beings. Abuses of the Lord's Supper reflect a distorted relationship with Christ, leading to broken relationships among believers.

---

2. Økland, *Women in Their Place*, 1.
3. Mitchell, *Rhetoric of Reconciliation*, xi.
4. Grillo, "African Rituals" 114.

7.1 The Ritual Context of 1 Corinthians 11:17–34

The longstanding and generally accepted view is that the Lord's Supper originally took place in the homes of believers and that it began as a communal, complete meal, as evidenced by Paul's reprimand about overeating and getting drunk (1 Cor 11:21).[5] There are, however, suggestions that early Christian meeting places were not limited to the homes of believers but included rented dining spaces, shops, workshops, and outdoor spaces.[6] Regardless of the location, Paul expected the celebration of the Lord's Supper to be honoured as a sacred meal that was invested with spiritual significance.[7]

According to Jorunn Økland, Paul expected that the gathering of the ἐκκλησία would be a sacred space where ritual practices could take place. In support of this assumption, Økland cites Paul's use of συνάγω, pointing out that συνάγω is "the term Paul uses when he wants to speak more precisely about the ritual gatherings of the *ekklesia*."[8] In addition, she highlights Paul's rebuke that the congregation was not celebrating the κυριακὸν δεῖπνον but, rather, ἴδιον δεῖπνον – that is, their own meals.[9] Økland suggests that Paul was encouraging a distinction between the οἰκία space and the ἐκκλησία space. According to Økland, one way to achieve this distinction was through the ritual meal, performed according to correct ritual procedures.[10] This ritual activity transforms the οἰκία space into "a sacred place with a meaningful, ordered territory."[11] Økland's suggestion that it was the context of worship that created the ἐκκλησία space seems convincing. This idea finds support in Paul's rebuke that the believers should celebrate the Lord's Supper rather than their own meals (1 Cor 11:20–21) and in his repeated use of ἀλλήλων (1 Cor 11:18, 20, 33, 34; 14:26). Thus, it is the presence of Christ, the gathering of believers, and the sacred activities that take place in the space that constitute the ἐκκλησία space.

---

5. Barclay, *Lord's Supper*, 99; Taussig, *In the Beginning*, 55; Murphy-O' Connor, *St Paul's Corinth*, 178-184.
6. See Adams, *Earliest Christian Meeting Places*, 24–30; Horrell, "Domestic Space," 349–369.
7. Jeremias, "This Is My Body," 197; Barclay, "Lord's Supper," 13.
8. Økland, *Women in Their Place*, 143.
9. Økland, 144.
10. Økland, 146.
11. Økland, 146.

Paul also refers to the ἐκκλησία as the temple of God (1 Cor 3:16–17). This reference calls to mind both the Jerusalem temple and the pagan temples in Corinth.[12] Traditionally, the temple was the place of God's dwelling, but now, under this new covenant, the new people of God become the new dwelling place of God through Jesus Christ.[13] Therefore, even though the gathering place might be a family home, the presence of Christ, the gathering of the people of God, and the cultic practices transform the οἰκία space into a sacred space that is suitable for ritual gathering. According to John Barclay, the Lord's Supper is a

> form of sacred exchange. The meal belongs not to the Corinthian assembly but to the Lord (κυριακὸν δεῖπον). As 10:16–17 had made clar, the cup and the bread that they share create community not only with one another but with Christ, just as meals devoted to δαιμόνια create sacred associations in other directions (10:19–22).[14]

The exact order of the Lord's Supper in the early church is uncertain; it could have been patterned after Graeco-Roman meals[15] or the Passover meal.[16] Either way, as noted by various scholars, Paul wants to encourage a more ritualized context by addressing the intent, structure, place, and timing of the meal, as well as the myths or narrative themes that should be emphasized during the Lord's Supper.[17] To this end, Paul reminds the Corinthian believers of the tradition he had passed on to them (1 Cor 11:23–26). It is now generally accepted that Paul's letters contain the earliest literary record of the Lord's Supper tradition.[18] However, this does not mean that he received this through

---

12. Brower, *God's Holy People*, 61.
13. Brower, 62.
14. Barclay, "Lord's Supper," 13.
15. Lampe, "Eucharist," 38; Ibita, "Conversation," 97–114.
16. Wright, *Faithfulness of God*, 1347; Jeremias, "This Is My Body," 196.
17. See Strecker, *Liminale Theologie*, 313–320; Turley, *Ritualized Revelation*, 133–167; Fuad, "Lord's Supper," 202–214; Grimes, *Ritual Criticism*; Smit, "Ritual Failure," 165–193.
18. Jeremias, "This Is My Body," 198; Marshall, *Last Supper*, 31; Knoch, "Do This in Memory," 3.

a direct revelation from Jesus; it was probably a tradition transmitted from pre-Pauline Christian sources.[19]

The two visible symbols in this meal are the bread that Jesus interprets as his body (1 Cor 11:24) and the cup, which was interpreted variously as the cup of the new covenant in the blood of Jesus (1 Cor 11:25) or the cup of thanksgiving (1 Cor 10:16). The ritual actions involved include giving thanks, breaking the bread, ingesting the symbols, reciting the ritual words, the mandate to remember, and the implied mandate to repeat the ritual. All this is done in the presence of the Lord, who is believed to be present at the meal. These ritual symbols point to a wealth of *significata* aimed at transforming the community.

The meanings of the bread and the cup are clear since they were interpreted, as Paul says, by Jesus himself. The bread signifies the body of Christ, which was broken for believers (1 Cor 11:24). According to Hooker, "Possibly the breaking symbolises what happens to Jesus' body in death: he is broken – for you; he dies – for you."[20] The broken bread signifies the fulfillment of Christ's self-giving for the atonement of the people he loves and calls to mind the sacrifice of the paschal lamb.[21] The cup, according to Paul, is the new covenant in the blood of Christ (1 Cor 11:25). The metaphor of the body and blood of Christ recalls the suffering, humiliation, and self-emptying love of Christ. However, these symbols also convey multiple ideas, relationships, and themes. Paul's extensive reference to the exodus narrative (1 Cor 10:1–22), his reference to the new covenant (1 Cor 11:25), and his reference to Christ as the "Passover lamb" (1 Cor 5:7) make it evident that Paul sees the Passover[22] as the framework to interpret the Lord's Supper. This interpretation is strengthened by the fact that later sources also situate the meal within the context of the Passover meal (Matt 26:19; Mark 14:16; Luke 22:13).

Theissen suggests that the sacraments of the Lord's Supper and baptism replaced the traditional sign language of Judaism, (temple practices, Torah

---

19. Jeremias, "This Is My Body," 198; Gardner, *1 Corinthians*, 508; Fee, *Corinthians*, 607; Conzelmann, *1 Corinthians*, 196; Marshall, *Last Supper*, 32; Witherington, *Conflict and Community*, 250.

20. Hooker, *Not Ashamed*, 22.

21. Thiselton, *Corinthians*, 874.

22. It is beyond the scope of this research to discuss whether or not the Lord's Supper was a Passover meal. For a discussion on this issue, see Thiselton, *Corinthians*, 871–878; Jeremias, *Eucharistic Words*, 15–88; Marshall, *Last Supper*, 57–75.

observance, covenantal signs like circumcision etc.) and that, in celebrating the meal during Passover, Jesus was offering an alternative to the temple rituals.[23] Thiselton agrees, observing that the body of Christ broken for you "now replaces the events or objects of redemption from Egypt made participatory and contemporary."[24] According to Thiselton, the words τὸ ὑπὲρ ὑμῶν – which is for you – echo the suffering servant of Isaiah 53, which reflects themes of identification and substitution. These Old Testament parallels indicate that the Passover provides the key framework for understanding the Lord's Supper. The central theme that emerges from Christ being the Passover lamb is deliverance and redemption from slavery. According to Hofius, "τὸ ὑπὲρ ὑμῶν specifies Jesus' self-surrender unto death as expiatory and reconciliatory event."[25] Paul envisions the deliverance from Egypt as a prefiguration of salvation in Christ, evident from the frequent analogies he draws between freedom from sin and freedom from slavery (Rom 6:3–14, 22; 8:15; 1 Cor 7:23; Gal 4:8, 24–31).

Unique to Paul's account of the Lord's Supper is the identification of the body of Christ with the ἐκκλησία. In 1 Corinthians 10:17, he says, "Because there is one loaf, we, who are many, are one body, for we all share the one loaf," and elaborates further on this idea in 1 Corinthians 12. Neyrey's description of the social body of Christ is very appropriate:

> The social body of the church is holy, the body of Christ (12:12; 6:15). Moreover, its holiness consists of being filled with a "holy" Spirit (12:4–11, 13; see 3:16 and 6:19). However, the holiness of the body is likewise perceived in terms of its wholeness, viz. unity. One of the functions of the Holy Spirit in 12:4–11 is to unify the cornucopia of gifts given to the body's diverse members.[26]

According to Neyrey, the greatest threat to the body of Christ is division.[27] This is suggested in Paul's emphasis on the divisions manifested among

---

23. Theissen, *Earliest Churches*, 124–127.
24. Thiselton, *Corinthians*, 877.
25. Hofius, "Lord's Supper," 98.
26. Neyrey, "Body Language," 157.
27. Neyrey, 157.

believers during the Lord's Supper. This raises the question: could the Lord's Supper be a means to remedy these schisms?

The significance of the elements in the Lord's Supper is indisputable. However, a question remains: Was there any perceived power in the actual elements of bread and the cup? Käsemann makes this comment on the "spiritual food" and "spiritual drink" in 1 Corinthians 10:3–4:

> The βρῶμα and πόμα πνευματικόν undoubtedly mean "food and drink which convey πνεῦμα". This is why it is immediately suggested that the rock which followed was spiritual, i.e. Christ himself, who is again identified with πνεῦμα in 2 Cor 3:17. The gift takes on the character of the Giver himself. The gift is at once instrument and effective power just because it is participation in the Giver himself."[28]

This view has been widely challenged based on the syntactical usage of κοινωνία in ordinary Greek[29] and to counter an interpretation that favours a doctrine of transubstantiation.[30] However, could Käsemann's view be substantiated by approaching this question from a ritual perspective?

Anthropologists support the idea of a possible relationship between the gift and giver or between the symbol and the deity. According to Turner, each symbol may transmit multiple themes. However, the efficacy of rituals lies in the fact that symbols in rituals are not just passive representations of ideas but are actively experienced as having real power and significance. Turner states that rituals are not just a combination of messages and actions but

> also a fusion of the powers believed to be inherent in the persons, objects, relationships, events, and histories represented by ritual symbols. It is a mobilisation of energies as well as messages. In this respect, the objects and activities in point are not merely things that stand for other things or something abstract, they participate in the powers and virtues they represent.[31]

---

28. Käsemann, *New Testament Themes*, 113.
29. Campbell, "κοινωνία," 367.
30. Willis, *Idol Meat in Corinth*, 17–64.
31. Turner, "Symbols in African Ritual," 1102.

This belief is undoubtedly present in African rituals, which might help to shed further light on this question. According to Mulago, a person's vital force or spirit can be channelled through symbols. However, he cautions that it is not the object itself – for example, the bread – but the vital force of the *significata* in the object that causes change.[32] Actions and words can externalize the vital force and make it known to third parties, and the symbols can transmit the vital force or characteristics of the *significata* to participants.[33] Therefore, symbols infused with spiritual power are an essential means for vital participation in the African religions because they contain and transmit this power to participants.

Transmission of spiritual power through symbols is a possibility in the Lord's Supper. Interpreting 1 Cor 11:17–34 text through the lens of African spirituality, rather than through post-Enlightenment rationalism, may enrich our understanding of Paul's instructions. A modified view of the sacramental nature of the elements is thus possible. Instead of transubstantiation – where it is believed that the elements become the body and blood of Christ – or a mere metaphorical interpretation, we propose that the elements can convey spiritual benefits when consumed within the correct ritual context because they are infused with the *pneuma* of Christ. This idea is discussed further below.

7.2 Vertical *Communitas* during the Lord's Supper

This primary focus of this section is sacred communion with Christ during the Lord's Supper and the spiritual consequences this creates. Consideration of the ancient spiritual world view is paramount for a faithful interpretation of this aspect of the Lord's Supper.

Edith Humphrey notes that belief in supernatural powers was part of the first-century Jewish and Graeco-Roman world views, as exemplified in Paul's writings.[34] She argues that although Paul frequently mentions the supernatural, spiritual powers, he appears to feel no need to explain these references, which suggests that he believed that his hearers would share his world view

---

32. Mulago, "Vital Participation," 152.
33. Mulago, 152.
34. Humphrey, "Apocalyptic as Theoria," 92.

and, therefore, understand these references. Thus, Paul's references to the spiritual world reflect his context.

Michael Gorman appropriately warns that "it would be a mistake to underestimate the so-called 'mystical' character of Paul's experience."[35] He notes that Paul's Damascus Road experience, where the exalted Christ appeared to him, was a "mystical" experience.[36] Further evidence of this spiritual world view is found in Paul's personal experiences: the Lord appeared to him (1 Cor 15:8–10), he received the gospel through a revelation (Gal 1:11–12), he travelled to Jerusalem in response to a revelation (Gal 2:1–2), he professed to speak in tongues (1 Cor 14:18), and, though speaking in the third person, confessed to being caught up to the third heaven (2 Cor 12:1–4).

Bultmann concedes that Paul had this spiritual world view when he says this of Paul:

> To be sure, it is scarcely permissible to say that he completely freed himself of the mystery-conception of sacrament as having magical effect; for he leaves vicarious baptism, which rest upon such conception, at least uncontested (1 Cor 15:29) and also shows himself influenced by it in his view of the Lord's Supper.[37]

In relation to the Lord's Supper, Bultmann further states that

> in Paul's conception of the *Lord's Supper* mystery ideas unites with his own view of the salvation-occurrence. Paul took over from the Hellenistic Church both the celebration of the Lord's supper and a conception of it as a sacrament which effects communion with the crucified and risen Christ by means of bread and wine, eaten and drunk.[38]

Clearly, Paul believed in the mystical effects of the Lord's Supper, but this belief is unlikely to have been borrowed from the Hellenistic church. Rather, these beliefs can be understood from the perspective of Paul's essentially Jewish spiritual world view, and this is corroborated by ritual theory.

---

35. Gorman, *Cruciformity*, 25.
36. Gorman, 25.
37. Bultmann, *Theology*, 311–312.
38. Bultmann, 313.

In his discussion of 2 Corinthians 5:16–17, Douglas Campbell underscores the importance of sharing in Paul's world view when endeavouring to interpret his letters.[39] Paul's new position "in Christ" forms the basis of his interpretation of reality. This epistemology is relational; Paul is part of the new creation and sees things according to the Spirit because he is now "in Christ." So, for Paul, "everything is not as it seems to the naked eye and one must 'believe' and 'know' that this 'veiled,' 'inner,' and unseen dimension within reality is, in fact, the most important one within its dynamics, and analyse accordingly."[40] Campbell's observation about Paul is also true of the African world view, which corresponds to the first century in many ways. An African reading would take these "mystical" aspects for granted, which facilitates interpreting Paul's directives concerning the correct celebration of the Lord's Supper in 1 Corinthians 11:17–34.

Paul's spiritual world view is reflected in his discussion of the Lord's Supper in several ways. First, Paul's insistence on the presence of Christ during the Lord's Supper points to the spiritual power infusing the meal. According to Paul, Jesus presides over the meal as the host and is personally present during the ritual.[41] This is evident in Paul's rebuke, where he claims that the Corinthians' behaviour demonstrates that they are not really partaking of the Lord's Supper (κυριακὸν δεῖπον) when they come together (1 Cor 11:20). Paul states that he received the tradition of the Lord's Supper from Jesus Christ (1 Cor 11:23) and that the elements are the body and blood of Christ (1 Cor 11:24–25). The *pneuma* of Christ is the spiritual power present that infuses the symbols, behaviours, and people as they participate in this meal.[42]

Second, Paul makes this blunt statement: "Is not the cup of thanksgiving for which we give thanks a participation in the blood of Christ? And is not the bread that we break a participation in the body of Christ?" (1 Cor 10:16). As discussed in an earlier chapter, when understood within the ritual context of this discussion and considering Paul's understanding of *pneuma*, we may view this as real participation with Christ. According to Paul, this participation happens through the bread and the cup.

---

39. Campbell, "Apocalyptic Epistemology," 68
40. Campbell, 68.
41. Lampe, "Eucharist," 43.
42. Turner, "Symbols in African Rituals," 1102.

Third, Paul warns that partaking in the bread and cup of the Lord in an unworthy manner can lead to judgement (κρίμα), which may take the form of illness or even death (1 Cor 11:27–30). Although this is commonly interpreted metaphorically, as referring to the congregation as the body of Christ, the ritual implications of Paul's assertion cannot be ignored. From a ritual perspective, incorrect participation in the symbols and behaviours required during a ritual can lead to judgement.[43]

Gruenwald's exploration of the rituals of Leviticus 16 may help to illustrate this point. Gruenwald states that the death of Aaron's sons (Lev 16:1) is an example of what happens when ritual regulations are not followed and demonstrates the risk of approaching a sacred place or touching a sacred object incorrectly.[44] He also suggests that rituals are only empowered to accomplish their desired objects when there is proper adherence to ritual demands, arguing that this was Paul's problem with the way the Corinthians celebrated the Lord's Supper.[45] During the Lord's Supper, judgement occurs after eating and drinking (1 Cor 10:29), which implies that the act of consuming does not have the desired effect – instead of uniting and strengthening the community, it leads to illness and death.[46]

The theological nature of this judgement is inferred from the ritual situation and its explanation. Thus, the judgement associated with the abuse of the Lord's Supper is also a result of despising the church of God – represented by the bread – by humiliating those who had nothing. This abuse of "weaker" believers amounts to despising Christ, who is the Lord of the Supper. As in 1 Corinthians 8, the "strong" wound the conscience of the "weak," thereby despising Christ himself, who died for them (1 Cor 8:12).

The next question to address is this: How does this vertical *communitas* occur? The ritual circumstances facilitate vertical *communitas*, and the blessing over the bread and the cup infuses these with *pneuma*, thus making them πνευματικὸν βρῶμα and πνευματικὸν ἔπιον (spiritual food and drink) (1 Cor

---

43. See Fuad, "Lord's Supper," 202–214; Smit, "Ritual Failure," 165–193.
44. Gruenwald, *Rituals and Ritual Theory*, 204.
45. Gruenwald, 249.
46. See also an insightful article by Chelcent Fuad, cited above, who, using Ronald Grimes's theory of ritual infelicity, makes a strong case for understanding the behaviour of the Corinthians during the Lord's Supper as ritual failure. According to Fuad, inappropriate behaviour includes social aspects – how they treated each other – and religious aspects – the defilement of the sacred meal. Faud, "Lord's Supper."

10:3–4). According to Gruenwald, "The blessing creates a ritual connection between the cup, the blood of Christ and the community."[47] Thus, the blessing creates the reality that generates the constitutive process that shapes the community that receives the ritual status of being allowed to participate in the blood of Christ.[48] For Gruenwald, the words of blessing have transformative power because they "[indicate] the ritual act of transferring to humans something that initially belonged to God."[49] Ritual theory suggests that the spiritual power of the *pneuma* of Christ infuses the elements.[50]

Explained in terms of ritual theory, the power called upon during the prayer is believed to infuse the sacrificial food.[51] As Mulago puts it, the "vital force" or spirit is channelled through the symbol.[52] Thus, in the Lord's Supper, the symbol becomes a means whereby the participant can appropriate the benefits and power of Christ's death and resurrection.

Paul's belief that the elements channel *pneuma* is evident in various ways. First, he compares the bread and the cup to the πνευματικὸν βρῶμα and πνευματικὸν ἔπιον (1 Cor 10:3–4) eaten by the wilderness generation. Some scholars will accept that πνευματικὸν here means provided by the Spirit of God, but not that it conveys something spiritual.[53] However, Thiselton suggests that we retain Paul's general usage of πνευματικόν when interpreting this verse.[54] As suggested earlier, this normal usage does not signify something immaterial. Paul's understanding of *pneuma* shares some similarities with the Stoic understanding of this concept. As Thiessen so aptly puts it, "It is capable of blending itself with different bodies, so that every part of the original body, while maintaining its own character, still participates fully in the mixture."[55] The bread and the cup, interpenetrated by the *pneuma* of Christ through thanksgiving and breaking, thus become a means to facilitate

---

47. Gruenwald, *Rituals and Ritual Theory*, 252.
48. Gruenwald, 253.
49. Gruenwald, 254.
50. See section 4.2.2 above; see also Turner, "Symbols in African Ritual," 1102; Mulago, "Vital Participation," 152.
51. Turner, 1102.
52. Mulago, "Vital Participation," 152.
53. See Fee, *Corinthians*, 495; Thiselton, *Corinthians*, 726.
54. Thiselton, *Corinthians*, 726.
55. Thiessen, "Rock Was Christ," 120.

communitas with Christ among believers and transform the community into the body of Christ.

Second, participation in the narrative of Christ crucified facilitates vertical *communitas*, and this union with Christ affects transformation in the community. According to Okoye, during the Lord's Supper, Christ "actually incorporates us into his sacrificial life by sanctifying our lives."[56] In 1 Corinthians 10:16–17, Paul affirms his belief that participation in the Lord's Supper is participating in Christ. This participation happens when believers enter the narrative of the Christ-event through rituals.

C. F. D. Moule suggests that the Lord's Supper, like baptism, is the repeated event that unites believers to Christ by uniting them with his death and resurrection.[57] Moule bases this conclusion on the fact that both rituals – baptism and the Lord's Supper – share one central myth: the death and resurrection of Jesus Christ.[58] Thus, just as in baptism, believers participate in Christ's death and resurrection, leading to their union with His life and their inclusion in the family of God, the Lord's Supper also reenacts this same core truth. Believers, in participating, accept that they are guilty of sin and that God is fair in his judgement, but they also accept the remedial death of Christ.[59] Thus, in eating together, believers appropriate the benefits of Christ's death and resurrection again.[60] Thiselton, agreeing with Moule, affirms that "to remember" means "pleading guilty, and pleading the body and blood of Christ under the weight of judgement and the glory of promise."[61]

However, this does not signify that the Lord's Supper is a repeated initiation rite but, rather, a means of continued transformation into the image of Christ. Moule argues that this repeated dying with Christ is necessary because of humanity's fallen nature and the fallenness of the cosmos.[62] Moule seems to have a more negative view of the fallen human condition and neglects Paul's description of the new nature of those who are baptized into Christ.

---

56. Okoye, "African Eucharistic Celebration," 235.
57. Moule, "Judgement Theme," 464.
58. Moule, 471.
59. Moule, 477.
60. Theissen, *Earliest Churches*, 124.
61. Thiselton, *Corinthians*, 880.
62. Moule, "Judgement Theme," 468.

He states, "Sin is prominent in the best of them."[63] Paul, however, adopts a more optimistic stance, asserting that believers are "dead to sin" (Rom 6:11) but must learn to live according to this reality. Paul emphasizes that believers are being transformed into the image of the Son (2 Cor 3:18).

While Moule is correct in saying that Paul holds this tension, I think that this tension is simultaneously "mortal and eternally alive *simul mortuus et vivens*,"[64] to use Barclay's helpful statement, which differs subtly from Luther's *simul justus et peccator*.[65] Believers are still destined to die physically, but they already share in the resurrection life of Christ and can hope in their own resurrection at the *parousia*. While in the body, believers obtain the new nature in Christ and, even though they may still face temptation, are no longer under the power of sin.[66]

According to Moule, this tension between the already and the not yet is expressed sacramentally in baptism – the unrepeated ritual – and the Lord's Supper – the renewal ritual.[67] In remembering (1 Cor 11:25), believers are not simply recalling that Jesus died but re-enacting that they have died with Christ and are now the new people of God. Concerning the interpretation of *anamnēsis* in this verse, Hooker rightly states,

> The English word suggests simply memory, but in fact, the actions of the eucharist are a proclamation; for the Jews, the Passover is not simply a remembrance of what took place once, long ago; it is the re-enactment of those past events in the present; and it is a looking forward to the final Passover, when the Messiah will come.[68]

Therefore, "remembering" Christ and retelling the story of "the night he was betrayed" (1 Cor 11:23) results in vertical *communitas* with Christ and leads to the transformation of the believer and the community. To "remember" Christ means allowing his death to constitute, shape, and transform

---

63. Moule, 468.
64. Barclay, *Paul and the Gift*, 502.
65. Barclay, 502.
66. Barclay, 503.
67. Moule, "Judgement Theme," 469.
68. Hooker, *Not Ashamed*, 23.

the individual and corporate identity of the church.⁶⁹ Participating in Christ through the Lord's Supper should transform believers into the *kenotic* likeness of Christ in the same way that baptism does. Baptism transforms believers into the likeness of Christ, while the Lord's Supper is a means of their continual transformation into the image of Christ.

In this passage, vertical *communitas* is reflected in the ritual language that Paul uses and in his insistence on Christ's presence during the meal. The themes of judgement also suggest that connection with the divine is at stake during the ritual. Vertical *communitas* takes place through the blessing, distribution, and partaking of the elements that convey the *pneuma* of Christ to believers. Participation in the narrative of Christ crucified facilitates vertical *communitas*. Paul views the Lord's Supper as a sacred ritual that requires the observance of acceptable ritual behaviour, where the symbols are infused with the *pneuma* of Christ, resulting in *communitas* with Christ.

7.3 Horizontal *Communitas* during the Lord's Supper

Scholars have endeavoured to label the communal relationships that Paul calls for in 1 Corinthians 11:17–34. Gerd Theissen suggests that "love-patriarchalism" would be an appropriate term. According to Theissen, Paul acknowledged "the class-specific differences within the community while minimising their manifestations."⁷⁰ Thus, Paul allowed for "a certain pre-eminence"⁷¹ for the rich, provided they acted in a loving, respectful way. Yung Suk Kim suggests that Paul called for egalitarian relationships that were shaped by the sacrificial death of Christ.⁷² Such relationships would counteract the hegemonic ideologies of the Roman Empire and honour the "weak" in the community.⁷³ Suzanne Watts Henderson proposes that Paul was calling on the rich to feed the poor, emphasizing the importance of sharing.⁷⁴ John Barclay suggests

---

69. Thiselton, *Corinthians*, 880.
70. Theissen, *Social Setting*, 164.
71. Theissen, 164.
72. Kim, *Christ's Body in Corinth*, 31.
73. Kim, 62.
74. Henderson, "If Anyone Hungers," 195–208. See also Ibita, "Conversation," 97–114.

that Paul called for "comprehensive solidarity, founded on mutual honour,"[75] arguing that this is evidenced in the words "for you" (1 Cor 11:24)[76] – referring to Christ's death that attributes infinite worth to all believers – and in Paul's instructions to the Corinthians to "wait for one another" (1 Cor 11:33 NRSV).[77] The Lord's Supper thus becomes an occasion where all members are recognized and honoured.[78]

This study suggests that *communitas* might be an apt way to describe the types of relationships that Paul advocated for. *Communitas* affirms union with Christ as the foundation of the relationship between believers. It underscores that believers share in the *pneuma* of Christ and that their relationship thus goes beyond shared ideologies or associations. These relationships are sacred because they are grounded in union with Christ, empowered by the Holy Spirit, and guided by an ethic of love.

This horizontal *communitas* is rooted in vertical *communitas* during the Lord's Supper. This connection is evident in Paul's ambiguous references to the body in 1 Corinthians 11:27–29. In these verses, Paul warns that believers who participate in the Supper in an unworthy manner are guilty of sinning against the body and blood of Christ. Therefore, he calls the Corinthians to examine themselves before they participate, stating that "all who eat and drink without discerning the body, eat and drink judgement against themselves" (1 Cor 11:29 NRSV).

There is general agreement that "the body and blood" in 1 Corinthians 11:27 refers to the body of Christ, but there is disagreement about the interpretation of "the body" in 1 Corinthians 11:29 as the body of believers. According to Marshall, "the body" in 1 Corinthians 11:29 should be understood as a shorthand for the "body and blood" as used in 1 Corinthians 11:27. He proposes that both instances refer to the offender "failing to realise that the bread and the cup represent the body and blood of Jesus."[79] Conzelmann suggests that "body" in 1 Corinthians 11:27 means an offence against the

---

75. Barclay, "Lord's Supper," 5.
76. Barclay, 15.
77. Barclay, 19.
78. Barclay, 21.
79. Marshall, *Last Supper*, 114.

elements and, ultimately, an offence against the Lord himself; thus, the person who eats in an unworthy manner is just as guilty as those who killed Christ.[80]

In this light, Paul's indictment against the Corinthians for participating in the Lord's Supper in an unworthy manner (1 Cor 11:27) is not limited to their current behaviour against those who have nothing but pertains to the entire salvation narrative. According to Fee, those who participate in an unworthy manner are just as culpable for the Lord's death as those who originally crucified him.[81] Failure to discern the body of Christ also entails a failure to discern the meaning of Christ's sacrificial death.[82] "The body" in 1 Corinthians 11:27 thus refers to the body of Christ as the source of the believing community. According to Higgins, the unity of the community during the Lord's Supper is a result of the believer's union "in Christ"; believers are baptized into the body of Christ.[83]

Fee,[84] Campbell,[85] Mitchell,[86] and Thiselton[87] suggest that 1 Corinthians 11:29 should be understood as referring to the congregation. They suggest that the absence of "the blood" in 1 Corinthians 11:29 supports this interpretation, while the context of communal σχίσματα in the Corinthian ἐκκλησία also strengthens the possibility. According to this view, the mistreatment of the poor constitutes a failure to discern the body of Christ, which is the church.[88] According to Fee, "the body" in 1 Corinthians 11:29 "deliberately recalls Paul's earlier interpretation of the bread (10:17), thus indicating that the concern is with the problem in Corinth itself, of the rich abusing the poor."[89] Brower argues that

> "discerning the body" is focused upon the people as the body of Christ. Therefore, if one has a proper discernment of the body of Christ, the holy communion is a sacred communal meal which

---

80. Conzelmann, *1 Corinthians*, 202.
81. Fee, *Corinthians*, 621.
82. Moule, "Judgement Theme," 472.
83. Higgins, *Lord's Supper*, 69.
84. Fee, *Corinthians*, 618–619.
85. Campbell, *1 Corinthians*, 191.
86. Mitchell, *Rhetoric of Reconciliation*, 265.
87. Thiselton, *Corinthians*, 890–891.
88. See Brower, *God's Holy People*, 74; Higgins, *Lord's Supper*, 69.
89. Fee, *Corinthians*, 623.

precludes independent and selfish action which does not take account of the body of Christ.[90]

Both interpretations of "the body" are vital for participating in horizontal *communitas* because the believers' existence "in Christ" enables them to experience *communitas* with one another. Several clues point to the fact that Paul desired *communitas* among the Corinthian believers.

First, as mentioned in section 6.5, Paul's use of κοινωνία in 1 Corinthians 10:17–34 denotes *communitas*. It was already noted that this κοινωνία results from the believer's joint participation in Christ. Thus, it is κοινωνία with Christ that creates the locale for horizontal *communitas*.

Second, the use of the body as a metaphor in 1 Corinthians 10:17 is also an important signal of *communitas*. According to Thiselton, "the body" in this context stands in contrast to the schisms in the Corinthian ἐκκλησία and points back to 1 Corinthians 1:13, where Paul asks, "Is Christ divided?"[91] In this sense, the focus is on the meaning of the ἐκκλησία as the body of Christ, which speaks to concepts of unity, mutual dependence, and mutual submission.

Third, further investigation of 1 Corinthians 10:17 and 1 Corinthians 11:17–34 reveals semantical pointers to *communitas*. The use of μετέχω (1 Cor 10:17), means "partaking along with others,"[92] or "we all share,"[93] or as Fee suggests, partaking together in "the single loaf, the body of Christ."[94] In this instance, μετέχω refers the believers' equal sharing in Christ, resulting in their unity as the body of Christ. This sharing precludes partaking at the table of demons because such sharing creates union with unbelievers and threatens the life of the holy community.[95]

Μετέχω denotes a vital aspect of *communitas*. According to Turner, people who experience *communitas* together are absolutely equal and thus

---

90. Brower, *God's Holy People*, 72.
91. Thiselton, *Corinthians*, 768.
92. Campbell, "κοινωνία," 352–380.
93. Thiselton, *Corinthians*, 768.
94. Fee, *Corinthians*, 518.
95. Ciampa and Rosner, *Corinthians*, 476.

share everything equally.⁹⁶ This is also reflected in African communalism. According to Mulago,

> The life of the individual is grasped as it is shared. The member of the tribe, the clan, the family knows that he does not live to himself but within the community. He knows that apart from the community, he would no longer have the means of existence.⁹⁷

This quote from Mulago sheds light on Paul's intention in his use of μετέχω in this context. Brower, commenting on 1 Corinthians 10:17, notes that "the diverse members of the body of Christ have their origin and owe their very existence to Christ."⁹⁸ This continued existence depends on continued sharing in Christ and sharing with one another.

Paul's use of συνέρχομαι (coming together) (1 Cor 11:17–18, 20, 33–34) also points to *communitas*. Συνέρχομαι frequently occurs in this discussion and, according to Fee, refers to their coming together as the ἐκκλησία.⁹⁹ This coming together is thus a gathering of people with a specific identity – the body of Christ – and a specific purpose. Their coming together should thus be an expression of their identity as the ἅγιος (holy ones), and the schisms that are taking place are a direct contradiction of who they are supposed to be. Therefore, incorrect behaviour during their gathering – that is, when they come together for their own purposes instead of for Christ – may lead to their condemnation (1 Cor 11:34).¹⁰⁰

Paul also uses ἀλλήλων (one another), to counsel the Corinthians to wait for one another when they come together to celebrate the Lord's Supper (1 Cor 11:33 NRSV). Ἀλλήλων is used in connection with relationships characterized by transcendence, solidarity, reciprocity, and mutuality.¹⁰¹ Paul frequently uses ἀλλήλων in his letters to encourage mutual relationships that are rooted in joint participation in Christ.¹⁰² Paul later expounds on this in his letter to the Romans, where he reminds believers that they are "members one

---

96. Turner, "Betwixt and Between," 238.
97. Mulago, "Vital Participation," 139.
98. Brower, *God's Holy People*, 75.
99. Fee, *Corinthians*, 594. See also Mitchell, *Rhetoric of Reconciliation*, 264.
100. Mitchell, 265.
101. Russell, "In the World," 224.
102. Lohfink, *Jesus and Community*, 99–106.

of another" (Rom 12:5 NRSV) and calls them to welcome one another (Rom 15:7) and live in harmony with one another (Rom 15:5). In Galatians, he says that believers must serve one another (Gal 5:13) and bear one another's burdens (Gal 6:2); and in his letter to the Thessalonians, Paul instructs them to comfort one another, be at peace with one another, and be good to one another (1 Thess 5:11–15). Ἀλλήλων expresses the selfless love and unity exemplified in the sacrifice of Christ.

Finally, *communitas* is revealed in the shared vocation of the ἐκκλησία. Paul reminds the Corinthians that the celebration of the Lord's Supper is a proclamation of Christ's death until he comes again (1 Cor 11:26). The ritual actions and words, along with the *communitas* among the believers, all serve to proclaim the gospel of Jesus Christ. This meal not only affirms and shapes their identity as the people of God but is also supposed to have a missional impact. Gorman states that the injustice and loveless behaviour present in the Corinthian church could have harmed the church's witness.[103] He notes that there must have been unbelievers who visited the meeting (1 Cor 14:16, 21–25) and that Paul's concern not to offend potential believers would have applied in this situation.[104] The believer's participation in the Lord's Supper is supposed to be the embodiment of the self-giving love of Christ, as well as a proclamation of the salvation that is available for all and a reminder of Christ's imminent return.

Peter Lampe suggest three possible ways that the proclamation of the Lord's death connects with the ethical problems in Corinth.[105] First, he suggests that Christ died for the "weak" believers (1 Cor 8:11) and that, therefore, the reality of his death for their sake should discourage their mistreatment. Second, he suggests that Christ's self-denial is an example to the Corinthians on how they should empty themselves and put the needs of others ahead of their own (Phil 2:4–7). Third, he looks to Romans 6:2–8, where believers die with Christ during the ritual of baptism. This dying-to-self determines how believers should live – a life of self-denial and active love for others.[106] All three of Lampe's suggestions are valid as they underscore the various aspects of

---

103. Gorman, *Becoming the Gospel*, 245.
104. Gorman, 245.
105. Lampe, "Eucharist," 44.
106. Lampe, 45.

participation in the cross of Christ during the ritual meal and affirm believers' *communitas* with one another.

7.4 Conclusion

In sum, Paul's intention in 1 Corinthians 11:17–34 was to correct the abuses of the Lord's Supper because he viewed it as a sacramental means to transform the community into greater Christlikeness. This implies that *communitas* with Christ is central to this discussion, and that *communitas* with fellow believers is an outcome of correct participation at the Lord's Table.

The ritual context of this passage is vital for its interpretation because the ritual of the Lord's Supper is the central subject. The exegetical meaning of the bread and the cup is laid out in the tradition that Paul received from the Lord (1 Cor 11:23–26). The bread was the body of Christ that was broken for them (1 Cor 11:24), and the cup was the new covenant in Christ's blood (1 Cor 11:25). Paul also interprets the bread as the church, which is the body of Christ (1 Cor 10:17). The ritual elements, actions, and words should be interpreted in the light of the Passover, where Christ is the Passover lamb (1 Cor 5:7), slain to deliver humanity from the power of sin.

Vertical *communitas* is possible because of the assumed presence of Christ, who is the host of the Supper (1 Cor 11:20). The ritual elements, actions, and words infuse the elements and the ritual with the *pneuma* of Christ, thus making the whole event a means for transformation. The *pneuma* facilitates *communitas* between Christ and believers, and among believers.

The possibility of judgement, manifested in the form of illness and death (1 Cor 11:29–31), also points to the sacred nature of the Lord's Supper; unworthy participation may be detrimental to the well-being of both individuals and the community.

The ritual of the Lord's Supper is based on the narrative of Christ crucified and, like baptism, it is an occasion to re-enact union in Christ's death and resurrection and to experience the new creation facilitated by the sacrifice of Christ. This union with Christ is repeated every time believers participate in the Lord's Supper and is a means of keeping believers in a state of cruciformity and enabling self-sacrificial love.

The best way to describe the types of relationships Paul calls for in Corinth is horizontal *communitas*. This sacred relationship is rooted in the believer's participation in Christ. Horizontal *communitas* is revealed in Paul's use of κοινωνία, μετέχω, συνέρχομαι, and ἀλλήλων, as well his use of the "body" metaphor. The ἐκκλησία as the body of Christ stands in contrast to the divisions in Corinth, underscoring the unity, mutual love, and reciprocity that Paul wanted to teach.

Horizontal *communitas* is also present in the shared vocation of the ἐκκλησία. It proclaims the Lord's death and points to his return at the *parousia* (1 Cor 11:26). The wrongful treatment of the "weak" in the community renders the ritual ineffective, denies the sacrifice of Christ, and destroys the church's mission to the unbelieving society. The ἐκκλησία should embody the *kenotic* love of Christ during their celebration of the Lord's Supper, which can attract new members to the community. This suggests a reciprocal relationship between observing the sacred ritual of the Lord's Supper and showing love to the "weak." Faithful observance of the ritual renders the Lord's Supper effective and shapes the community into an ethos of Christlike love, thus enabling greater empathy for the "weak." Conversely, mistreatment of the "weak" renders the ritual of the Lord's Supper ineffective, which impedes the transformation of the community into Christlike love.

Correct participation in the Lord's Supper anticipates the eschatological salvation of the *parousia*. This summary of the tradition that Paul passed on to them ties in with his warning in 1 Corinthians 10. The Corinthians were still in a liminal situation, awaiting the day of Christ's return, and judgement was still in the future.[107] Paul's reminder offers hope to those who are "in Christ" but also serves as a warning to those participating unworthily in the Lord's Supper.[108]

This research suggests that using the lens of African spirituality – with its focus on spirituality and communalism – offers a deeper understanding of the mystical character of the Lord's Supper. The African concept of vital participation, which is discussed in section 3.1, sheds light on participation between Christ and believers during the ritual. This is reflected in the earlier discussion of vertical *communitas* with Christ and the judgement that results from participating in an unworthy manner. The aspects of the presence of Christ, the sacred space, and the ritual actions and words all affirm the

---

107. Fee, *Corinthians*, 617.
108. Coutsoumpos, *Lord's Supper*, 124.

sacramental character of the meal. As the discussion of horizontal *communitas* during the Lord's Supper has shown, vital participation also highlights the possibility that believers are united with one another as they are united with Christ and share in the *pneuma* of Christ. The concept that vital force can be channelled through symbols offers a possible way to interpret the symbols of the bread and the cup. Spiritual benefits may be imparted to believers as they receive the elements through the blessing over these elements in the presence of Christ within the ritual context. This ritual setting allows the elements to become a means to convey the *pneuma* of Christ and facilitate participation with both Christ and one another. It is this vital participation that transforms believers as they are incorporated into the life, death, resurrection, and *kenotic* life of Christ.

Our study of 1 Corinthians 11:17–34 has provided the following insights regarding the Lord's Supper as a ritual for holiness transformation:

First, the Lord's Supper can help believers to grow in holiness because it is the locale where believers re-enact their union with Christ through the ritual process. During this *communitas* with Christ, believers accept their guilt as sinners and receive, once again, the provision Christ made by his death and resurrection. This is also an opportunity for believers to receive a fresh infilling of the Holy Spirit through participation in the elements of bread and wine, which serve as a means of grace that conveys the benefits of salvation to believers.

Second, the Lord's Supper is the locale where believers are united as this body of Christ. Their joint participation signifies that they receive the same Spirit of Christ and are, therefore, included in this family of Christ. This union is based on real kinship because they all share in the nature and benefits of Christ. The Lord's Supper thus becomes the level ground where true transcendence, mutuality, and equality are made possible. It is also the space where believers are prepared to live ethical lives, patterned after the *kenotic* life of Christ, governed by the law of love, and free from self-centred ambitions and actions.

Third, the abuse and mistreatment of "weak" members in the church undermines the church's holiness because there is a reciprocal relationship between horizontal and vertical *communitas* during the Lord's Supper.

Finally, the Lord's Supper provides a means for continued renewal of the believer's union with Christ. This renewal is important as believers learn to live moral and ethical lives in accordance with their identity as God's holy people. Therefore, the Lord's Supper is a way for believers to live out in their daily lives who they already are in Christ.

Part 4

Application and Conclusions

This section considers the role of inculturation in applying the conclusions about ritual meals from 1 Corinthians 8:1–11:1 and 1 Corinthians 11:17–34 within the African cultural context. This exercise is pivotal because it applies the research to the fundamental questions within the African cultural context and will, hopefully, lead to congruency in worship and practice among African believers. This exercise will explore elements of continuity and discontinuity between ritual meals to ancestors and the Lord's Supper. This section seeks to discover whether the Lord's Supper can address the spiritual and practical needs of African believers while avoiding syncretism. It will also explore how the Lord's Supper can be a means of affirming their identity as both African and Christian, while also moulding their character and behaviour towards greater Christlikeness.

Chapter 8 explores inculturation by addressing two key questions: Should ancestors be included in the celebration of the Lord's Supper? And how can the celebration be made more relevant to African cultural sensibilities? The chapter examines the concept of *communitas* as as a means of fostering holiness within the community. It concludes that ancestors may be acknowledged as fellow worshippers in the Lord's Supper, but attributing to them roles or worship that belong solely to God or Jesus Christ constitutes idolatry. Additionally, Chapter 8 presents practical considerations for adapting the Lord's Supper to the African cultural context.

Chapter 9 provides a summary and conclusions for this study. First, it highlights the similarities between the African cultural worldview and Paul's perspective, showing how these parallels enhance our understanding of Paul's discussion of ritual meals in Corinth by emphasizing their sacramental nature. Second, the chapter underscores the role of *communitas* during the Lord's Supper. This *communitas* has the power to transform the believing community into the holy people they are called to be.

CHAPTER 8

Inculturation of the Lord's Supper for the African Context

8.0 Introduction

This section will inculturate the Lord's Supper for the African context by facilitating communication between the Bible and the African context.[1] The process of inculturating the gospel requires knowledge of and respect for the context in question. Inculturation is not limited to the African context because every culture must undergo a process of engaging with the gospel to determine how to reconcile cultural identity with Christian identity. The problem arises when one cultural expression of the gospel is viewed as the normative form. Unfortunately, early missions often disregarded the African cultural context and created the impression that the gospel is powerless to meet the spiritual needs of African believers.

Earlier, I proposed that the Lord's Supper could be more comprehensively utilized to meet African believers' spiritual needs and transform the community to greater Christlikeness. There are, of course, dangers of distorting Scripture and syncretism; however, when Scripture remains central, this can positively impact the community. I will, therefore, proceed with caution and trust that this study will contribute to the ongoing conversation concerning the contextualization of the Lord's Supper for the African context.

---

1. Amadi, "Inculturating the Eucharist," 28.

8.1 Inculturation of the Lord's Supper for the African Context

The Lord's Supper has been successfully contextualized for the African context. Wessel Bentley gives an example of how the Methodist Church of South Africa used the Lord's Supper as a means of reconciliation during and after the devastation caused by apartheid.[2] According to Bentley, during the apartheid era, there were attempts to split the church along racial lines, but the Methodist Church rejected these efforts and affirmed that they were a single and undivided family.[3] This stance allowed the congregation to unite people divided by race, social status, and the country's laws around the Lord's Table. Bentley observes, "People who had fundamental differences in their political views still found themselves kneeling side by side at the Table in Church. This pronouncement was a pivotal moment in the life of Methodist movement in South Africa and the way it understood and celebrated the Sacrament."[4]

Bentley goes on to explain that the Lord's Table became a space where the church could show solidarity with those who had experienced violence and marginalization in society. He cites the example of the Central Methodist Mission in downtown Johannesburg, which welcomed and ministered to the homeless, victims of abuse, and immigrants suffering from the onslaught of xenophobia. According to Bentley, the Lord's Supper was offered daily to all who wished to participate. The message, according to Bentley, was that

> although they are cast out by society at large, there is a place for all at the Lord's Table and it is through this Sacrament that that they and all who kneel alongside them are seen in equal measures of love and grace by the Almighty.[5]

This example from South Africa demonstrates how the Lord's Supper can be adapted to a local context in ways that impact and transform community life. The celebration of the Lord's Supper provided a ritual space where

---

2. Apartheid, a political system instituted by the White National Party in 1948, segregated the people of South Africa along racial lines. "The Population Registration Act of 1950 authorised officials to categorise people by their 'race.' The population was divided into white and non-white, the non-whites into Coloured, Indian, and Bantu; Bantu and Coloured into still further subgroups." Isichei, *History of Christianity*, 303.

3. Bentley, "Holy Communion," 1.

4. Bentley, 2.

5. Bentley, 2.

racial and political divisions were confronted and an attitude of love – rather than hatred and unforgiveness – was encouraged. The Lord's Supper thus proved effective in transforming generations of racial and political tension and creating a new community in which everyone is equal in Christ. The long-lasting impact of this transformation is demonstrated by the fact that the Methodist Church in South Africa still strives to live out its mission as a "one and undivided" church.[6]

Although the process of contextualizing the Lord's Supper is complicated, churches can effectively utilize this process for the holiness transformation of the body of Christ. In his attempt to inculturate the Lord's Supper for a Catholic diocese in Zimbabwe, Anthony Amadi warns that the language, rites and symbol must be meaningful to the community. This should be more than translating from European Languages but "there is need to create new text that originate from the cultural life of the people."[7] Bearing this in mind, we proceed with our attempt to inculturate the Lord's Supper while endeavouring to remain faithful to the gospel.

8.2 Inclusion of the Ancestors?

Chapter 3 of this thesis discusses the vitally important role that ancestors play in the daily lives of Africans. It also reveals that ancestral veneration is still practised among believers in the twenty-first century. However, before discussing whether inclusion of ancestors during the celebration of the Lord's Supper is possible and advisable, we must answer one vital question: Do ancestral ritual meals constitute worship, or are these merely paying homage to departed loved ones? Several scholars argue that the ancestral cult is simply a means of including the living-dead in family life[8] and that it can be offensive to suggest that Africans worship their ancestors.[9]

Scholars who advocate for the inclusion of ancestors in Christian worship do so on the basis that ancestral veneration is merely a means of honouring departed loved ones. Aylward Shorter suggests that ancestral veneration

---

6. Bentley, 1.
7. Amadi, "Inculturating the Eucharist," 204.
8. See the following examples: Muhindo, "Cloud of Witnesses," 49–68; Shorter, "Ancestor Veneration," 27–37; Kenyatta, *Facing Mount Kenya*, 265.
9. Mbiti, *African Religions and Philosophy*, 9.

enables Africans to enjoy continuity beyond death in family life.[10] According to Shorter, the belief that ancestors coexist with the supreme being shows that they do not practise idolatry because ancestors receive their power from God. Kofi Opoku extends this idea by suggesting that "ancestors help to confirm the belief in the living God."[11] Another approach is that of Edwin Zulu, who suggests that ancestral veneration can be viewed as fulfilment of the fifth commandment because it enables children to honour their parents even after death.[12]

It is thus necessary for this research to address this question, in view of these varying opinions. Gift Mtukwa explores this question and concludes that the ancestral cult should be viewed as worship.[13] Mtukwa makes this assertion on the basis that ancestors are viewed as intermediaries between God and humans, a role that should be reserved only for Christ. He also notes that many prayers made by practitioners make no reference to the Creator God but are addressed only to ancestors. Mtukwa also points to the prominence of fear that motivates ancestral rituals and suggests that this fear is an indication that the cult is not just intended to maintain friendly family relations but is a means to appease angry spirits.[14]

According to Fowl, fear and insecurity are dispositions that may lead people into idolatry.[15] He states that "the first act of idolatry begins with seeking security in something other than the Lord. The second occurs in the formal idolatry in making treaties."[16] The examples mentioned in chapter 3 not only demonstrate that this fear is present in ancestral veneration but also show that the living make treaties with the deceased to ensure well-being in life. Thus, instead of finding hope and security in God, they turn to ancestors, and this constitutes idolatry, as illustrated by the example from the wilderness generation.

The religious context of ancestral ritual meals provides clues as to whether what is intended is an act of worship or social interaction. This is because,

---

10. Shorter, "Ancestor Veneration," 27.
11. Opoku, "African Traditional Religion," 75.
12. Zulu, "Reverence for Ancestors," 476–482.
13. Mtukwa, "Ancestral Cult," 6.
14. Mtukwa, 7.
15. Fowl, *Idolatry*, 75.
16. Fowl, 82.

as Grillo states, rituals are eloquent expressions that convey critical religious ideas.[17] In addressing this question, it is helpful to consider a specific example.

The sacrificial rituals of the North Sotho community of South Africa offer an example of the religious context of ritual meals. During these sacrificial rituals, sacrificial meals are offered to propitiate the ancestors and prayers are made "for the sick, asking for rain in times of drought and famine, telling of general difficulties and asking for relief, praying for the alleviation of an epidemic as well as giving thanks to ancestors for a good harvest."[18] The traditional healer usually oversees these rituals and acts as an intermediary between the living and the dead. Finally, a sacred meal consisting of maize and traditional beer is placed as a sacrifice on the grave or shrine of the departed.[19] During the ritual, the ancestors are informed of the sacrifices that have been brought, and words of praise and petitions are offered. Participants are then invited to share the meal with the ancestors. At the end of the ritual, everyone present is invited to join the celebrations by feasting on the leftover meat.[20] Throughout the ceremony, singing and dancing are used to invoke the ancestral spirits.

The example of sacrificial rituals has an obviously religious context: it includes sacred space, religious leaders who oversee the rituals, sacrifices, prayers, praises of the departed, and acts of worship through singing, dancing, and offerings. In addition, there is also a narrative that is directed to the ancestors. Finally, it is the ancestors, not the Creator God, who are petitioned for life's necessities. These components, which are common in most ancestral rituals,[21] suggest a context of worship rather than merely an act of respect.

Therefore, we conclude that ancestral veneration can be construed as idolatry when believers turn to created beings rather than God for security and well-being in life. It is also problematic when practitioners approach ancestors, instead of Christ, as the intermediaries between God and humans. The elaborate ritual regulations of sacred space, the presence of religious leaders, and the singing, prayers, and petitions all suggest that a worship context

---

17. Grillo, "African Rituals," 114.
18. Sekhukune, "Symbolism," 66.
19. Sekhukhune, 66.
20. Sekhukhune, 66
21. For more examples, see Hamer, "Myth," 327–339; Christensen, *An African Tree*, 33.

is intended. If idolatry is taking place, this could also create opportunities for demonic powers, who operate behind idols, to infiltrate the church. In the discussion of the nature of idolatry in section 6.2, we noted that Paul warns the Corinthians that although idols are nothing, there are demonic powers behind them and they can become a means for demonic powers to divert the believer's attention away from God. The fear and perceived calamity associated with the neglect of ancestors in the African context suggest that there may be more at work during ancestral veneration than just honouring departed loved ones.

However, the question remains: Could there be any benefit in including the ancestors in the Lord's Supper? Sithembele Sipuka explains that among the Xhosa believers in South Africa, believers respond in two ways to the relationship with ancestors:

> There is one group that consciously denies the value of ancestors and consequently the value of sacrifice to them. Yet as we have tried to show, this group unconsciously still has regard for ancestors because it continues to make animal killings that are associated with traditional ancestral sacrifice, even though they do not call it sacrifice but *Idinila* (a dinner). The other group consciously participates in both traditions of sacrifice because it sees one tradition as catering for one type of needs, while the other caters for another type of needs. As expressed by Tlhagale, the understanding this group has is that ancestral sacrifice is for "health, well-being, peace, reconciliation, favour, while Christ's sacrifice is for the forgiveness of sins committed by humankind."[22]

Sipuka's solution to this problem of two sacrificial meals is to include the ancestors during the celebration of the Lord's Supper. He states that "if the ancestors can be openly included in the Eucharistic sacrifice, then there would be no need for Xhosa Catholics to be involved in two types of sacrifices, i.e. the ancestral and the Eucharistic sacrifices."[23]

---

22. Sipuka, "Sacrifice of the Mass," 244.
23. Sipuka, 245.

Thus, Sipuka suggests that the Lord's Supper should be one meal, where both the ancestors and God can be honoured. He suggests that this can be done by inviting ancestors to participate in worshipping God, thanking them for their contributions to the lives of the living, and requesting that they pray for the living because they are closer to God than the living.[24] Sipuka's argument is predicated on a sacrificial view of the Lord's Supper, which is more closely aligned with the Roman Catholic context. However, his work affirms the need for contextualization across Christian denominations in Africa and provides helpful discussion points.

Although Sipuka's suggestion would go a long way towards alleviating the problem of two types of ritual meals for two different groups, it creates a problem of syncretism, which could result in idolatry. In chapter 5, we defined idolatry as unfaithfulness to God by worshipping other gods, approaching God through the wrong medium (that is, anything other than Jesus Christ), or misrepresenting God through wrong intentions or wrong actions. Praying to ancestors during the Lord's Supper and asking them to convey prayers to God constitutes approaching God through the wrong medium and is, therefore, an unacceptable addition to the Lord's Supper.

The second problem with Sipuka's suggestion is that requesting better living conditions from ancestors or crediting them with bestowing blessings in life also constitutes idolatry. It was such practices of the wilderness generation that Paul warns against in 1 Corinthians 10:1–13. The Israelites had turned their back on God, who delivered them from Egypt, to offer praise and thanksgiving to the golden calf. They told Aaron to make gods that would go before them (Exod 32:1) and later credited the golden calf with bringing them out of Egypt (32:4). This dependence on sources other than God for well-being or crediting created beings or created things for blessings violates the covenant with God. The Song of Moses proclaims that although God cared for his people like a father in the wilderness, they made him jealous by worshipping strange gods (Deut 32:7–16). Similarly, crediting or petitioning creatures instead of the Creator for our daily necessities constitutes idolatry (Rom 1:21–22).

However, in view of texts such as Revelation 5:8 and Revelation 8:3, along with the practice of praying with the saints or the use of icons, prevalent in

---

24. Sipuka, 249.

Roman Catholic traditions in the West and Orthodox Christianity in the East, it seems exegetically problematic to completely dismiss any possibility of acknowledging ancestors in Christian worship. This raises a question: Can ancestors be compared to Roman Catholic saints? According to Edison Kalengyo, African ancestors cannot be equated with saints in the Roman Catholic tradition because these ancestors are believed to have more power than the saints. Kalengyo states that in many African traditions, ancestors do not act as mere intermediaries to God but are seen by many as "deities capable of responding independently to prayers/petitions of the living"[25] to whom sacrifices are offered. This view of the ancestors motivates ritual meals to them and creates fear of incurring their displeasure. Our survey of ritual meals to ancestors in chapter 3 affirms this high view of ancestors; although practitioners profess that ancestors are intermediaries to God, their actions suggest something more. I agree with Kalengyo that treating the ancestors like departed saints is not satisfactory since this does not take account of the pivotal role played by these ancestors in African communities.

In this context, I also found Fowl's discussion, based on the work of Jean-Luc Marion,[26] helpful. According to Marion, the key factor in idolatry is the focus of the worshipper's attention or "gaze." This gaze "reflects a desire on the part of the subject to know, acquire, comprehend, or control the object of one's gazing."[27] The gaze is primarily about establishing an intimate relationship and includes the desire to know the divine. Thus, idolatry takes place when the gaze is captivated by the creature rather than the Creator. In this way, any person, environment, or object may lead to idolatry if it does not direct the gaze to God. The research on worship practices during ancestral veneration demonstrates that the focus is not on God but the ancestors since all prayers and sacrifices are offered to them. If the ultimate focus of the ritual is on the ancestors rather than God, this constitutes idolatry.

Kalengyo suggests that ancestors could be present during the Lord's Supper in the same manner that the "great cloud of witnesses" referred to in Hebrews 12:1 – whom he refers to as departed faithful ancestors – are part of church life. He suggests that ancestors should be acknowledged by including

---

25. Kalengyo, "Cloud of Witnesses," 61.
26. Marion, *God without Being*.
27. Fowl, *Idolatry*, 25.

them in the liturgy during the celebration. Kalengyo cites examples from the liturgy of a church in Kenya:

> We stand together with Christians throughout the centuries, and throughout the world today. We heartily thank you for our faithful ancestors and all who have passed through death to a new life of joy in our heavenly home.[28]

Such prayers are not idolatrous as they are directed to God. However, the question arises whether such inclusion would satisfy the underlying motivation for ritual meals to ancestors. It seems that such a watered-down acknowledgement of the African ancestors would be seen as paramount to ritual failure and would not meet the spiritual needs that motivate these ritual meals to ancestors. Therefore, it is necessary to challenge this high view of ancestors and, instead, teach believers that Christ is the only source through whom life can be found.

Thus, we conclude that including ancestors in the worship context of the Lord's Supper might be permissible if ancestors are addressed as fellow worshippers and God remains the focus of worship. However, given Africans' high view of the ancestors, such an approach does not seem feasible. This research demonstrates that the motivation for ancestral veneration is not to worship God but to appease the ancestors. The example cited from the Xhosa believers in South Africa demonstrates that the purpose of ritual meals to ancestors is to meet their needs for well-being in life and avert calamity, which requires that specific rituals be successfully carried out. Treating the ancestors as fellow saints would not meet the needs that drive ancestral veneration.

Therefore, it is important to focus on God as the sole source for life, through Jesus Christ, during the Lord's Supper. This is essential because it will help to transform the world view that fears calamity when ancestors are not venerated. In the quest for inculturation, it is important to remember that the objective is not to preserve everything in traditional religion but to ensure that the gospel message remains the focal point of all mission endeavours.[29] The primary identity of African believers – like the Corinthian believers – is that they are the ἅγιος in Jesus Christ. The study of εἰδωλόθυτα in section 6.1

---

28. Kalengyo, "Cloud of Witnesses," 63.
29. Ezeanya, "Spirit World," 30–46.

revealed that the Corinthians faced the same dilemma as African Christians. There were numerous opportunities to participate in εἰδωλόθυτα, and participation was crucial for their identity and status in society. However, Paul teaches that allegiance to Christ and fellow believers should take precedence. He also advises them to keep their liminal situation in mind as they navigate the intricacies of their cultural context. The African traditional mindset tends to focus on the present; however, as followers of Christ, believers must live in expectation of the *parousia*. Such an expectation may require a revision of the understanding of the nature and role of ancestors vis-à-vis God because continuing with the practice of ritual meals to ancestors could lead to falling away from Christ. However, this does not mean that inculturation is impossible. There are many ways in which the Lord's Supper may be contextualized for the African context.[30]

8.3 Communication of the *Sacra* during the Lord's Supper

The Lord's Table is a liminal space, brimming with the potential to effect transformation in the community. However, there needs to be more intentionality in the celebration. Transformation depends on the communication of the *sacra* during the ritual. We explained earlier that the *sacra* are the sacred information, myths, or ideologies communicated to participants during the liminal period. This sacred information serves as the divine mandate that encourages the correct relationships and behaviours in the community. We also mentioned that the *sacra* comprise three main components: exhibitions, actions, and instructions. Effective communication of the *sacra* provokes participants to think about their context and challenge the status quo. Christian churches have used the Lord's Supper rather effectively in the past. The Supper was conducted with an emphasis on self-reflection and confession, and this practice found roots in the church. However, a broader spectrum of transformation is possible if the teaching is geared towards a more comprehensive understanding of the meaning of the Lord's Supper.

30.

The celebration of the Lord's Supper must thus be accompanied by sound teaching.[31] The Lord's Supper is a liminal sphere where time converges. Participants look to the crucifixion and resurrection of Christ in the past, appropriate the blessings and benefits Christ gives in the present, and anticipate, with joy and thanksgiving, the return of Christ (1 Cor 11:23–26).

In order to be relevant, the teaching that takes place should be applied to the congregation's context. For example, we mentioned earlier that while Africans practise ritual meals to ancestors to meet their needs for health, wealth, and well-being, the Lord's Supper is only for the forgiveness of sins.[32] This situation can be remedied if the Lord's Supper also addresses the concrete needs of people. The key emphasis, in order to address fear, should be that Christ overcomes all spiritual powers in his death and resurrection (Col 2:15).

One of the motivations for continued sacrifices to ancestors is fear of incurring the wrath of the ancestors by neglecting them or fear of malevolent spiritual powers. These malevolent powers are believed to hurt humans through the use of sorcery and witchcraft. Concerning ancestors, Triebel rightly asserts that

> everyone who neglects the relationship to his or her ancestors endangers his or her life, indeed the life of the whole community. The wrath of the ancestors can cause misfortune, illness, hunger, and death. It is therefore necessary to ensure their favor and benevolence towards the living and thus to preserve the stream of life.[33]

The teaching of the Lord's Supper should thus include the affirmation of the supremacy of Christ over supernatural powers.[34] The Lord's Supper is an opportunity to affirm belief and awareness of the work of the Holy Spirit in the lives of believers. It is also an opportunity to denounce the work and power of the devil. In his resurrection, Christ has overcome all evil powers (Phil 2:8–11; Col 2:15). Since believers are united with Christ by their faith and through their baptism, they share in this victory of Christ. If believers re-enact their union with Christ every time they partake in the Lord's Supper,

---

31. Barclay, *Lord's Supper*, 10.
32. Sipuka, "Sacrifice of the Mass," 244.
33. Triebel, "Living Together," 189.
34. wa Gatumu, *Supernatural Powers*, 212.

they appropriate the power of the Holy Spirit and, thereby, enjoy victory over the powers.

Second, the equality of all human beings should be affirmed during the Lord's Supper. It is a space of horizontal *communitas*, where all hierarchy and social differentiation disappear and the people of God can come together as one family in Christ (1 Cor 10:16–17). It is an affirmation that all members of the family, not just those of the same kin, are equally loved and welcomed by the Father.

This horizontal *communitas* in the celebration of the Lord's Supper should be especially emphasized in the African church, given the political and social humiliation suffered on the continent. The dehumanizing after-effects of colonization, poverty, and diseases, as well as the hierarchical legacy of culture that diminishes certain groups of people based on gender, age, or tribe, make it essential to emphasize the equality of all people in Christ. Unfortunately, past celebrations have often affirmed marginalizing structures instead of challenging them. Attempting to address social inequality in daily life can be controversial and may be viewed as an attack on people's cultures. However, in the liminal environment of the Lord's Supper, social taboos fall away. The ritually sanctioned space allows for cultural revision and encourages new bodily knowledge.[35] Paul's outcry against the Corinthians is appropriate for this context: they preferred to affirm, rather than challenge, the structures and axioms of their society that were contrary to the values of Christ's kingdom.

Third, the celebration of the Lord's Supper can be an occasion where believers intentionally receive the power of the Holy Spirit to face practical challenges in their daily lives. Thus, this power would be for more than just the forgiveness of sins and would include power for all of life. Sipuka suggests that concrete prayers can be made during the celebration of the Lord's Supper: prayers for healing, protection against evil spirits, rain, fertility of the land, employment, and peace and harmony in families and nations.[36] In this way, Christ will be lifted up as the source for all life.

This affirmation, when made within a ritual setting, has a greater capacity to bring about change than doctrinal teachings alone, which have proven insufficient given the persistent dependence on the ancestral cult.

---

35. Turner, "Betwixt and Between," 239.
36. Sipuka, "Sacrifice of the Mass," 257.

Fourth, the Lord's Supper should be utilized as an opportunity for growth in holiness. This can be done by emphasizing *communitas* with Christ and fellow believers. This point is discussed in the section below.

8.4 *Communitas* during the Lord's Supper

During the Lord's Supper, teaching should underscore *communitas* with Christ and fellow believers. For this concept to be successfully conveyed, the sacred nature of the celebration should be emphasized. Since Africans revere the sacred, it is important to create an atmosphere of respect.[37] In ATR, this is achieved through strict rules during the ritual meals. These rules include washings before participation and rules regarding the roles and procedures during the ritual. These regulations underscore the sacredness of the occasion and the elevation of ancestors above the living. Preparation for the Lord's Supper may include personal and communal prayers of confession or responsive readings that would help to prepare the congregation for an encounter with Jesus Christ.

The Lord's Supper affords the perfect opportunity to teach and impress upon believers the significance of being in Christ. When believers partake in the elements of the bread and the cup, they are united in the death and resurrection of Christ. They receive the holiness of Christ and receive the Holy Spirit and are equipped to live a life of holiness.

It is also important to emphasize that participation in Christ leads to a *kenotic* life (Phil 2:1–11). This emphasis is necessary because the general emphasis in many African Pentecostal churches is on the prosperity gospel. Impoverished and marginalized Africans want to know how Christianity can elevate their lives. However, an overemphasis on physical benefits may lead to attitudes of self-elevation, self-gratification, and materialism, distort Scripture, and even feed into a culture of corruption.[38]

Therefore, it is vital to call believers to live anti-structurally with regard to a mindset focused on prosperity. This requires balancing the message of

---

37. Okoye, "African Eucharistic Celebration," 228–242.

38. For a discussion on a biblical response to the scourge of corruption in Mozambique, Africa, see Chambo, "Metadidonai, 163–208"

empowerment for life through participation in Christ with an emphasis on humility and integrity as exemplified in the *kenotic* life of Christ.

Another example where the Lord's Supper has been contextualized comes from Nairobi, Kenya.[39] This example is positive in that it demonstrates how the Lord's Supper was used to counter the minimalist interpretation that sees it as merely as a remembrance and extend its significance to a celebration of transformation. Unfortunately, this also has negative aspects as it focuses on the socio-economic situation in Africa and, as a result, the pastors allowed societal structures such as the scourge of poverty and the need for wealth and prosperity to influence their interpretation of the Lord's Supper. Thus, pastors taught parishioners that all forms of suffering can be eradicated and that they could gain an advantage in life by participating in the Lord's Supper.[40]

David Oyedepo, founder and pastor of the Winner's Chapel in Nairobi, exemplifies this method of contextualization and the possible pitfalls it might create. In his book *The Miracle Meal*, Oyedepo explains that the Lord's Supper is a mysterious meal that can help believers in all areas of life.[41] He suggests that the Lord's Supper can be used to heal the body, advance a person's business, and help to gain supremacy in life. Oyedepo promises his followers that "when you understand the mystery of the communion table, you gain mastery, you become a master and this puts you in charge!"[42] Such teachings misuse the Lord's Supper to gratify a need for power and superiority instead of encouraging the *kenotic* love of Christ. This interpretation of the Lord's Supper calls to mind the abuse of the Lord's Supper in Corinth (1 Cor 11:17–34), where the meal was used to gratify the greed and self-interest of the "strong."

This example from the Winner's Chapel demonstrates some essential truths concerning the celebration of the Lord's Supper in Africa. First, it reveals the great need among African people for practical, relevant religion that addresses their daily needs. The Winner's Chapel has been operating successfully in thirty-eight African countries, and many other Pentecostal denominations also preach the same message with far more success than traditional missionary churches.

---

39. Gifford, "Healing in African Pentecostalism," 253.
40. Gifford, 253.
41. Oyedepo, *Miracle Meal*, 33.
42. Oyedepo, 37.

Second, it highlights the possible pitfalls of inculturation. The principal goal of inculturation must be to strengthen the relationships between humans and God and prepare them to be agents of the gospel. Giving central place to created things, rather than the Creator, constitutes idolatry and may incur the wrath of God (Rom 1:25).

Finally, this example underscores the vital importance of sound exegesis when attempting to contextualize the Lord's Supper. Using the Lord's Supper solely to meet physical needs can lead to narcissistic worship, where believers have no interest in union with Christ.

Communitas with Christ should thus be taught as empowerment for holy living – to live an abundant life by the power of the Holy Spirit while exemplifying the *kenotic* love of Christ. As suggested earlier, while prayers for needs should be made, this must be done in the humility that Christ demonstrated when he said, "Yet not what I will, but what you will" (Mark 14:36; see also Luke 22:42). *Communitas* with Christ should transform believers into the likeness of Christ.

The Lord's Supper is also an opportunity to espouse horizontal *communitas*. This comes naturally to Africans, who are community oriented. The Lord's Supper can unite those who share in the meal. One way in which it can be applied to the communal sensibilities of Africans is to include opportunities for thanksgiving, celebration, and dancing together.

Emphasis needs to be placed on the family of God, sharing, and acceptance of one another.[43] Mutual love can be encouraged by expounding on the love of Christ as demonstrated in his self-sacrificial example on the cross. Christ's love is demonstrated in the Lord's Supper because he gave himself completely for the people he loves.[44] The Lord's Supper is an opportunity for believers to be transformed by that same love.

Real relatedness, based on participation in Christ and participating together in the Holy Spirit, should be underscored. Here, the language of kinship would be very effective. Believers will understand that they are a family because they all share in the same Spirit and share equally in the benefits of being in Christ.

---

43. Amadi, "Inculturating the Eucharist," 211.
44. Okonkwo, "Eucharist," 110.

This hospitality may also be extended to people who are not yet part of the believing community by offering an open table during the celebration of the Lord's Supper. The African philosophy of communalism offers a model where the stranger is always welcome at the Lord's Table and people are invited into kinship in Christ. In this way, the celebration of the Lord's Supper becomes both a proclamation of the Lord's death and an embodiedment of God's mission to the world.

8.5 Practical Considerations

The practical implications for the celebration of the Lord's Supper will vary from context to context. Some practical considerations include the frequency of the celebration, locations, types of elements used, and even the design of the worship space.

The question of frequency is important. Sipuka suggests that the problem faced by the Catholic Church among the Xhosa people is that the celebration happens too frequently – almost daily – which diminishes the sacredness of the event.[45] This is because African ritual meals usually take place on special occasions, and Sipuka thinks that this factor should be considered when planning the Lord's Supper. He suggests that limiting the celebration to Sundays may may add more gravitas to the celebration.

The opposite is true among the Baptist churches of South Africa, where, according to Ian Simms's research, the Lord's Supper appears to "occupy an increasingly discrepant position in the corporate testimony of the Baptist Church."[46] According to Simms, the South African Baptist Church celebrates the Lord's Supper once or twice a month.[47] Simms's survey demonstrates that 71.6 percent of members surveyed believed that a more frequent celebration would reduce the meaning of the ritual. However, 25.8 percent wanted to celebrate the Lord's Supper more frequently because they wanted to be reminded of their salvation and worship God.[48] Thus, it is crucial for congregations to consider their context when deciding on frequency. A regular cycle

---

45. Sipuka, "Sacrifice of the Mass," 253.
46. Simms, "From Sign to Symbol," 2.
47. Simms, 60.
48. Simms, 60.

that underscores the sacredness and importance of the Lord's Supper for life would lead to a more effective celebration that fosters holiness transformation.

The types of elements used during the Lord's Supper should also be considered. Sipuka suggests that traditional African elements – such as maize bread and *umqombothi* (traditional African beer), which are used during Xhosa ritual meals – should be used.[49] Another example of the use of local produce comes from the Church of Jesus Christ on Earth in Nkamba, Congo (previously known as Zaire).[50] This indigenous church, which was founded by a prophet named Simon Kimbangu, contextualizes the elements by using cakes made with maize flour, potato flour, or banana flour, along with honey diluted in water to represent the blood of Christ.[51] There is a need to be flexible with regard to the elements. For example, some societies do not eat bread, and others do not have access to grape juice or wine. This was the case in the Church of the Nazarene in Mozambique during the civil war and the period of communism. During this time, this denomination did not celebrate the Lord's Supper because they had no access to the traditional elements of bread, wine, or juice.

A consideration of location and ritual circumstances is also essential. In section 3.5, I noted the importance of sacred space in ATR because these spaces are viewed as the dwelling places of the divine and, therefore, treated with great reverence. This suggests that care is needed to create an environment with a sacred atmosphere. The Supper is a communal meal where participants encounter Christ and one another, and while this does not have to take place in a church building, the circumstances are important. For example, believers may gather around a hospital bed or in the home of a believer, as in Corinth. However, it must be a sanctioned space where it can be the "Lord's Table," not merely the people's table.

8.6 Conclusion

Inculturation of the Lord's Supper for the African context has proved to be a complex endeavour. The examples from African Pentecostal churches

---

49. Sipuka, "Sacrifice of the Mass," 251.
50. Olowola, "African Independent Churches," 287.
51. Olowola, 296.

underscore the real danger of blindly applying the Lord's Supper to African sensibilities, needs, and situations. We concluded that including the ancestors during the ritual of the Lord's Supper is only advisable if these ancestors can be viewed as fellow worshippers of God. However, is unlikely to be accepted in an African context because current beliefs and practices indicate a very high view of the ancestors, and ritual practices suggest that worship is taking place during ancestral veneration. This indicates that ritual meals to ancestors constitute idolatry. Christ should be the only medium to approach God the Father and the only object of worship. We also emphasized the vital importance of teaching during the celebration to ensure that participants experience the full transformational benefits of celebrating the Lord's Supper together. Participants should be taught that *communitas* with Christ can result in transformation into the *kenotic* image of Christ. Self-elevation and self-gratification are contrary to the self-giving love of Christ, which is enacted in the Lord's Supper.

Practical considerations such as frequency, location, and the types of elements used should depend on the needs and the context. Care should always be taken to ensure that it is the *Lord's* Supper that is celebrated and not a meal of the people.

CHAPTER 9

Summary and Conclusions

9.1 Summary

In this book, I sought to address the continued practice of ritual meals to ancestors among some African believers through a reflexive theological study of ritual meals in 1 Corinthians 8:1–11:1 and 1 Corinthians 11:17–34. The premise of this study was that if Paul attributes a similar function to the Lord's Table as to ritual meals in pagan temples (1 Cor 10:16–17),[1] then his discussion of ritual meals may answer some of the questions that arise in the African cultural context. This study also questions whether the Lord's Supper has been utilized to its fullest potential as a ritual for transforming people into God's holy people in African and other churches with a "low church" practice.

I argue that ritual meals possess generative power to transform communities due to the liminal circumstances, the *communitas,* and the communication of the *sacra* that occurs during the ritual process. I use Victor Turner's ritual theory of liminality, paired with inculturation methods, to examine 1 Corinthians 8:1–11:1 and 1 Corinthians 11:17–34.

Part 1 introduced Victor Turner's ritual theory and elaborated on the African cultural world view as the framework for this research. The aspects of Turner's theory that proved most helpful for this study were the concepts of liminality and *communitas*. The two components of *communitas* – the vertical dimension, relating to the divine, and the horizontal dimension, relating to fellow participants – create a fertile environment for transformation. An

---

1. Ehrensperger, "Eat or Not to Eat," 114–133.

essential aspect of Turner's method is his insistence that religious phenomena should be studied by considering both qualitative and quantitative data. He proposes that full and sympathetic consideration of belief and the supernatural powers believed to be operative during the ritual would prevent a reductionist evaluation of rituals.

In chapter 3, I suggested that the African cultural context may enhance our analysis of ritual meals in Corinth because the African cultural context has much in common with Paul's world view. For Paul, believers live in a liminal "between-the-times" space. Similarly, the African world view is liminal because it believes that that humans live between the physical and the spiritual realms and that *communitas* is possible between the living and the powers that inhabit the spiritual realm. Ritual meals facilitate *communitas* with both the spiritual world and fellow believers. This concept of *communitas* is seen as vital participation. Thus, the African context has potential to shed light on the ritual meals in Corinth.

Part 2 addressed liminality and *communitas* in Paul's letters. I argued that Paul saw holiness as an essential characteristic of liminal living. He believed that God's principal objective during the liminal time was to create a holy people who would impact the cosmos for Christ by living anti-structurally with regard to the surrounding pagan cultural context. Liminality was defined as living between the times – that is, between the old age and the age of the Spirit that was inaugurated by Christ's death and resurrection and will culminate at the *parousia*. Liminality also has a spatial or cosmological dimension as it indicates the believer's existence between the realms of the flesh and the spirit.

Communitas is evidenced in Paul's "in Christ" language. Stowers's proposal that Paul uses Jewish concepts of patrilineal lineage to describe what is meant by participation in Christ was most helpful. Stowers argues that Paul and his contemporaries believed that *pneuma* had real substance. The *Pneuma* of Christ is thus transferred to believers during baptism, resulting in actual relatedness because believers share the same *Pneuma* with Christ and fellow believers in the same way that Abraham and his descendants shared the same seed. Believers participate in Christ's death, resurrection, and crucifixion through baptism. This participation results in transforming the nature or being of believers, enabling them to relate to God and others as they ought to.

Horizontal *communitas*, referring to the relationship among believers, describes how believers relate to one another as real kin because they all share the same *Pneuma* with Christ and each other. This mutual participation enables sacred, egalitarian relationships, patterned after Christ's *kenotic* love, that transcend all human divisions and barriers.

We described holiness as living in a reconciled, faithful relationship (*communitas*) with God and others through Jesus Christ. For Paul, the primary manifestation of sin in fallen humanity is idolatry, leading to social disintegration. However, the liminal time is also plagued by the operation of supernatural powers that seek to tempt humanity. Therefore, believers should live in faithfulness to their identity as the ἅγιος in Christ, sanctified by the Holy Spirit in anticipation of the *parousia* of Christ.

An examination of ritual meals in 1 Corinthians 8:1–11:1 revealed that Paul's primary concern in this passage is the holiness of the community threatened by idolatry (1 Cor 10:13–14). Idolatry is defined as unfaithfulness to God by worshipping other gods, approaching God through the wrong medium (that is, anything other than Jesus Christ), or misrepresenting God through wrong intentions or wrong actions that may lead to a *habitus* that is contrary to the cross of Christ. Idolatry was the sin that threatened both the wilderness generation and the Corinthian ἐκκλησία. Moreover, participation in pagan temples violates *communitas* with Christ and fellow believers. It creates fellowship with unbelievers and orients believers towards the honour-shame culture of the surrounding society instead of Christ's *kenotic* love. This negative orientation may lead to the abuse of fellow believers, as evidenced in Paul's concerns for the well-being of the "weak" believers. If approaching God through the wrong mediums – that is, through means other than Jesus Christ – constitutes idolatry, then continued ritual meals to honour ancestors among African believers should be interpreted as idolatrous if ancestors – alongside Jesus Christ – are accepted as mediators between God and humans.

Paul's intention in 1 Corinthians 11:17–34 was to correct the abuse of the Lord's Supper because he saw this as a sacramental means to transform the community into greater Christlikeness. *Communitas* with Christ is central to this discussion, while *communitas* with fellow believers is an outcome of correct participation in the Lord's Table. Utilizing the African world view as a lens to study 1 Corinthians 11:17–34 was helpful because it underscored the mystical character and ritual nature of the Lord's Supper. These factors allowed us to uncover the potential of the Lord's Supper as a ritual to transform the community, rather than merely viewing it as a ceremony to affirm the identity of the believing community.

An important indicator of the transformative potential of the Lord's Supper is that, like baptism, it is based on the same narrative of Christ crucified. This suggests that the Lord's Supper is an occasion to re-enact our union in Christ's death and resurrection, as well as in the new creation accomplished in baptism. This re-enactment transforms participants by affirming their union with Christ, stimulating cruciformity, and enabling self-sacrificial love. Even those who are not followers of Christ can experience this transformation when they encounter the love and welcome of Christ and his church during the Lord's Supper. In this way, the Lord's Supper can become a saving sacrament. The best way to describe the types of relationships Paul calls for in Corinth is horizontal *communitas*. This sacred, egalitarian relationship is rooted in the believers' *communitas* with Christ. Such a demonstration of selfless love among believers, especially during the celebration of the Lord's Supper, would have a missional impact, attracting people to the church as they lived in anticipation of the *parousia*.

In summary, Paul's admonitions concerning ritual meals in 1 Corinthians 8:1–11:1 and 1 Corinthians 11:17–34 are best understood within their ritual context. Our use of the African world view and ritual context alerts us to the sacramental nature of ritual meals in Corinth, underscoring the relationship with God through Christ. This also helped us uncover the transformational potential of the Lord's Supper for the holiness of the community. Participating in the Lord's Supper in a worthy manner should transform both individuals and the community, leading them to live in *kenotic* love (horizontal *communitas*) with one another. Such sacred relationships amplify the witness of the ἐκκλησία as they proclaim the Lord's death until the *parousia*.

9.2 Conclusions and Contributions

This study brings together the African cultural context with the discussion of meals in the Corinthian ἐκκλησία, thereby shedding light on both. This is an exercise in theological reflective reading of Scripture. It explores what might be gained by reading ritual meals in Corinth through an African cultural lens. Reading these texts through the heuristic lens of ATR is important because the African world view is much closer to that of Paul than to post-Enlightenment rationalism and can, therefore, offer a fresh perspective. This study also underscores the need for appropriate inculturation of the gospel for the African context without falling prey to either syncretism or theological imperialism.

This approach privileges the spiritual world view and underscores the significance of the presence of Christ during the celebration of the Lord's Supper. Conversely, it warns of the risk of engaging with demons by participating in pagan ritual meals and prompts the reader to pay closer attention to Paul's spiritual world view when interpreting his admonitions concerning ritual meals in Corinth.

First, this study challenges the view that Paul's intentions in 1 Corinthians 8:1–11:1 and 11:17–34 were primarily for the social well-being of the ἐκκλησία. Focusing on the ritual context and underscoring the sacramental nature of his discussions suggests that Paul's greatest fear was that, in both instances, what was at stake was *communitas* with Christ and, consequently, the salvation of the Corinthians. The mistreatment of the "weak" was a symptom of their defective relationship with Christ, and participation in the Lord's Supper served not only as a metaphor for ideal relationships but also as the locale where sacred relationships are created and can grow. This is clear from the fact that these passages are found in the section of Corinthians where Paul addresses the worship practices of the church. Paul also uses many ritual references and cites the *topos* from the wilderness generation, indicating that the relationship with Christ is at the heart of his discussion. Paul also refers to the abuse of fellow believers as "sin against Christ" (1 Cor 8:12). In 1 Corinthians 11:20, he states that they are not really eating the Lord's Supper. All this suggests that Paul feared that the Corinthians' behaviour was violating their relationship with Christ.

Second, *communitas* can be considered a possible way to describe the relationships Paul advocates in Corinth because it privileges vertical *communitas* as the foundation for good relationships among believers. It highlights the sacred relationship with Christ and includes the practical aspects of egalitarianism and justice in human relationships. Conversely, injustice and abuse of fellow believers destroy *communitas* with Christ and make horizontal *communitas* impossible. It is thus the believer's union with Christ that makes sacred relationships with one another possible. Believers "in Christ" share the *Pneuma* of Christ, are joined together in the narrative of Christ crucified and share in the holiness of Christ. In Christ, believers die to self, receive the *kenotic* love of Christ, and are enabled to love as Christ loves.

Third, and most important for this study, the use of African "vital participation" contributes to the discussion of Paul's use of "in Christ" in his letters because it highlights the spiritual aspects of this discussion. The African philosophy of spirituality and communalism revealed in "vital participation" correlates with much of what Paul says and thus offers insights into the meaning of participation in Christ and how this participation takes place. Vital participation is the link that unites vertically and horizontally the living, and the realm of the ancestors. It involves a union between the living, the ancestors, and all that belong to them. Vital participation is enabled by the sharing of *ntu* – that is, the life-force – that resides in all people and things. This life-force results in real relatedness or kinship between people and the spiritual world, making sacred relationships possible. Seen in the light of vital participation, Paul's "in Christ" language denotes real union and relatedness between Christ and believers and, consequently, also among believers. This union is enabled by the *Pneuma* of Christ that resides in all believers, creating the diverse family of God. Sacred, egalitarian relationships are thus a result of the union of believers with Christ and one another by the power of the Holy Spirit.

This study provides tentative answers to two questions from the African cultural context. First, do continued practices of ritual meals to ancestors constitute idolatry? Second, can the Lord's Supper be used as a means of transformation for holiness in African and non-African evangelical churches?

In response to the first question, in the light of 1 Corinthians 8:1–11:1, it appears that ritual meals in honour of ancestors can be described as idolatrous because, as chapter 3 demonstrates, ancestors function as intermediaries between God and the living. From our discussion in chapter 8, we concluded that ritual meals to ancestors constitute worship because of the religious context and the ancestral cult's elaborate proceedings and ritual demands, the presence of religious leaders, and prayers, petitions, singing, and dancing – all directed at the ancestors. If participation in the ancestral cult can be classified as idolatry, this poses a real threat to those who still practise it. According to Paul, idols may not be real, but there are demonic powers behind them. Although ancestors are not idols themselves, the idolatrous circumstances and acts of worship create opportunities for demonic forces to gain access to the church. Participants thus become vulnerable to these powers that seek to infiltrate the church. Participation can transform the ethos of the community into one that is contrary to the self-sacrificial life of Christ. Participation may also lead to believers falling away. Christians live in a liminal situation until the *parousia* of Christ and must, therefore, remain faithful to Christ by avoiding idolatry.

The second question concerns the use of the Lord's Supper as a means of transformation for holiness. Based on the Lord's Supper discussion in 1 Corinthians 11:17-34, we can conclude that transformation is possible during the Lord's Supper because of the generative capacity created by ritual conditions. The presence of Christ, the elements, the ritual words, and the fellowship of the believers all create a liminal environment that facilitates transformation. Transformation happens when believers participate in the narrative of Christ's crucifixion and resurrection. They are also transformed as they receive the spiritual benefits of Christ's *Pneuma* through partaking in the bread and wine.

When the Lord's Supper is approached in a manner similar to ritual meals to ancestors, with the spiritual presence of Christ assumed, this may lead to more effective practices in evangelical church. It will then become for them not just a remembrance or recollection of Christ's death but a re-enactment that can reconstitute individuals and the community, leading to greater Christlikeness. In this way, it becomes a sanctifying sacrament that is celebrated more frequently and will be a more powerful proclamation of Christ's death until the *parousia*.

Participation in the Lord's Supper in this manner also facilitates horizontal *communitas*. This sacred relationship is rooted in the believer's participation in Christ. The ἐκκλησία, as the body of Christ, stands in contrast to divisions and emphasizes the unity, mutual love, and reciprocity that Paul teaches.

9.3 Further Studies

This study focused on analyzing just two passages – 1 Corinthians 8:1–11:1 and 1 Corinthians 11:17-34 – through a ritual lens, revealing sacramental aspects of Paul's gospel. It would also be helpful to use ritual theory and the African spiritual world view to study other ritual texts in the rest of Paul's letters. This could help to affirm the findings pertaining to ritual passages in this study and contribute further to the discussion concerning the central themes of Paul's theology. While privileging the sacramental and reading these two Pauline passages through an African lens had provided important insights into the meaning of participation "in Christ," there is much more to be explored in this very complex concept in Paul's writings.

Africa is a vast continent, where ATR find expression in various ways. While this thesis is based upon some key commonalities in ATR, along with some specific sample studies, it might be profitable for further research in other specific African geographical areas not included here to test the conclusions reached by this research. It would also be useful to undertake specific ethnographic research into the African cultural context of specific people groups to generate new data that could significantly enhance this discussion.

It could also be profitable to examine how culture may impact the theology of the sacraments. Views shaped by the cultural vagaries of post-medieval European philosophies seem inadequate to capture the essence of Pauline and African spirituality. The Lord's Supper is more than an act of remembrance, and the bread and wine are more than mere symbols. In the Lord's Supper, Christ is present by his Holy Spirit, and the elements and ritual conditions create the locale where believers can experience union with Christ and appropriate the benefits of his death and resurrection once again. Thus, it becomes a sanctifying sacrament that continues to transform believers into greater Christlikeness.

In light of the African philosophy of communalism and hospitality, it would also be helpful to investigate the concept of an open table during the Lord's Supper. This discussion would challenge the Western individualism that lends itself to a closed table and emphasize the Lord's Table as a place where the nations and the generations are welcomed and transformed to be one holy family of God.

9.4 Implications for the Church Today

This study has demonstrated the capacity of ritual meals to transform believers and the community. This capacity was seen in both meals offered to idols and the Lord's Supper. This points to a real danger for some African believers who engage in the practice of ritual meals to ancestors as they risk drifting into idolatry, which could lead to the loss of their *communitas* with Christ. Therefore, for the well-being of the African church, it is clear that there is a need for continued engagement with both this cultural practice and Scripture.

In addition, this study also suggests that the Lord's Supper can be used more effectively, especially in "low church" Protestant Christianity, to transform the holy community within the church. Thus, there is a need for both Western practical theologians and African theologians to rethink the significance of the Lord's Supper. The post-Enlightenment view of the Lord's Supper in Protestantism risks robbing this sacrament of its transformative capacity and reduces it to an empty ceremony that merely maintains the status quo. Ritual participation in the broken body and blood of Christ can transform the church to be an expression of Christ's sacrificial love in the face of injustice and marginalization in the world.

Bibliography

Primary Sources

Aland, Kurt, Barbara Aland, Johannes Karavidopoulos, Carlo M. Martini, and Bruce M. Metzger, eds. *Novum Testamentum Graece*. 28th ed. Stuttgart: Deutsche Bibelgesellschaft, 2012.

Dio Chrysostom. *Discourses 12-30*. Translated by J. W. Cohoon. LCL. Cambridge: Harvard University Press, 1939.

Lucian. *The Carousal (Symposium)*. Translated by A. M. Harmon. LCL. Cambridge: Harvard University Press, 1913.

Plato. *Symposium*. Translated by W. R. Lamb. LCL. Cambridge: Harvard University Press, 1925.

Plutarch. *Moralia, Table Talk*. Translated by P. A. Clement and H. B. Hoffleit. LCL. Vol. 8. Cambridge: Harvard University Press, 1969.

Xenophon. *Symposium*. Translated by E. C. Marchant and O. J. Todd. LCL. Cambridge: Harvard University Press, 2013.

Secondary Sources

Adams, Edward. "Abraham's Faith and Gentile Disobedience: Textual Links between Romans 1 and 4." *JSNT* 65 (1997): 47-66.

———. *The Earliest Christian Meeting Places: Almost Exclusively Houses?* London: T&T Clark, 2013.

Adegbola, E. Adeolu. "The Theological Basis of Ethics." In *Biblical Revelation and African Beliefs*, edited by Kwesi Dickson and Paul Ellingworth, 116-136. Maryknoll: Orbis Books, 1969.

Adewuya, J. Ayodeji. "2 Corinthians 7:1 against the Backdrop of African Purification Rites." In *1 and 2 Corinthians*, (Texts @ Contexts Series) edited by Yung Suk Kim, 67-78. Minneapolis: Fortress, 2013.

———. *Holiness and Community in 2 Cor 6:14–7:1: Paul's View of Communal Holiness in the Corinthian Correspondence.* New York: Lang, 2001.

———. "Paul's Understanding of Holiness in 1 & 2 Corinthians: An African Perspective." *Lexington Theological Quarterly* 39, no. 2 (2004): 93–115.

———. "Revisiting 1 Corinthians 11:27–34: Paul's Discussion of the Lord's Supper and African Meals." *JSNT* 30, no. 1 (2007): 95–112.

Ainslie, Andrew. "Harnessing the Ancestors: Mutuality, Uncertainty and Ritual Practice in the Eastern Cape Province, South Africa." *Africa* 84, no. 4 (2014): 530–552.

Amadi, Anthony Igbokwe. "Inculturating the Eucharist in the Catholic Diocese of Mutare, Zimbabwe." PhD diss., University of South Africa, 2008.

Babcock, Barbara A. "Reflexivity: Definitions and Discriminations." *Semiotica* 30 (1980): 1–14.

Banda, Collium. "The Sufficiency of Christ in Africa: A Christological Challenge from African Traditional Religions." MA thesis, University of South Africa, 2005.

Barclay, John M. G. "The Lord's Supper and the Lion's Share: The Negotiation of Transactional Orders in 1 Corinthians 11:17–34." Unpublished paper, used with permission.

———. *Paul and the Gift.* Grand Rapids: Eerdmans, 2015.

———. *Pauline Churches and Diaspora Jews.* Grand Rapids: Eerdmans, 2011.

———. "Thessalonica and Corinth: Social Contrast in Pauline Christianity." *JSNT* 47 (1992): 49–74.

Barclay, William. *The Lord's Supper.* Philadelphia: Westminster, 1967.

Barrett, C. K. "Things Sacrificed to Idols." *NTS* 11, no. 2 (1965): 138–153.

Barry, John D., ed. *The Lexham Bible Dictionary.* Bellingham: Lexham, 2016.

Bartlett, David L. *Romans.* WeBC. Louisville: Westminster John Knox, 1995.

Barton, Stephen C. "Paul's Sense of Place: An Anthological Approach to Community Formation in Corinth." *NTS* 32 (1986): 225–246.

———. "Sanctification and Oneness in 1 Corinthians with Implications for the Case of 'Mixed Marriages' (1 Corinthians 7:12–16)." *NTS* 63 (2017): 38–55.

Bates, Matthew W. "Beyond Hays's Echoes of Scripture in the Letters of Paul: A Proposed Diachronic Intertextuality with Romans 10:16 as a Test Case." In *Paul and Scripture: Extending the Conversation*, edited by Christopher D. Stanley, 263–292. Atlanta: SBL, 2012.

Bediako, Kwame. *Christianity in Africa: The Renewal of a Non-Western Religion.* Edinburgh: Edinburgh University Press, 1995.

———. *Theology and Identity: The Impact of Culture upon Christian Thought in the Second Century and Modern Africa.* Oxford: Regnum Books, 1992.

Beker, J. Christiaan. *Paul's Apocalyptic Gospel: The Coming Triumph of God.* Minneapolis: Fortress, 1982.

Bell, Catherine M. *Ritual: Perspectives and Dimensions*. Oxford: Oxford University Press, 1997.

Bentley, Wessel. "The Reconciliatory Role of Holy Communion in the Methodist Tradition." *Verbum et Ecclesia* 32 (2011): 1–6.

Berry, Jan. "Whose Threshold? Women's Strategies of Ritualization." *Feminist Theology* 14, no. 3 (2006): 273–288.

Blackwell, Ben C., John K. Goodrich, and Jason Maston, eds. *Paul and the Apocalyptic Imagination*. Minneapolis: Fortress, 2016.

Blidstein, Moshe. *Purity, Community, and Ritual in Early Christian Literature*. Oxford: Oxford University Press, 2017.

Brower, K. E. *Living as God's Holy People: Holiness and Community in Paul*. Carlisle: Paternoster, 2009.

Brower, K. E., and Andy Johnson, eds. *Holiness and Ecclesiology in the New Testament*. Grand Rapids: Eerdmans, 2007.

Brower Latz, Andrew, and Arseny Ermakov, eds. *Purity: Essays in Bible and Theology*. Eugene: Pickwick, 2014.

Bruce, F. F. *The Epistle to the Galatians: A Commentary on the Greek Text*. NIGTC. Grand Rapids: Eerdmans, 1982.

———. *Paul, Apostle of the Heart Set Free*. Grand Rapids: Eerdmans, 2000.

Bucher, Hubert. *Spirits and Power: An Analysis of Shona Cosmology*. Cape Town: Oxford University Press, 1980.

Bultmann, Rudolf. "The Significance of the Old Testament for Christian Faith." In *The Old Testament and Christian Faith*, edited by Bernhard W. Anderson, 8–35. New York: Harper & Row, 1963.

———. *Theology of the New Testament*. Translated by Kendrick Grobel. New York: Scribner's Sons, 1951.

Bynum, Caroline Walker. "Women's Stories, Women's Symbols: A Critique of Victor Turner's Theory of Liminality." In *Fragmentation and Redemption: Essays on Gender and the Human Body in Medieval Religion*, 27–52. New York: Zone Books, 1992.

Caird, G. B. *Principalities and Powers: A Study in Pauline Theology*. Eugene: Wipf & Stock, 2003.

Campbell, Charles. *1 Corinthians*. Belief: A Theological Commentary on the Bible. Louisville: Westminster John Knox, 2017.

Campbell, Constantine R. *Paul and Union with Christ: An Exegetical and Theological Study*. Grand Rapids: Zondervan, 2012.

Campbell, Douglas A. "Apocalyptic Epistemology: The Sine Qua Non of Valid Pauline Interpretation." In *Paul and the Apocalyptic Imagination*, edited by Ben C. Blackwell, John K. Goodrich, and Jason Maston, 65–86. Minneapolis: Fortress, 2016.

———. *The Deliverance of God: An Apocalyptic Rereading of Justification in Paul.* Grand Rapids: Eerdmans, 2009.

———. *The Quest for Paul's Gospel: A Suggested Strategy.* Edinburgh: T&T Clark, 2005.

Campbell, J. Y. "κοινωνία and Its Cognates in the New Testament." *JBL* 51, no. 4 (1932): 352–380.

Chambo, Alesandra (Samantha). "Explorations of the Doctrine of Christian Holiness in the Teaching of Significant Leaders in the Church of the Nazarene in Southern Africa and the Need for Contextualization." MA diss., Nazarene Theological College, 2014.

Chambo, Filimao Manuel. "Metadidonai as Ethical Principle on Material Possessions according to the Gospel of Luke (3:10–14) and the Book of Acts." PhD diss., University of Johannesburg, 2008.

Cheung, A. T. *Idol Food in Corinth: Jewish Background and Pauline Legacy.* Sheffield: Sheffield Academic, 1999.

Chow, John K. *Patronage and Power: A Study of Social Networks in Corinth.* Library of New Testament Studies 75. Sheffield: Sheffield Academic, 1992.

Christensen, Thomas G. *An African Tree of Life.* Maryknoll: Orbis Books, 1990.

Ciampa, Roy E., and Brian S. Rosner. *The First Letter to the Corinthians.* Grand Rapids: Eerdmans, 2010.

Collier, Gary D. "'That We Might Not Crave Evil': The Structure and Argument of 1 Corinthians 10:1–13." *JSNT* 55 (1994): 55–75.

Collins, Raymond F. *First Corinthians.* SP 7. Collegeville: Liturgical Press, 1999.

Conzelmann, H. *1 Corinthians.* Translated by James W. Leitch. Philadelphia: Fortress, 1975.

———. *An Outline of the Theology of the New Testament.* Translated by John Bowden. New York: Harper & Row, 1969.

Cooper, Alan. "Ps 24:7–10: Mythology and Exegesis." *JBL* 102, no. 1 (1983): 37–60.

Coutsoumpos, Panayotis. *Paul and the Lord's Supper: A Socio-Historical Investigation.* StBibLit 84. New York: Lang, 2005.

Cullmann, Oscar. *Christ and Time: The Primitive Christian Conception of Time and History.* Translated by Floyd V. Filson. Rev. ed. Philadelphia: Westminster, 1948.

Davies, J. P. "What to Expect When You're Expecting: Maternity, Salvation History, and the 'Apocalyptic Paul.'" *JSNT* 38, no. 3 (2016): 301–315.

Davis, James A. "The Interaction between Individual Ethical Conscience and Community Ethical Consciousness in 1 Corinthians." *HBT* 10 (1988): 1–18.

Deasley, Alex R. G. *1 Corinthians: A Commentary in the Wesleyan Tradition.* NBBC. Kansas City: Beacon Hill, 2021.

De Boer, Martinus C. de. *Paul: Theologian of God's Apocalypse: Essays on Paul and Apocalyptic.* Eugene: Cascade Books, 2020.

Deflem, Mathieu. "Ritual, Anti-structure, and Religion: A Discussion of Victor Turner's Processual Symbolic Analysis." *JSSR* 30 (1991): 1–25.

DeMaris, Richard E. "Corinthian Religion and Baptism for the Dead (1 Corinthians 15:29): Insights from Archaeology and Anthropology." *JBL* 114 (1995): 661–682.

———. *The New Testament in Its Ritual World*. New York: Routledge, 2008.

deSilva, David A. *Honor, Patronage, Kinship, and Purity: Unlocking New Testament Culture*. Downers Grove: InterVarsity Press, 2015.

Devisch, René. "Divination in Africa." In *The Wiley-Blackwell Companion to African Religions*, edited by Elias Kifon Bongmba, 79–96. Chichester: Wiley-Blackwell, 2012.

Douglas, Mary. *Purity and Danger: An Analysis of Concepts of Pollution and Taboo*. New York: Praeger, 1966.

Dube, Musa W. "Postcolonial Feminist Perspectives on African Religions." In *The Wiley-Blackwell Companion to African Religions*, edited by Elias Kifon Bongmba, 127–139. Chichester: Wiley-Blackwell, 2012.

Dunn, James D. G. *The Cambridge Companion to St Paul*. Cambridge: Cambridge University Press, 2003.

———. "'The Lord, the Giver of Life': The Gift of the Spirit as Both Life-Giving and Empowering." In *The Spirit and Christ in the New Testament and Christian Theology: Essays in Honor of Max Turner*, edited by I. Howard Marshall, Volker Rabens, and Cornelis Bennema, 1–17. Grand Rapids: Eerdmans, 2012.

Ehrensperger, Kathy. "To Eat or Not to Eat – Is This the Question? Table Disputes in Corinth." In *Decisive Meals: Table Politics in Biblical Literature*, edited by Kathy Ehrensperger, Nathan MacDonald, and Luzia Sutter Rehmann, 114–133. New York: Bloomsbury, 2012.

Elliott, John H. *What Is Social-Scientific Criticism?* Minneapolis: Fortress, 1993.

Elliott, Neil. *The Arrogance of Nations: Reading Romans in the Shadow of Empire*. Minneapolis: Fortress, 2008.

Elwell, Walter A., and Philip Wesley, eds. *Tyndale Bible Dictionary*. Tyndale Reference Library. Wheaton: Tyndale, 2001.

Engberg-Pedersen, Troels. *Cosmology and Self in the Apostle Paul: The Material Spirit*. Oxford: Oxford University Press, 2010.

Engelke, Matthew. "The Problem of Belief: Evans-Pritchard and Victor Turner on 'The Inner Life.'" *AT* 18, no. 6 (2002): 3–8.

Engels, Donald. *Roman Corinth: An Alternative Model for the Classical City*. Chicago: University of Chicago Press, 1990.

Ezeanya, Stephen N. "God, Spirits and the Spirit World." In *Biblical Revelation and African Beliefs*, edited by Kwesi Dickson and Paul Ellingworth, 30–46. Maryknoll: Orbis Books, 1969.

Ezzy, Douglas. "Faith and Social Science: Contrasting Victor and Edith Turner's Analysis of Spiritual Realities." In *Victor Turner and Contemporary Cultural Performance*, edited by Graham St John, 309–323. New York: Berghahn Books, 2008.

Fee, Gordon D. *The First Epistle to the Corinthians*. Grand Rapids: Eerdmans, 1987.

———. *God's Empowering Presence: The Holy Spirit in the Letters of Paul.* Grand Rapids: Baker Academic, 2011.

———. *Paul, the Spirit, and the People of God.* Peabody: Hendrickson, 2001.

Finney, Mark T. *Honour and Conflict in the Ancient World: 1 Corinthians in Its Greco-Roman Social Setting.* London: T&T Clark, 2012.

Forbes, Chris. "Pauline Demonology and/or Cosmology? Principalities, Powers and the Elements of the World in Their Hellenistic Context." *JSNT* 24, no. 3 (2002): 51–73.

———. "Paul's Principalities and Powers: Demythologising Apocalyptic?" *JSNT* 23, no. 82 (2001): 61–88.

Ford, J. M. "Rabbinic Humour behind Baptism for the Dead (1 Cor XV:29)." *Studia Evangelica* 4 (1968): 400–403.

Fowl, Stephen E. *Idolatry*. Waco: Baylor University Press, 2019.

Freud, Sigmund. *The Interpretation of Dreams*. Translated by James Strachey and Angela Richards. Harmondsworth: Penguin Books, 1991.

Fuad, Chelcent. "The Practice of the Lord's Supper in 1 Corinthians 11:17–34 as a Socio-Religious Ritual Failure." *ExpTim* 130, no. 5 (2019): 202–214.

Gäckle, Volker. *Die Starken und die Schwachen in Korinth und Rom: Zu Herkunft und Funktion der Antithese in 1 Kor 8, 1–11, und in Röm 14, 1–15, 13.* Tübingen: Mohr Siebeck, 2004.

Gardner, Paul. *1 Corinthians*. ZECNT. Edited by Clinton E. Arnold. Grand Rapids: Zondervan, 2018.

———. *The Gifts of God and the Authentication of a Christian: An Exegetical Study of 1 Corinthians 8–11:1.* Lanham: University Press of America, 1994.

Gardner, Percy. *The Religious Experience of Saint Paul.* New York: G. P. Putnam's Sons, 1913.

Gaston, Thomas, and Andrew Perry. "Christological Monotheism: 1 Cor 8:6 and the Shema." *HBT* 39 (2017): 176–196.

Gatumu, Kabiro wa. *The Pauline Concept of Supernatural Powers: A Reading from the African Worldview.* Eugene: Wipf & Stock, 2008.

Gifford, Paul. "Healing in African Pentecostalism: The 'Victorious Living' of David Oyedepo." In *Global Pentecostal and Charismatic Healing*, edited by Candy Gunther Brown, 251–266. Oxford: Oxford University Press, 2011.

Ginsburskaya, Mila. "Purity and Impurity in the Hebrew Bible." In *Purity: Essays in Bible and Theology*, 3–29. edited by Andrew Brower Latz and Arseny Ermakov. Eugene: Pickwick, 2014.

Glanville, Mark R., and Luke Glanville. *Refuge Reimagined: Biblical Kinship in Global Politics*. Downers Grove: IVP Academic, 2021.

Goh, Menghun. "The Issue of Eidōlothyta." In *1 and 2 Corinthians* (Texts @ Contexts Series), edited by Yung Suk Kim, 79–96. Minneapolis: Fortress, 2013.

Gooch, Paul W. "'Conscience' in 1 Corinthians 8 and 10." *NTS* 33 (1987): 244–254.

Gooch, Peter D. *Dangerous Food: 1 Corinthians 8–10 in Its Context*. Waterloo: Wilfrid Laurier University Press, 1993.

Gorman, Michael J. *Apostle of the Crucified Lord: A Theological Introduction to Paul and His Letters*. Grand Rapids: Eerdmans, 2017.

———. *Becoming the Gospel: Paul, Participation, and Mission*. Grand Rapids: Eerdmans, 2015.

———. *Cruciformity: Paul's Narrative Spirituality of the Cross*. Grand Rapids: Eerdmans, 2001.

———. *Inhabiting the Cruciform God: Kenosis, Justification, and Theosis in Paul's Narrative Soteriology*. Grand Rapids: Eerdmans, 2009.

———. "'You Shall Be Cruciform for I Am Cruciform': Paul's Trinitarian Reconstruction of Holiness." In *Holiness and Ecclesiology in the New Testament*, edited by K. E. Brower and Andy Johnson, 148–166. Grand Rapids: Eerdmans, 2007.

Gottlieb, Roger S. *This Sacred Earth: Religion, Nature, Environment*. New York: Routledge, 1996.

Greathouse, William M., and George Lyons. *Romans 1–8: A Commentary in the Wesleyan Tradition*. NBBC. Kansas City: Beacon Hill, 2008.

Grillo, Laura S. "African Rituals." In *The Wiley-Blackwell Companion to African Religions*, edited by Elias Kifon Bongmba, 112–126. Chichester: Wiley-Blackwell, 2012.

Grimes, Ronald L. *Deeply into the Bone: Re-inventing Rites of Passage*. Berkeley: University of California Press, 2000.

———. *Ritual Criticism: Case Studies in Its Practice, Essays on Its Theory*. Columbia: University of South Carolina Press, 1990.

Gruenwald, Ithamar. *Rituals and Ritual Theory in Ancient Israel*. Leiden: Brill, 2003.

Hamer, John. "Commensality, Process and the Moral Order: An Example from Southern Ethiopia." *Africa* 64, no. 1 (1994): 126–44.

———. "Myth, Ritual and the Authority of Elder's Authority in an Ethiopian Society." *Africa* 46, no. 4 (1976): 327–339.

Hays, Richard B. "The Conversion of the Imagination: Scripture and Eschatology in 1 Corinthians." *NTS* 45 (1999): 391–412.

———. *Echoes of Scripture in the Letters of Paul*. New Haven: Yale University Press, 1989.

———. *First Corinthians*. IBC. Louisville: John Knox Press, 1997.
———. *Reading with the Grain of Scripture*. Grand Rapids: Eerdmans, 2020.
———. "Three Dramatic Roles: The Law in Romans 3–4." In *Paul and the Mosaic Law: The Third Durham-Tübingen Research Symposium on Earliest Christianity and Judaism*, edited by James D. G. Dunn, 151–164. Tübingen: Mohr Siebeck, 1996.
———. "What Is 'Real Participation in Christ'? A Dialogue with E. P. Sanders on Pauline Soteriology." In *Redefining First-Century Jewish and Christian Identities: Essays in Honor of Ed Parish Sanders*, edited by Fabian E. Udoh, 336–351. Indiana: University of Notre Dame Press, 2008.
Henderson, Suzanne Watts. "'If Anyone Hungers . . .': An Integrated Reading of 1 Cor 11:17–34." *NTS* 48 (2002): 195–208.
Higgins, A. J. B. *The Lord's Supper in the New Testament*. SBT. Chicago: Regnery, 1952.
Hodge, Caroline Johnson. *If Sons, Then Heirs: A Study of Kinship and Ethnicity in the Letters of Paul*. New York: Oxford University Press, 2007.
Hofius, Otfried. "The Lord's Supper and the Lord's Supper Tradition: Reflection on 1 Corinthians 11:23b–25." In *One Loaf, One Cup: Ecumenical Studies of 1 Cor 11 and Other Eucharistic Texts*, edited by Ben F. Meyer, 75–115. Macon: Mercer University Press, 1993.
Hollander, Harm W. "The Idea of Fellowship in 1 Corinthians 10:14–22." *NTS* 55, no. 4 (2009): 456–470.
Hooker, Morna D. *Continuity and Discontinuity: Early Christianity in Its Jewish Setting*. London: Epworth, 1986.
———. *From Adam to Christ: Essays on Paul*. Cambridge: Cambridge University Press, 1990.
———. *Not Ashamed of the Gospel: New Testament Interpretations of the Death of Christ*. Eugene: Wipf & Stock, 1994.
Horrell, David. "Domestic Space and Christian Meeting at Corinth: Imagining New Contexts and the Buildings East of the Theatre." *NTS* 50 (2004): 349–369.
———. *The Social Ethos of the Corinthian Correspondence: Interests and Ideology from 1 Corinthians to 1 Clement*. Edinburgh: T&T Clark, 1996.
———. *Solidarity and Difference: A Contemporary Reading of Paul's Ethics*. London: T&T Clark, 2005.
Horsley, Richard A. *1 Corinthians*. Nashville: Abingdon, 1998.
———. "Consciousness and Freedom among the Corinthians: 1 Corinthians 8–10." *CBQ* 40 (1978): 574–589.
———, ed. *Paul and Politics: Ekklesia, Israel, Imperium, Interpretation*. Harrisburg: Trinity, 2000.
Horváth, Agnes. "Tricking into the Position of the Outcast: A Case Study in the Emergence and Effects of Communist Power." *PP* 19, no. 2 (1998): 331–347.

Humphrey, Edith M. "Apocalyptic as Theoria in the Letters of St. Paul: A New Perspective on Apocalyptic as Mother of Theology." In *Paul and the Apocalyptic Imagination*, edited by Ben C. Blackwell, John K. Goodrich, and Jason Maston, 87–110. Minneapolis: Fortress, 2016.

Hurtado, Larry W. *At the Origins of Christian Worship: The Context and Character of Earliest Christian Devotion*. Cambridge: Eerdmans, 2000.

———. *One God, One Lord: Early Christian Devotion and Ancient Jewish Monotheism*. Minnesota: Fortress, 1988.

Ibita, Ma Marilou S. "A Conversation with the Story of the Lord's Supper in 1 Corinthians 11:17–34: Engaging the Scripture Text and the Filipino Christians' Context." In *1 and 2 Corinthians* (Texts @ Context Series), edited by Yung Suk Kim, 97–114. Minneapolis: Fortress, 2013.

Idowu, E. Bolaji. "Introduction." In *Biblical Revelation and African Beliefs*, edited by Kwesi Dickson and Paul Ellingworth, 9–16. Maryknoll: Orbis Books, 1969.

Isichei, Elizabeth. *A History of Christianity in Africa: From Antiquity to the Present*. Grand Rapids: Eerdmans, 1995.

Jamir, Lanuwabang. *Exclusion and Judgment in Fellowship Meals: The Socio-historical Background of 1 Corinthians 11:17–34*. Eugene: Pickwick, 2016.

Janzen, J. Gerald. "The Character of the Calf and Its Cult in Exodus 32." *CBQ* 52 (1990): 597–607.

Jeremias, Joachim. *The Eucharistic Words of Jesus*. 2nd ed. London: SCM, 1973.

———. *Infant Baptism in the First Four Centuries*. London: SCM, 1960.

———. "This Is My Body." *ExpTim* 83 (1972): 196–203.

Johnson, Luke Timothy. *Religious Experience in Earliest Christianity: A Missing Dimension in New Testament Studies*. Minneapolis: Fortress, 1998.

Kahl, B. *Galatians Re-Imagined: Reading with the Eyes of the Vanquished*. Minneapolis: Fortress, 2010.

Kalengyo, Edison Muhindo. "'Cloud of Witnesses' in Hebrews 12:1 and Ganda Ancestors: An Incarnational Reflection." *Neot* 43 (2009): 49–68.

Kalu, Ogbu U. "Gods as Policemen: Religion and Social Control in Igboland." In *Religious Plurality in Africa: Essays in Honour of John S. Mbiti*, edited by Jacob K. Olupona and Sulayman S. Nyang, 109–132. New York: de Gruyter, 1993.

Käsemann, Ernst. *Essays on New Testament Themes*. Translated by W. J. Montague. London: SCM, 1964.

———. *Perspectives on Paul*. Translated by M. Kohl. Philadelphia: Fortress, 1971.

Kenyatta, Jomo. *Facing Mount Kenya: The Traditional Life of the Gikuyu*. Nairobi: Kenway, 1978.

Kepe, Thembela, Gillian McGregor, and Philipa Irvine. "Rights of 'Passage' and Contested Land Use: Gendered Conflict over Urban Space during Ritual Performance in South Africa." *Applied Geography* 57 (2015): 91–99.

Khoza, Reuel J. *Attuned Leadership: African Humanism as Compass.* Johannesburg: Penguin Books, 2012.

Kim, Yung Suk. *Christ's Body in Corinth: The Politics of a Metaphor.* Minneapolis: Fortress, 2014.

Kittel, Gerhard, and Gerhard Friedrich, eds. *Theological Dictionary of the New Testament: Abridged in One Volume.* Translated by G. W. Bromiley. Grand Rapids: Eerdmans, 1985.

Knoch, Otto. "'Do This in Memory of Me!' (Luke 22:20; 1 Corinthians 11:24ff.): The Celebration of the Eucharist in the Primitive Christian Communities." In *One Loaf, One Cup: Ecumenical Studies of 1 Cor 11 and Other Eucharistic Texts*, edited by Ben F. Meyer, 1–10. Macon: Mercer University Press, 1993.

Kunene, Musa. *Communal Holiness in the Gospel of John.* Carlisle: Langham Academic, 2012.

Lampe, Peter. "The Eucharist: Identifying with Christ on the Cross." *Int* 48 (1994): 36–49.

Lane, William L. "Covenant: The Key to Paul's Conflict with Corinth." *TynBul* 33 (1982): 3–29.

Last, Richard. *The Pauline Church and the Corinthian* Ekklēsia*: Greco-Roman Associations in Comparative Context.* New York: Cambridge University Press, 2016.

Lee, Jung Young. "Interpreting the Demonic Powers in Pauline Thought." *NovT* 12 (1970): 54–69.

Leese, J. J. Johnson. *Christ, Creation and the Cosmic Goal of Redemption: A Study of Pauline Creation Theology as Read by Irenaeus and Applied to Ecotheology.* New York: T&T Clark, 2018.

Leopold, Anita Maria, and Jeppe Sinding Jensen, eds. *Syncretism in Religion: A Reader.* London: Routledge, 2004.

Lincoln, Andrew T. *Paradise Now and Not Yet: Studies in the Role of the Heavenly Dimension in Paul's Thought with Special Reference to His Eschatology.* SNTSMS 43. Cambridge: Cambridge University Press, 1981.

Lints, Richard. *Identity and Idolatry: The Image of God and Its Inversion.* NSBT 36. Downers Grove: InterVarsity Press, 2015.

Lohfink, Gerhard. *Jesus and Community.* Philadelphia: Fortress, 1982.

Longenecker, Richard N. *Biblical Exegesis in the Apostolic Period.* Grand Rapids: Eerdmans, 1975.

Lucas, Alec J. *Evocations of the Calf? Romans 1:18–2:11 and the Substructure of Psalm 106 (105).* Berlin: de Gruyter, 2014.

MacDonald, Margaret Y. "Ritual in the Pauline Churches." In *Social-Scientific Approaches to New Testament Interpretation*, edited by David Horrell, 233–248. Edinburgh: T&T Clark, 1999.

Malcolm, Matthew R. "Premature Triumphalism in Corinth." *ExpTim* 128, no. 3 (2016): 115–125.

———. *The World of 1 Corinthians: An Exegetical Source Book of Literary and Visual Backgrounds*. Milton Keynes: Paternoster, 2012.

Maluleke, Tinyiko Sam. "Half a Century of African Christian Theologies: Elements of the Emerging Agenda for the Twenty-First Century." *JTSA* 99 (1997): 4–23.

Marcus, Joel. "Idolatry in the New Testament." In *The Word Leaps the Gap: Essays on Scripture and Theology in Honor of Richard B Hays*, edited by J. Ross Wagner, C. Kavin Rowe, and A. Katherine Grieb, 107–131. Grand Rapids: Eerdmans, 2008.

Marion, Jean-Luc. *God without Being*. Translated by Thomas A. Carlson. Chicago: University of Chicago Press, 1991.

Marshall, I. Howard. *Last Supper and Lord's Supper*. Grand Rapids: Eerdmans, 1981.

Martin, Brice L. *Christ and the Law in Paul*. NovTSup 62. Leiden: Brill, 1989.

Martin, Dale B. *The Corinthian Body*. New Haven: Yale University Press, 1995.

Martyn, J. Louis. *Theological Issues in the Letters of Paul*. Nashville: Abingdon, 1997.

Mazibuko, Nokuthula Caritus. "Llobolo, the Bride Price That Comes 'At a Price' and the Narratives of Gender Violence in Mamelodi, a South African Township." *Gender & Behaviour* 14, no. 2 (2016): 7373–7378.

Mbiti, John S. *African Religions and Philosophy*. 2nd rev. ed. Johannesburg: Heinemann, 1989.

———. "African Views of the Universe." In *This Sacred Earth: Religion, Nature, Environment*, edited by Roger S. Gottlieb. New York: Routledge, 1996.

———. *Concepts of God in Africa*. New York: Praeger, 1970.

———. *The Prayers of African Religion*. Maryknoll: Orbis Books, 1975.

McDonough, Sean M. *Christ as Creator: Origins of a New Testament Doctrine*. New York: Oxford University Press, 2009.

———. "Through Whom? Messianic and Demonic Mediation in 1 Corinthians 8-10" In Christ as Creator: Origins of a New Testament Doctrine, Oxford Scholarship Online: January 2010.

Meeks, Wayne A. "'And Rose Up to Play': Midrash and Paraenesis in 1 Corinthians 10:1–22." *JSNT* 16 (1982): 64–78.

———. *The First Urban Christians: The Social World of the Apostle Paul*. New Haven: Yale University Press, 1983.

———. "The Image of the Androgyne: Some Uses of a Symbol in Earliest Christianity." In *In Search of the Early Christians*, edited by Allen Hilton, and Gregory Snyder, 165–208. New Haven: Yale University Press, 2002.

Menkiti, Ifeanyi A. "Person and Community in African Traditional Thought." In *African Philosophy*, 3rd ed., edited by Richard Wright. Lanham: University Press of America, 1984.

Milgrom, Jacob. *Leviticus: A Book of Ritual and Ethics*. Minneapolis: Fortress, 2004.

Mitchell, Margaret M. *Paul and the Rhetoric of Reconciliation: An Exegetical Investigation of the Language and Composition of 1 Corinthians*. Louisville: Westminster John Knox, 1992.

Morris, Leon. *The Epistle to the Romans*. Grand Rapids: Eerdmans, 1988.

Moses, Robert E. "Love Overflowing in Complete Knowledge at Corinth: Paul's Message Concerning Idol Food." *Int* 72 (2018): 17–28.

Moule, C. F. D. "The Judgement Theme in the Sacraments." In *The Background of the New Testament and Its Eschatology*, edited by W. D. Davies and D. Dube. Cambridge: Cambridge University Press, 1956.

Mtukwa, Gift. "Ancestral Cult and the Church in Africa." *AJWT* 1 (2014): 1–12.

Mudimbe, V. Y., and Susan Mbula Kilonzo. "Philosophy of Religion on African Ways of Believing." In *The Wiley-Blackwell Companion to African Religions*, edited by Elias Kifon Bongmba, 41–61. Chichester: Wiley-Blackwell, 2012.

Mulago, Vincent. "Vital Participation." In *Biblical Revelation and African Beliefs*, edited by Kwesi Dickson and Paul Ellingworth, 137–158. Maryknoll: Orbis Books, 1969.

Murphy-O'Connor, Jerome. *Keys to First Corinthians: Revisiting the Major Issues*. Oxford: Oxford University Press, 2009.

———. *St. Paul's Corinth: Text and Archaeology*. Collegeville: Liturgical Press, 2002.

Musopole, Augustine C. *Being Human in Africa: Toward an African Christian Anthropology*. New York: Lang, 1994.

Muzorewa, Gwinyai. *The Origins and Development of African Theology*. Maryknoll: Orbis Books, 1958.

Nasuti, Harry P. "The Woes of the Prophets and the Rights of the Apostle: The Internal Dynamics of 1 Corinthians 9." *CBQ* 50, no. 2 (1988): 246–264.

Nche, G. C., L. N. Okwuosa, and T. C. Nwaoga. "Revisiting the Concept of Inculturation in a Modern Africa: A Reflection on Salient Issues." *HTS Teologiese Studies/Theological Studies* 72 (2016): 1–6.

Newton, Derek. *Deity and Diet*. Sheffield: Sheffield Academic, 1998.

Newton, Michael. *The Concept of Purity at Qumran and in the Letters of Paul*. Cambridge: Cambridge University Press, 1985.

Neyrey, Jerome. "Body Language in 1 Corinthians." *Semeia* 35 (1986): 129–170.

Nwoke, Mary Basil. "Bride Price and Implications for Women's Rights in Nigeria: Psychological Perspective." *Gender & Behaviour* 7, no. 1 (2009): 2078–86.

Nyiawung, Mbengu D. "Contextualising Biblical Exegesis: What Is the African Biblical Hermeneutic Approach?" *HTS Theological Studies* 69, no. 1 (2013): 1–9.

Oakes, Peter. *Empire, Economics, and the New Testament.* Grand Rapids: Eerdmans, 2020.

———. "Made Holy by the Holy Spirit: Holiness and Ecclesiology in Romans." In *Holiness and Ecclesiology in the New Testament*, edited by K. E. Brower and Andy Johnson, 167–183. Grand Rapids: Eerdmans, 2007.

Ok, Jannette H. *Constructing Ethnic Identity in 1 Peter: Who You Are No Longer.* London: T&T Clark, 2021.

Økland, Jorunn. *Women in Their Place: Paul and the Corinthian Discourse of Gender and Sanctuary Space.* London: T&T Clark, 2004.

Okonkwo, Izunna. "Eucharist and the African Communalism." *AFER* 52, nos. 2–3 (2010): 105–118.

Okoye, C. J. "A Relevant African Eucharistic Celebration." *AFER* 42 (2000): 228–242.

Olowola, Cornelius. "An Introduction to African Independent Churches." In *Issues in African Christian Theology*, edited by Samuel Ngewa, Mark Shaw, and Tite Tienou, 286–305. Nairobi: East African Educational Publishers, 1998.

Olupona, Jacob K. *African Religions: A Very Short Introduction.* Oxford: Oxford University Press, 2014.

Opoku, Kofi Asare. "African Traditional Religion: An Enduring Heritage." In *Religious Plurality in Africa: Essays in Honour* of John S. Mbiti, edited by Jacob K. Olupona and Sulayman S. Nyang, 67–82. New York: de Gruyter, 1993.

Oropeza, B. J. "Apostasy in the Wilderness: Paul's Message to the Corinthians in a State of Eschatological Liminality." *JSNT* 75 (1999): 69–86.

———. *Paul and Apostasy: Eschatology, Perseverance and Falling Away in the Corinthian Congregation.* Tübingen: Mohr Siebeck, 2000.

Ortner, Sherry B. "Theory in Anthropology since the Sixties." *CSSH* 26 (1984): 126–166.

Oyedepo, David O. *The Miracle Meal.* Nigeria: Dominion, 2002.

Pariyo, George, David Bishai, Kathryn Falb, and Michelle Hindin. "Bride Price and Sexual Risk Taking in Uganda: Original Research Article." *AJRH* 13, no. 1 (2009): 147–158.

Patterson, Jane Lancaster. *Keeping the Feast: Metaphors of Sacrifice in 1 Corinthians and Philippians.* Atlanta: SBL, 2015.

Pearson, Birger A. *The Pneumatikos-Psychikos Terminology in 1 Corinthians: A Study in the Theology of the Corinthian Opponents of Paul and Its Relation to Gnosticism.* Missoula: Scholar Press, 1973.

Philip, George. *Paul and Common Meal: Re-Socialization of the Christian Community.* New Delhi: Christian World Imprints, 2017.

Phua, Richard. *Idolatry and Authority: A Study of 1 Corinthians 8:1–11:1 in the Light of the Jewish Diaspora.* New York: T&T Clark, 2005.

Pierce, C. A. *Conscience in the New Testament.* London: SCM, 1958.

Plevnik, Joseph. *Paul and the End Time?* WATSA. New York: Paulist, 2009.

Pobee, John S. "African Theology Revisited." In *Religious Plurality in Africa: Essays in Honour of John S. Mbiti*, edited by Jacob Olupona and Sulayman Nyang, 135–144. New York: de Gruyter, 1993.

Rasmussen, Susan J. "Spirit Possession in Africa." In *The Wiley-Blackwell Companion to African Religions*, edited by Elias Kifon Bongmba, 184–197. Chichester: Wiley-Blackwell, 2012.

Reasoner, Mark. *The Strong and the Weak: Romans 14:1–15:13 in Context.* Cambridge: Cambridge University Press, 1999.

Robertson, Nyk. "The Power and Subjection of Liminality and Borderlands of Non-Binary Folx." *Gender Forum*, suppl. special issue: Early Career Researchers VI 69 (2018): 45–59.

Rogers, Trent A. *God and the Idols: Representations of God in 1 Corinthians 8–10.* Tübingen: Mohr Siebeck, 2016.

Rosaldo, Renato. *Culture and Truth: The Remaking of Social Analysis.* Boston: Beacon, 2008.

Rosaldo, Renato, Smadar Lavie, and Kirin Narayan, eds. *Creativity/Anthropology.* Ithaca: Cornell University Press, 2018.

Rosner, Brian S. *Paul and the Law: Keeping the Commandments of God.* NSBT 31. Downers Grove: InterVarsity Press, 2013.

Russell, Annette Suzanne. "In the World But Not of the World: The Liminal Life of Pre-Constantine Christian Communities." PhD diss., University of California, 2013.

Salamone, Frank A., and Marjorie M. Snipes, eds. *The Intellectual Legacy of Victor and Edith Turner.* Lanham: Lexington Books, 2018.

Sampley, J. Paul. *Walking between the Times.* Minneapolis: Fortress, 1991.

Sanders, E. P. *Paul and Palestinian Judaism: A Comparison of Patterns of Religion.* 40th anniversary ed. Minneapolis: Fortress, 2017.

Sandnes, Karl Olav. *Belly and Body in the Pauline Epistles.* SNTSMS 120. Cambridge: Cambridge University Press, 2004.

Schweitzer, Albert. *The Mysticism of Paul the Apostle.* Translated by William Montgomery. 2nd ed. London: Adam & Charles Black, 1953.

Sekhukhune, Phatudi D. "Symbolism of Food and Drink: A Survey on Rituals and Other Forms of Ceremonial Interaction." *SAJE* 16, no. 2 (1993): 64–68.

Shorter, Aylward. "Conflicting Attitudes to Ancestor Veneration in Africa." *AFER* 11, no. 1 (1969): 27–37.

Simms, Ian Melville. "From Sign to Symbol: Re-integrating Communion into the Common Life of Baptists in South Africa." MA thesis, University of South Africa, 1999.

Simões, Tchilissila Alicerces, and Isabel Marques Alberto. "Family Rituals and Routines in the Developmental Trajectory of Urban Southern Angolan Families." *JBP* 45 (2019): 454–493.

Simpson, Diane. "Syncretism in Two African Cultures." *Totem* 2 (1995): 61–64.

Sipuka, Sithembele. "The Sacrifice of the Mass and the Concept of Sacrifice among the Xhosa: Towards an Inculturated Understanding of the Eucharist." PhD diss., University of South Africa, 2000.

Smart, James D. "The Eschatological Interpretation of Psalm 24." *JBL* 52, no. 2/3 (1933): 175–180.

Smit, Joop. *About the Idol Offerings: Rhetoric, Social Context and Theology of Paul's Discourse in First Corinthians 8:1–11:1*. Hadleigh: Peeters, 2001.

———. "'Do Not Be Idolaters': Paul's Rhetoric in First Corinthians 10:1–22." *NovT* 39, no. 1 (1997): 40–53.

Smit, Peter-Ben. "Ritual Failure, Ritual Negotiation, and Paul's Argument in 1 Corinthians 11:17–34." *JSPL* 3 (2013): 165–193.

Smith, Dennis E., and Hal E. Taussig. *Many Tables: The Eucharist in the New Testament and Liturgy Today*. London: Trinity, 1990.

Söding, Thomas. "Starke und Schwache der Götzenopferstreit in 1 Kor 8–10 als Paradigma paulinischer Ethik." *Zeitschrift für die neutestamentliche Wissenschaft und die Kunde der älteren Kirche* 85 (1994): 69–92.

St John, Graham, ed. *Victor Turner and Contemporary Cultural Performance*. New York: Berghahn, 2008.

Stargel, Linda M. *The Construction of Exodus Identity in Ancient Israel: A Social Identity Approach*. Eugene: Pickwick, 2018.

Stendahl, Krister. "The Apostle Paul and the Introspective Conscience of the West." *HTR* 56 (1963): 199–215.

Still, E. Coye, III. "Paul's Aims regarding εἰδωλόθυτα: A New Proposal for Interpreting 1 Corinthians 8:1--11:1." *NovT* 44, no. 4 (2002): 333–342.

Stowers, Stanley K. "Elusive Coherence: Ritual and Rhetoric in 1 Corinthians 10–11." In *Reimagining Christian Origins: A Colloquium Honoring Burton L. Mack*, edited by Burton L. Mack, Elizabeth A. Castelli, and Hal Taussig, 68–83. Valley Forge: Trinity, 1996.

———. "What is 'Pauline Participation in Christ'?" In *Redefining First-Century Jewish and Christian Identities: Essays in Honor of Ed Parish Sanders*, edited by Fabian E. Udoh, 352–371. Indiana: University of Notre Dame Press, 2008.

Strayer, Robert. "Mission History in Africa: New Perspectives on an Encounter." *ASR* 19 (1976): 1–15.

Strecker, Christian. *Die Liminale Theologie Des Paulus: Zugänge Zur Paulinischen Theologie Aus Kulturanthropologischer Perspektive*. Göttingen: Vandenhoeck & Ruprecht, 1999.

Swanson, James. *Dictionary of Biblical Languages with Semantic Domains: Greek (New Testament)*. Oak Harbor: Logos Research Systems, 1997.

Talbott, Rick F. *Jesus, Paul, and Power: Rhetoric, Ritual and Metaphor in Ancient Mediterranean Christianity*. Eugene: Cascade Books, 2010.

Taussig, Hal. *In the Beginning Was the Meal: Social Experimentation and Early Christian Identity*. Minneapolis: Fortress, 2009.

Theissen, Gerd. *The Religion of the Earliest Churches: Creating a Symbolic World*. Minneapolis: Fortress, 1999.

———. *The Social Setting of Pauline Christianity: Essays on Corinth*. Translated by John Howard Schütz. Edinburgh: T & T Clark, 1982.

———. "Social Stratification in the Corinthian Community: A Contribution to the Sociology of Early Hellenistic Christianity." In *Christianity at Corinth: The Quest for the Pauline Church*, edited by Edward Adams and David G. Horrell, 97–106. Lousiville: Westminster John Knox, 2004.

Thiessen, Matthew. "'The Rock Was Christ': The Fluidity of Christ's Body in 1 Corinthians 10:4." *JSNT* 36, no. 2 (2013): 103–126.

Thiselton, Anthony C. *The First Epistle to the Corinthians: A Commentary on the Greek Text*. Grand Rapids: Eerdmans, 2013.

———. "Realized Eschatology at Corinth." *NTS* 24, no. 4 (1978): 510–526.

Thomas, Linda. "South African Independent Churches, Syncretism, and Black Theology." *JRT* 2 (1997): 39–50.

Thomassen, Bjørn. "The Uses and Meaning of Liminality." *IPA* 2, no. 1 (2009): 5–27.

Tibbs, Clint. *Religious Experience of Pneuma: Communication with the Spirit World in 1 Corinthians 12 and 14*. Tübingen: Mohr Siebeck, 2006.

Tomson, Peter J. *Paul and the Jewish Law: Halakha in the Letters of the Apostle to the Gentiles*. Minneapolis: Fortress, 1990.

Trail, Ronald. *An Exegetical Summary of 1 Corinthians 10–16*. 2nd ed. Dallas: SIL International, 2008.

Triebel, Johannes. "Living Together with the Ancestors: Ancestor Veneration in Africa as a Challenge for Missiology." *Missiology* 30, no. 2 (2002): 187–197.

Turley, Stephen Richard. *The Ritualized Revelation of the Messianic Age: Washings and Meals in Galatians and 1 Corinthians*. London: T&T Clark, 2015.

Turner, Edith L. B. *Communitas: The Anthropology of Collective Joy*. Basingstoke: Palgrave Macmillan, 2012.

Turner, Harold W. "The Primal Religions of the World and Their Study." In *Australian Essays in World Religions*, edited by Victor Hays, 27–37. Bedford Park: Australian Association for World Religions, 1977.

Turner, Victor W. "Betwixt and Between: The Liminal Period in *Rites de Passage*." RCR 4 (1979): 234–243.

———. *Blazing the Trail: Way Marks in the Exploration of Symbols*. Edited by Edith Turner. Tucson: University of Arizona Press, 1992.

———. "Dramatic Ritual/Ritual Drama: Performative and Reflexive Anthropology." *Kenyon Review* 1, no. 3 (1979), 80–93.

———. *The Forest of Symbols: Aspects of Ndembu Ritual*. London: Cornell University Press, 1967.

———. *Revelation and Divination in Ndembu Ritual*. Ithaca: Cornell University Press, 1975.

———. *The Ritual Process: Structure and Anti-Structure*. Chicago: Aldine, 1969.

———. *Schism and Continuity in an African Society: A Study of Ndembu Village Life*. Oxford: Washington, DC: Berg, 1996.

———. "Social Dramas and Stories about Them." *CI* 7 (1980): 141–168.

———. "Symbols in African Ritual." *Science* 179 (1973): 1100–1105.

Turner, Victor W., and International African Institute. *The Drums of Affliction: A Study of Religious Processes among the Ndembu of Zambia*. London: Oxford University Press with International African Institute in Association, 1968.

Tutu, Desmond Mpilo. *God Is Not a Christian: and Other Provocations*. New York: Harper Collins, 2011.

Ukpong, Justin S. "Developments in Biblical Interpretation in Africa: Historical and Hermeneutical Directions." In *The Bible in Africa: Transaction, Trajectories and Trends*, edited by Gerald O. West and Musa W. Dube, 11–28. Leiden: Brill, 2000.

Uzukwu, E. Elochukwu. "Reconciliation and Inculturation: a Nigerian (Igbo) Orientation." *AFER* 25, no. 5 (1983): 275–279.

Van Gennep, Arnold. *The Rites of Passage*. Translated by M. B. Vizedom and G. L. Caffee. Chicago: University of Chicago Press, 1960.

Vos, Geerhardus. *The Pauline Eschatology*. New Jersey: Princeton University Press, 1930. Repr., Phillipsburg: P&R Publishing, 1994.

Wagner, J. Ross. "Paul and Scripture." In *The Blackwell Companion to Paul*, edited by Stephen Westerholm, 154–171. Chichester: Wiley-Blackwell, 2011.

Walters, James C. "Paul and the Politics of Meals in Roman Corinth." In *Corinth in Context*, edited by Steve J. Friesen, Daniel N. Schowalter, and James Walters, 343–364. Leiden: Brill, 2010.

Weber, Donald. "From Limen to Border: A Meditation on the Legacy of Victor Turner for American Cultural Studies." *AQ* 47, no. 3 (1995): 525–536.

White, Joel R. "'Baptized on Account of the Dead': The Meaning of 1 Corinthians 15:29 in Its Context." *JBL* 116 (1997): 487–499.

Whittle, Sarah. "Purity in Paul." In *Purity: Essays in Bible and Theology*, edited by Andrew Brower Latz and Arseny Ermakov. Eugene: Pickwick, 2014.

Willis, Wendell Lee. *Idol Meat in Corinth: The Pauline Argument in 1 Corinthians 8 and 10.* Eugene: Wipf & Stock, 2004.

Wink, Walter. *Engaging the Powers: Discernment and Resistance in a World of Domination.* Minneapolis: Fortress, 1992.

———. *Naming the Powers: The Language of Power in the New Testament.* Philadelphia: Fortress, 1984.

Winter, Bruce. "Carnal Conduct and Sanctification in 1 Corinthians: *Simul Sanctus et Peccator*?" In *Holiness and Ecclesiology in the New Testament*, edited by K. E. Brower and Andy Johnson, 184–200. Grand Rapids: Eerdmans, 2007.

———. "Theological and Ethical Responses to Religious Pluralism – 1 Corinthians 8–10." *TynBul* 41, no. 2 (1990): 209–226.

Witherington, Ben. *Conflict and Community in Corinth: A Socio-Rhetorical Commentary on 1 and 2 Corinthians.* Grand Rapids: Eerdmans, 1995.

———. *Jesus, Paul and the End of the World: A Comparative Study in New Testament Eschatology.* Downers Grove: InterVarsity Press, 1992.

———. *Paul's Narrative Thought World: The Tapestry of Tragedy and Triumph.* Louisville: Westminster John Knox, 1994.

Wright, N. T. *Paul.* Minneapolis: Fortress, 2009.

———. *Paul and the Faithfulness of God.* Minneapolis: Fortress, 2013.

Yeo, Khiok-Khng. *Rhetorical Interaction in 1 Corinthians 8 and 10: A Formal Analysis with Preliminary Suggestions for a Chinese, Cross-Cultural Hermeneutic.* Leiden: Brill, 1995.

Zuesse, Evan M. *Ritual Cosmos: The Sanctification of Life in African Religions.* Athens: Ohio University Press, 1987.

Zulu, Edwin. "Reverence for Ancestors in Africa: Interpretation of the 5th Commandment from an African Perspective." *Scriptura* 81 (2002): 476–482.

Langham Literature, with its publishing work, is a ministry of Langham Partnership.

Langham Partnership is a global fellowship working in pursuit of the vision God entrusted to its founder John Stott –

> *to facilitate the growth of the church in maturity and Christ-likeness through raising the standards of biblical preaching and teaching.*

Our vision is to see churches in the Majority World equipped for mission and growing to maturity in Christ through the ministry of pastors and leaders who believe, teach and live by the word of God.

Our mission is to strengthen the ministry of the word of God through:
- nurturing national movements for biblical preaching
- fostering the creation and distribution of evangelical literature
- enhancing evangelical theological education

especially in countries where churches are under-resourced.

Our ministry

Langham Preaching partners with national leaders to nurture indigenous biblical preaching movements for pastors and lay preachers all around the world. With the support of a team of trainers from many countries, a multi-level programme of seminars provides practical training, and is followed by a programme for training local facilitators. Local preachers' groups and national and regional networks ensure continuity and ongoing development, seeking to build vigorous movements committed to Bible exposition.

Langham Literature provides Majority World preachers, scholars and seminary libraries with evangelical books and electronic resources through publishing and distribution, grants and discounts. The programme also fosters the creation of indigenous evangelical books in many languages, through writer's grants, strengthening local evangelical publishing houses, and investment in major regional literature projects, such as one volume Bible commentaries like the *Africa Bible Commentary* and the *South Asia Bible Commentary*.

Langham Scholars provides financial support for evangelical doctoral students from the Majority World so that, when they return home, they may train pastors and other Christian leaders with sound, biblical and theological teaching. This programme equips those who equip others. Langham Scholars also works in partnership with Majority World seminaries in strengthening evangelical theological education. A growing number of Langham Scholars study in high quality doctoral programmes in the Majority World itself. As well as teaching the next generation of pastors, graduated Langham Scholars exercise significant influence through their writing and leadership.

To learn more about Langham Partnership and the work we do visit **langham.org**

www.ingramcontent.com/pod-product-compliance
Lightning Source LLC
Chambersburg PA
CBHW051539230426
43669CB00015B/2654

Dr. Chambo's work is a groundbreaking and deeply reflective study that powerfully reimagines the Lord's Supper as a dynamic, sacred ritual capable of transforming individuals and communities. By bridging Pauline theology, ritual theory, and African spirituality, Samantha reveals the rich, sacramental depth of 1 Corinthians 8:1–11:1 and 11:17–34 and offers a compelling framework for how the Lord's Supper can be lived and celebrated in today's African church context and beyond.

With clarity and careful research, the author illuminates how the Lord's Supper not only memorializes Christ's death but also actively shapes the church's shared life and witness. Readers will come away with a richer grasp of the Lord's Supper's sacred dimensions and its ongoing power to transform both individual believers and the entire Christian community. This insightful exploration of 1 Corinthians 8:1–11:1 and 11:17–34 offers an invaluable contribution to both biblical scholarship and practical theology.

J. Ayodeji Adewuya, PhD
Professor of New Testament,
Pentecostal Theological Seminary, Tennessee, USA

What if Paul's discussion about meat offered to idols and the Lord's Table were read through the lens of African Traditional Religions? By examining the African notion of "vital participation," Samantha Chambo illuminates Paul's "in Christ" language and the significance of the Lord's Table. Because of the seriousness with which Paul takes participation with Christ in the Lord's Table, the author warns Christians against participation in ritual meals to ancestors.

Dr. Chambo challenges us to rethink the notion of participation in Christ, the meaning and significance of the Lord's Table, and the shaping of *communitas* for the health and well-being of the *ekklesia*, both inside and outside of Africa. An important study that steers the path between syncretism and "theological imperialism."

Kent Brower, PhD
Senior Research Fellow in Biblical Studies,
Honourary Research Fellow, University of Manchester,
Nazarene Theological College, Manchester, UK

This innovative and stimulating study by Dr. Chambo brings Paul's discussion of ritual meals in 1 Corinthians 8–11 into dialogue with the African cultural context of ritual practices and spirituality. It skillfully applies and extends Victor Turner's ritual theory by exploring the concepts of liminality and *communitas* in Pauline teaching and offers significant implications for understanding the Lord's Supper as a transformative practice for Christian communities both in the African context and worldwide.

Svetlana Khobnya, PhD
Senior Lecturer in Biblical Studies,
Nazarene Theological College, Manchester, UK